JULIUS CAESAR

BROADVIEW / INTERNET SHAKESPEARE EDITIONS

Broadview Editions Series Editor
L.W. Conolly
Internet Shakespeare Editions Coordinating Editor
Michael Best
Internet Shakespeare Editions Textual Editor
Eric Rasmussen

JULIUS CAESAR

William Shakespeare

EDITED BY

John D. Cox

BROADVIEW / INTERNET SHAKESPEARE EDITIONS

Library and Archives Canada Cataloguing in Publication

Shakespeare, William, 1564–1616
    Julius Caesar / William Shakespeare ; edited by John D. Cox.

(Broadview Internet Shakespeare editions)
Includes bibliographical references.
ISBN 978-1-55481-050-5

    I. Cox, John D., 1945– II. Internet Shakespeare Editions
III. Title. IV. Series: Broadview Internet Shakespeare editions

PR2808.A2C69 2012   822.3'3   C2012-906045-3

Broadview Press is an independent, international publishing house, incorporated in 1985.

We welcome comments and suggestions regarding any aspect of our publications —
please feel free to contact us at the addresses below or at broadview@broadviewpress.com /
www.broadviewpress.com.

North America

Post Office Box 1243
Peterborough, Ontario
Canada K9J 7H5

2215 Kenmore Ave.
Buffalo, New York
USA 14207
tel: (705) 743-8990
fax: (705) 743-8353
customerservice
@broadviewpress.com

UK, Europe, Central Asia,
Middle East, Africa, India and
Southeast Asia

Eurospan Group
3 Henrietta St., London
WC2E 8LU, UK
tel: 44 (0) 1767 604972
fax: 44 (0) 1767 601640
eurospan
@turpin-distribution.com

Australia and New Zealand

NewSouth Books
c/o TL Distribution
15-23 Helles Ave.
Moorebank, NSW
Australia 2170
tel: (02) 8778 9999
fax: (02) 8778 9944
orders@tldistribution.com.
au

Copy-edited by Denis Johnston
Book design by Michel Vrana.

This book is printed on paper containing 100% post-consumer fibre.

Printed in Canada

For Michael Best

CONTENTS

FOREWORD

The Internet Shakespeare Editions (http://internetshakespeare. uvic.ca) and Broadview Press are pleased to collaborate on a series of Shakespeare Editions in book form, creating for each volume an "integrated text" designed to meet the needs of today's students. The texts, introductions, and other materials for these editions are drawn from those prepared by leading scholars for the Internet Shakespeare editions, modified to suit the demands of publication in book form. The print editions are integrated with the fuller resources and research materials that are available electronically on the site of the Internet Shakespeare Editions. Consistent with other volumes in the Broadview Editions series, each of these Shakespeare editions includes a wide range of background materials, providing information on the staging of the play, as well as on its historical and intellectual context, in addition to the text itself, introduction, chronology, and bibliography; all these will be found in more complex form on the website.

The Internet Shakespeare Editions, a non-profit organization founded in 1996, creates and publishes works for the student, scholar, actor, and general reader in a form native to the medium of the Internet: scholarly, fully annotated texts of Shakespeare's plays, multimedia explorations of the context of Shakespeare's life and works, and records of his plays in performance. The Internet Shakespeare Editions is affiliated with the University of Victoria.

The Broadview Editions series was founded in 1992 under the title "Broadview Literary Texts." Under the guidance of executive editors Julia Gaunce and Marjorie Mather, of series editors Eugene Benson and Leonard Conolly, and of managing editors Barbara Conolly and Tara Lowes, it has grown to include several hundred volumes— lesser-known works of cultural significance as well as canonical texts. Designed with the needs of undergraduate students in mind, the series has also appealed widely to scholars—and to readers in general.

Michael Best, Coordinating Editor, University of Victoria
Eric Rasmussen, General Textual Editor, University of Nevada, Reno
Don LePan, President, Broadview Press

ACKNOWLEDGEMENTS

I started work on the Internet Shakespeare Edition of *Julius Caesar* at the Folger Shakespeare Library in Washington, DC, in the spring of 2007, and I am grateful to the Folger's talented staff for their assistance and support. Librarians at Hope College's Van Wylen Library capably picked up where the Folger's left off, when my time in Washington reached its end. The early stages of resolving issues regarding the text of *Julius Caesar* were immeasurably assisted by Don Bailey, whose eagle-eyed consulting for the Internet Shakespeare Editions has no equal. I am grateful to Eric Rasmussen, ISE textual editor, for timely and collegial advice and suggestions. Jonathan Hope generously checked my notes about grammar and usage, helpfully supplying a descriptive linguistic treatment that omitted semantic and stylistic issues addressed by Edwin Abbott's more traditional approach. Alan Dessen helped me think about stage directions, and Paul Werstine encouraged my attempts to describe my decisions about the text.

Quotations from plays by Shakespeare other than *Julius Caesar* are from David Bevington's *Complete Works*, 5th edition, 2004. The brief essays on Shakespeare's life and Shakespeares's theater are reprinted from the Broadview edition of *As You Like It*, courtesy of David Bevington. The appendices are edited from online scanned versions of early printed books, downloaded from http://www.perseus.tufts.edu/ for the ISE *Julius Caesar* in July and November, 2008.

I am grateful to the vision and commitment of Broadview Press to make this edition possible. Leonard Conolly, Denis Johnston, Marjorie Mather, and Tara Trueman have all worked helpfully to bring the Broadview Press edition to fruition. I owe most to Michael Best, risk-taking and award-winning "onlie begetter" of the Internet Shakespeare Editions, to whom this Broadview edition is dedicated. Michael has corresponded tirelessly, offered limitless useful suggestions, and changed course graciously when he saw the need to do so.

INTRODUCTION

HISTORY AND TRAGEDY

Julius Caesar is the first play Shakespeare based on Sir Thomas North's translation of Plutarch's *Lives of the Noble Grecians and Romans*, which gave him a fresh sense of what he could do with history in drama. Datable with considerable certainty to 1599, *Julius Caesar* immediately followed a sequence of four English history plays, *Richard II* to *Henry V*, and that series had been preceded by another four-part sequence and by *King John*. *Julius Caesar* decenters its title character in the manner of Shakespeare's plays on Henry VI and Henry IV. Titled for the last great hero of the Roman Republic, whose bloody political murder is staged in horrific detail, the play nonetheless depicts Caesar's death in just the eighth of eighteen scenes and in the third of only three scenes in which the famous conqueror appears. Shakespeare goes out of his way, moreover, to emphasize Caesar's weaknesses, both physical and psychological. To be sure, *Julius Caesar* immediately preceded *Hamlet*, the first of Shakespeare's four major tragedies, and the running title of the play in the earliest printed edition designates it a tragedy. Critics have therefore wondered if perhaps Caesar's principal opponent, Brutus, is the tragic hero, rather than Caesar himself. Brutus appears as early as the play's second scene, he is present all but seven scenes, and the play ends with his death. Yet the play is titled for Caesar, and Brutus is defeated by those who aim to avenge Caesar's death. A useful way to resolve the debate about the tragic hero in *Julius Caesar* is to recognize that the play has many more characteristics of Shakespeare's history plays than of his tragedies. The play's lack of a hero like Hamlet or Lear makes sense if we think of the history plays Shakespeare had just finished rather than the tragedies he was about to undertake.

We know quite certainly that the play was first produced in 1599, because no references to it occur before that year, and because we have an eyewitness account by a Swiss visitor to London, Thomas Platter, who attended Shakespeare's play when it was performed in the newly-built Globe Theatre on the south bank of the Thames (Schanzer, "Platter," 466). Some references in the play itself seem to echo works published in early 1599, suggesting that Shakespeare likely composed it shortly before it was performed (Taylor).

One of the hallmarks of Shakespeare's English history plays is that they focus consistently and almost exclusively on politics conceived as the effort of ambitious men to acquire or maintain political power (Cox 97–160). This is certainly true of *Julius Caesar*. The title character is the most famously ambitious politician of ancient Rome, and he is opposed by another patrician, Brutus, who successfully leads still other Roman aristocrats against Caesar. Brutus in turn is opposed by Antony, who first appears in Caesar's company (1.2), and who eventually, in alliance with Octavius and Lepidus, triumphs over Brutus. At the end of *Julius Caesar*, the future appears to belong to these three, but Octavius alone will eventually go on to vindicate Caesar by defeating the other two and becoming "sole sir o' th' world," in Cleopatra's phrase (*Antony and Cleopatra*, 5.2.119), and eventually the first Roman emperor.

John Velz describes the pattern of events in *Julius Caesar* as "undular," or wavelike, and this pattern is more akin to the English history plays Shakespeare had just been writing than to the tragedies he was about to undertake. Moreover, the undular pattern recedes into an unknown past as the action commences, and events similarly open into an unknown future as the play closes, following the invariable pattern of Shakespeare's history plays. "The pattern is larger than the play," as Velz puts it ("Undular" 21), as if history is defined by waves of political successes and failures, and *Julius Caesar* simply selects a particular sequence of this continuum. The tribunes disperse the Roman commoners ("plebeians") who have gathered for Caesar's triumph in the play's opening scene, because the tribunes favor Pompey, whom Caesar has recently overthrown (1.1.38–56, TLN 44–62). Yet the conflict between Pompey and Caesar is presented without explanatory background, as if patrician competition of this sort were a fact of Roman political life. The past is made even more opaque by Brutus's opposition to Caesar, for Brutus does not favor Pompey as the tribunes do; rather, Brutus thinks Caesar poses a threat to the Republic, which is Brutus's chief concern (2.1.10–34, TLN 626–50). Many questions are thus left unanswered. What motivated the rivalry between Pompey and Caesar in the first place? Did Pompey also oppose Caesar out of republican sympathies? Was Pompey also a threat to the Republic?

The ending of *Julius Caesar* works similarly to raise questions about the future that the play itself gives us no basis for answering. Though Brutus's conflict with Caesar originated in Rome, seat of the Roman

Republic, the play's concluding battle takes place far from Rome, and no end to conflict is in sight. Octavius's final triumphant words seem to vindicate Caesar, because Antony and Octavius have successfully joined forces to defeat Caesar's enemies, and Antony has actually called Octavius "Caesar" shortly before (5.1.24, TLN 2355). But rivalry between Antony and Octavius is palpable from the beginning of their alliance, and Octavius's last line concedes little to Antony: "let's away / To part the glories of this happy day" (5.5.80–81, TLN 2729–30). While Octavius at least acknowledges that Antony deserves a share of the "glory," he is very far from deferring to Antony, though Antony was the first to take on the conspirators after Caesar's assassination, and Antony is a generation older than Octavius. The tension between these two triumphant patricians therefore continues into an unknown future as the play ends, recalling the play's dual focus at the outset on Caesar's recent success in his competition with Pompey and on budding tension between Brutus and Cassius (1.2).

The open-endedness of *Julius Caesar* is a quality that the play shares with Shakespeare's history plays, because it derives from Shakespeare's sense of secular history itself (Kastan 41). When Shakespeare was first establishing his pattern for writing history plays, the only dramatizations of history that he knew were regional productions of biblical history, and David Kastan points out that in these ambitious, sometimes days-long cycles of plays, history is interpreted as a discrete sequence of events in which God interacts providentially with humankind (4–5). The biblical plays' definitive revelation of divine action in history determines their episodic, non-linear quality and also their absolute beginning (creation) and ending (doomsday). Shakespeare's plays about secular history are, by contrast, open-ended, because their action is insistently continuous with events that precede and follow them in the endless continuum of secular time. Shakespeare's history plays therefore reveal not the hand of God but the shaping influence of human action in the perpetual contest for power. The open-ended structure of *Julius Caesar* insists that revealing events will continue after the play ends, making the significance of the history we have just witnessed impossible to determine in the play itself.

In addition to emphasizing the continuum of time in their structure, Kastan argues, Shakespeare's history plays also emphasize time thematically, and this is true of *Julius Caesar* as well. Velz points out that the image of wave action is twice associated with passing time ("Undular" 23–24): Antony laments Caesar as "the noblest man / That ever lived in the tide of times" (3.1.256–57, TLN 1485), and Brutus urges Cassius to immediate action by arguing that "There is a tide in the affairs of men" which favors the conspirators at Philippi, so they must seize the opportunity and attack Antony and Octavius at once (4.3.218, TLN 2217). Brutus turns out to be mistaken in this proposed strategy, as he nearly always is in conflicts with Cassius, but nothing challenges Brutus's generalization about time and human action. Cassius dies on his birthday, as he points out, making his life seem fruitless and futile: "where I did begin, there shall I end" (5.3.24, TLN 2504). He is afloat on a full sea, in Brutus's image, and they have lost their venture (4.3.222–24, TLN 2221–23). But in this respect they are like all the other patrician competitors in *Julius Caesar*, in that all are part of time's undular action, rising and falling with the endless tide of political history.

CHARACTERIZATION

While the memorable characters whom Shakespeare imagined in *Julius Caesar* owe a great deal to Plutarch's *Lives* as translated by Sir Thomas North (1579), Shakespeare substantially remade them to suit his own purpose. Where Caesar himself is concerned, Shakespeare selected details from Plutarch's account and invented others to create a much less impressive character than the one in the *Lives*. Whereas Plutarch starts with Caesar's valiant young manhood (as he does with Alexander), Shakespeare shows us Caesar only in his final days and mostly through the eyes of those who are his competitors for power in Rome. Again, whereas Plutarch reports that Caesar saved himself "with great hazard" by swimming across the harbor in Alexandria, while holding his most prized books out of the water with one hand (Appendix A1, p. 193), Cassius's account of his rescuing Caesar while they were swimming across the Tiber (1.2.100–15, TLN 198–213) impugns Caesar's endurance, and Cassius fills out the portrait of Caesar's physical vulnerability with Cassius's claim that Caesar depended on Cassius when he contracted a fever in Spain (1.2.119–28, TLN 217–26), that Caesar is hard of hearing (1.2.213, TLN 315; a detail not in Plutarch), and that he has the "falling sickness" or epilepsy (1.2.251, TLN 358; Appendix A1, p. 190), a disease that Elizabethans associated with deafness. Shakespeare also invented Caesar's belief in his wife's barrenness (1.2.7–9, TLN 95–97), a detail that could as easily reflect Caesar's disability as his wife's, though Caesar characteristically fails to see the situation that way.

Shakespeare weakens Caesar physically in order to suggest that his bodily vulnerabilities exemplify his psychological and moral failings. The swimming episode is a good example. Though Caesar at one time called out pitiably to Cassius to help him, he now treats Cassius as "a wretched creature," who "must bend his body / If Caesar carelessly but nod on him" (1.2.117–18, TLN 215–16). In other words, Caesar has become so arrogant that he has conveniently forgotten what he owes to Cassius. Because Cassius himself is ambitious, and because he is trying in this speech to solicit Brutus's aid in the conspiracy, it is impossible to know how accurately he is reporting the event, or even if it happened at all, but his report of it nonetheless initiates a damning pattern in Shakespeare's portrait of Caesar.

A surprising part of that pattern is the repeated suggestion that Caesar has to work hard to suppress fear—a suggestion barely inferable from Plutarch. On the morning of his assassination, Caesar patronizingly tells his wife, Calpurnia, that he is not afraid, in response to her expressed fear of wonders reported in the streets of Rome:

> Cowards die many times before their deaths;
> The valiant never taste of death but once.
> Of all the wonders that I yet have heard,
> It seems to me most strange that men should fear,
> Seeing that death, a necessary end,
> Will come when it will come. (2.2.32–37, TLN 1020–25)

Caesar has no sooner assured Calpurnia that death holds no fear for him than he demands of an entering servant what the augurers have said. In other words, Caesar is more afraid of the future than his bold words suggest, and his fear is confirmed by his vacillation about going to the senate. Moreover, his declaration to Calpurnia that he is not afraid is complemented by three similar declarations on Caesar's part that have no precedent in Plutarch (1.2.198–214, 2.2.10–12, 41–48, TLN 300–14, 997–99, 1031–38). Repeatedly insisting on one's possession of a particular virtue can be a clue to internal tension over that very virtue, as Shakespeare would famously suggest by means of Queen Gertrude in the next play he wrote: "The lady doth protest too much, methinks" (*Hamlet*, 3.2.228). Gertrude's perception that the player queen declares her fidelity to her husband too strongly is itself a hint of Gertrude's own struggle with her conscience regarding her unfaithfulness to old Hamlet.

Shakespeare conveys this kind of imperfect self-knowledge even more strongly for Brutus, Caesar's principal competitor, than for Caesar himself. In Brutus's case, the issue is not fear but deep-seated agitation that continually disrupts his belief in his own stoic calm. Early in his conversation with Cassius, Brutus frankly acknowledges that he is "vexed ... with passions of some difference ... / Which give some soil, perhaps, to my behaviors" (1.2.39–42, TLN 131–34), but as the competition becomes keener, he seems to suppress this self-insight in favor of expressed assertions regarding his stoic imperturbability. Plutarch again provided the hint: Brutus "framed his manners of life by the rules of virtue and study of philosophy" (Appendix A2, p. 205), and he "did so frame and fashion his countenance and looks, that no man could discern he had anything to trouble his mind. But when night came that he was in his own house, then he was clean changed" (Appendix A2, p. 211). Acting on this intimation, Shakespeare wrote the wakeful night-time scene in Brutus's orchard (2.1), when Portia begs him to tell her what is troubling him, and he at first denies that anything is. Brutus's refusal to listen to his wife is one of many parallels that Shakespeare created between Brutus and Caesar in 2.1 and 2.2, respectively.

Shakespeare goes beyond Plutarch, however, in suggesting that a divisive struggle with himself consistently underlies Brutus's façade of philosophic serenity. Cassius raises a question about Brutus's self-knowledge at their first meeting, when Brutus acknowledges being vexed with passion. In spite of this admission, Brutus increasingly acts as if his great-souled nobility puts him above every human foible, including Caesar's ambition and Cassius's obvious envy of Caesar: "I love / The name of honor more than I fear death" (1.2.88–89, TLN 186–87). Moreover, he is unaware that his pride in patrician self-possession is the very means Cassius uses to persuade him to join the conspiracy, as Cassius trenchantly remarks to himself when Brutus leaves him: "Well, Brutus, thou art noble, yet I see / Thy honorable mettle may be wrought / From that it is disposed" (1.2.301–03, TLN 415–17). Cassius's inability to lead the conspiracy without Brutus makes Cassius the lesser man of the two, yet Cassius's ability to manipulate Brutus by means of Brutus's misplaced confidence in his own judgment is a devastating irony in their relationship, and especially in Brutus's character, when we first meet the two of them.

Sometimes borrowing from Plutarch and sometimes inventing, Shakespeare repeatedly shows Brutus mistakenly overruling Cassius because Brutus believes in his own superior assessment of every situation. Brutus instantly rejects Cassius's urging that the conspirators take an oath together, insisting that honesty, virtue, and "th'insuppressive mettle of our spirits" make an oath ignoble (2.1.115–41, TLN 745–71). Brutus does not acknowledge that his harangue against oath-taking is an affront to Cassius, and Cassius seems so anxious to retain Brutus's approval that he does not object. Brutus overrules Cassius's suggestion that Cicero be included in the conspiracy (2.1.151, TLN 782), and he peremptorily objects to Cassius's urging that Antony be assassinated with Caesar (2.1.163–69, TLN 795–99). Allowing Antony to live is one of Brutus's most momentous political miscalculations, as subsequent events make clear, and his insistence that the assassination can somehow be a sacred act, when it is in fact a brutal political murder, is typical of the disjunction between his stoic idealism and the reality that constantly agitates him, both externally and internally.

Though Plutarch mentions a quarrel between Brutus and Cassius, Shakespeare interprets their quarrel near Sardis as a trenchant revelation of Brutus's lack of self-knowledge (4.3). Like his original, Shakespeare's Cassius is "choleric" or hot-tempered (Appendix A2, pp. 207, 220), as Brutus is well aware. When Cassius objects that Brutus has treated him dishonorably, Brutus immediately accuses Cassius of dishonesty (4.3.9–12, TLN 1978–81)—a retort made either out of obtuse self-righteousness or with the design to make Cassius even angrier, or perhaps both. Brutus mocks Cassius for his "rash choler," urging him to "Go show your slaves how choleric you are, / And make your bondmen tremble" (4.3.40–51, TLN 2012–17). Beside himself with rage and frustration, Cassius draws his dagger and urges that Brutus might as well kill him in fact, since he is already killing him with his words. Brutus replies by ordering Cassius to calm down, self-righteously emphasizing his own self-control, as he sees it, in contrast to Cassius's quick temper (4.3.107–13, TLN 2087–93). The result is that Brutus uses his façade of self-restraint to dominate Cassius.

If he truly cared as little for external events as his stoicism counsels him, he would not show so much as a "hasty spark" (4.3.112, TLN 2093), but even more, he would not boast of his power over himself, nor would he care so deeply to agitate and humiliate his co-conspirator, whom he treats as if he were his keenest rival.

The resolution of the quarrel between these two has been much admired (Johnson 8.836), but among other things it confirms Brutus's continued dominance of Cassius by Brutus's resourceful insistence on his own moral superiority. When Brutus again unguardedly admits his inner turmoil (4.3.144, TLN 2131), Cassius tweaks him with a failure to be consistently stoic: "Of your philosophy you make no use, / If you give place to accidental evils" (4.3.145–46, TLN 2132–33), only to have Brutus come back with his hardest-hitting comment thus far: "No man bears sorrow better. Portia is dead" (4.3.158, TLN 2134). Brutus has to know that this information, conveyed in this way, will make Cassius completely deferential out of concern for him, as in fact it does, and Brutus presses his advantage by urging that Cassius "Speak no more of her" (TLN 2149). Having pulled Cassius toward him with the announcement of Portia's death, Brutus immediately pushes him away again by ordering him not to talk about it any more. Both comments maintain Brutus's dominance and keep Cassius off balance. Confirming this strategy is Brutus's odd solicitation of news about Portia from the newly-arrived Messala—as if Brutus did not already know of his wife's death. When Messala reports it, Brutus responds with perfect stoic rectitude (4.3.190-92, TLN 2186–88), thereby eliciting astonished admiration for his godlike endurance from both Messala and Cassius (4.3.193–95, TLN 2189–91). This is surely the very reaction Brutus had counted on, as Geoffrey Miles suggests in his analysis of Brutus's stoic constancy as an "unnatural" suppression of feeling that is "artful" in its impression on others (143).

Brutus's smothered feelings betray him in domestic settings, as well as political ones, as Shakespeare makes brilliantly clear in Brutus's relationship with the boy Lucius, who has no precedent in Plutarch. Lucius is the only person who unequivocally defers to Brutus, and he therefore seems to call forth feelings of solicitude in Brutus that Brutus shows to no one else, even his wife, who challenges him forthrightly (2.1.238ff, TLN 874 ff.). Yet Brutus believes he should give way to no feeling, as the stoic philosopher and ex-slave, Epictetus, recommends:

In the case of everything attractive or useful or that you are fond of, remember to say just what sort of thing it is, beginning with the least little things. If you are fond of a jug, say "I am fond of a jug!" For then, when it is broken you will not be upset. If you kiss your child or your wife, say that you are kissing a human being; for when it dies you will not be upset. (12)

Brutus disguises his affection for Lucius with peremptoriness, calling sternly for the lad's prompt attention in the small hours of the morning and demanding that he fetch a taper (2.1.5–8, TLN 616–24). When they are encamped near Sardis, Brutus again demands the boy's attention late at night, insisting that Lucius play his lute while Brutus reads. Yet noticing Lucius's tiredness, Brutus is irresistibly drawn to care for him (4.3.242–43, TLN 2248–49). When Lucius falls asleep while trying to play, Brutus tenderly removes the lute, so Lucius will not accidentally damage it (4.3.270-73, TLN 2282–84).

These gestures of care are ambivalent, however, because they are accompanied by glances at Brutus's stoic habit of suppressing all feeling. When Brutus finds a book he had been looking for in the pocket of his gown, Lucius makes clear that Brutus had blamed him for the book's disappearance: "I was sure your lordship did not give it me" (4.3.255, TLN 2264). When Brutus calls out, after the ghost's departure, Lucius suddenly wakes, and assuming that Brutus had scolded him, he blames his lute: "The strings, my lord, are false" (4.3.292, TLN 2305). Lucius would not instinctively defend himself if he were not in the habit of needing to, and Brutus seems to treat him with alternate tenderness and severity in order to correct the former in himself with the latter. As if commenting unconsciously on his ambivalence about Lucius, Brutus urges the conspirators: "And let our hearts, as subtle masters do, / Stir up their servants to an act of rage / And after seem to chide 'em" (2.1.176–78, TLN 808–10).

Perhaps Shakespeare's most important insight from Plutarch concerns patrician competitiveness. Caesar and Brutus are keen rivals in *Julius Caesar*, and Shakespeare's incisive characterization of these two as alter egos in their stoic ambition and vulnerability is a comment on their aristocratic emulation, which motivates all the main characters in *Julius Caesar*. Shakespeare encountered this kind of contest in Plutarch, who describes Alexander as determined to conquer something his father could not, and he repeats this motif in his story of the young Caesar, who wept in frustration when he read of Alexander's deeds, because Alexander had conquered so much more than Caesar had at the same age (Appendix A1, p. 188). The parallel episodes point to a similar conception of upper-class male rivalry in both Greece and Rome. The difference, Gordon Braden argues, is that when Rome's territorial ambition produced ever-diminishing returns, the patrician warrior was compelled to turn inward for something to conquer, as Plutarch wrote of Caesar, whose desire for "glory" made him discontented with what he had achieved: "This humour [disposition] of his was no other but an emulation with himself as with another man" (Appendix A1, pp. 195-96). This distinctively Roman development helps to account for the widespread ideal of stoic perfectionism in Roman culture. The stoic sage, Braden concludes, "is so far ahead in the competition that he can never be caught" (23). Shakespeare seems to have drawn the same conclusion about stoicism from his reading and conceivably from what he knew of competition at the Elizabethan court, where neo-stoicism was the height of fashion in the 1590s.

The brilliance of Shakespeare's inventive characterization in *Julius Caesar* is heightened by the way the playwright complements character and history in this Roman history play. Cassius compares himself favorably to Aeneas (1.2.112–15, TLN 210–13), whose story as the founder of Roman history was authoritatively rendered for Shakespeare and his contemporaries in Virgil's *Aeneid*. Virgil interprets the goal of Roman history as the advent of Caesar Augustus, who appears in *Julius Caesar* as Octavius. For Virgil, Augustus is another Aeneas, providentially refounding Rome after the civil wars as a city of peace and the center of civilization. This is not how Shakespeare imagines either Aeneas or Octavius in *Julius Caesar*. Cassius's evocation of Aeneas as "our great ancestor" (1.2.112, TLN 210) is self-serving and petty, strategically deflating Julius Caesar's reputation in order to ascertain Brutus's willingness to join the conspiracy. Before the sudden arrival of Octavius's servant in 3.1, no one has so much as mentioned his master, whom the conspirators do not think of as a risk to them. Despite their underestimation of him, Octavius has the last word in the play, having triumphed with Antony over those who destroyed Caesar. Yet Octavius's triumph does not reveal the ultimate meaning of Roman history, as it implicitly does in the *Aeneid*; rather, Octavius's success merely marks another stage in the endless struggle for power that stretches into unknown time before the play begins, when Julius Caesar and Pompey were rivals, and into unknown time after the play ends, when the rivalry between Octavius and Antony will inevitably continue, with no hint of what lies thereafter. In short, Roman history in *Julius Caesar* is marked by endless competition among relentless patrician rivals, who seem to serve no other destiny than their own ambition, no matter how strongly or how often they may proclaim their belief in higher ideals both to themselves and to others.

RHETORIC AND POETIC LANGUAGE

Shakespeare's rhetorical skill is on rich display in the poetry of *Julius Caesar*, especially in the set-piece orations by Brutus and Antony, for which Shakespeare had no model in Plutarch. Wolfgang Müller and John Velz ("*Orator*") have shown in various ways how much more broadly Shakespeare applied classical oratory than those two famous speeches. Rhetoric governs the play's animal imagery, for example, noted by Caroline Spurgeon (346), for speakers use this imagery almost exclusively to characterize others, and since the images nearly always appear in various ways as insults, they implicitly reveal the speaker's sense of himself as a superior human to an inferior animal. Cassius uses a series of deliberate rhetorical images in persuading Casca to join the conspiracy (1.3.104–06, TLN 544–52). Four animal images (wolf, sheep, lion, "hinds" [deer]) in two opposed pairs parallel a concluding image of fire to make Cassius's point that Caesar's ambition depends on Roman submissiveness. The first image (1.3.104–05, TLN 545–46) may derive from a proverb, "He that makes himself a sheep shall be eaten by the wolf" (Dent S300), but Shakespeare changes the emphasis to have Cassius say that Caesar is a wolf only because the Romans are sheep. By the same token, Caesar is a mighty fire only because the Romans allow themselves to be combustible straws and other base matter. "Base" is a socially loaded adjective that is especially designed to appeal to Casca's sense of his own social worth: if you want to be a real patrician, Cassius implies, reject that predator Caesar and the weak prey who submit to him, and join us genuine noblemen who oppose him.

Antony similarly directs scorn against another in his comparison of Lepidus to an ass and a horse (4.1.21–40, TLN 1873–96). Unlike Cassius, however, Antony is not trying to persuade his companion, Octavius, to anything in this speech; Antony is sorting out the power relations between the triumvirs who have assigned themselves to punish Caesar's assassins. In the process of deciding who should be put to death, Octavius asserts his dominance by proscribing Lepidus's brother and ordering Antony to add the brother's name to the list. Lepidus asserts himself so far as to insist that Antony's brother, Publius, also be proscribed, but Lepidus's affront to Antony, instead of Octavius, tacitly reinforces Octavius's dominance. Though Antony acquiesces in his brother's proscription, he establishes his dominance over Lepidus by ordering him to fetch Caesar's will, and when Lepidus meekly departs in compliance, Antony launches into two insulting animal similes against Lepidus. Octavius demurs, but only to challenge Antony and keep him in his place, not to defend Lepidus from Antony's crude assault, which insists that Lepidus is no more than their beast of burden or their horse to be managed: "Do not talk of him / But as a property" (4.1.39–40, TLN 1895–96). Antony establishes his status with Octavius by making Lepidus out to be a pack animal.

Shakespeare invents another animal simile in Brutus's description of Cassius, and this simile has still another rhetorical function: to indicate Brutus's barely suppressed fury while he self-righteously compares Cassius to a "deceitful jade [horse]" (4.2.23–27, TLN 1930–39). Brutus's implicit pride in his own "plain and simple faith" (4.2.22, TLN 1933) is one example among many in *Julius Caesar* of a patrician warrior protesting his own virtue too much. Brutus's image implies that he is the rider, and Cassius is the kind of horse who shows a great deal of spirit before a competition, only to fade when his rider needs him most. "They should endure the bloody spur" (4.2.25, TLN 1937) is an especially angry clause, indicating not only what Brutus thinks Cassius should do but also what Brutus would, in effect, like to do to him. Brutus is not just comparing Cassius to a horse; Brutus is venting rage that he believes, in keeping with stoic assumptions, he should not feel, and the bitterness of his simile expresses the strain he is under. His effort to portray Cassius as an animal and himself as a superior human being actually reveals his vexed passions in a way he does not suspect.

In addition to animal imagery, G. Wilson Knight noted a pattern of body images (37–48), including especially blood (45–48), and Leo Kirschbaum developed Knight's remarks in an influential essay on blood in *Julius Caesar*, though Kirschbaum addressed staging rather than language. Noting that Shakespeare's plays call for no less stage blood than those of his contemporaries, Kirschbaum points out that bloody deeds in *Julius Caesar* are not metaphorical but literal and theatrical (520). His primary example is Brutus's urging the conspirators to bathe their hands in Caesar's blood after the assassination—another of Shakespeare's inventions (523). Its effect, Kirschbaum, argues, is to present in the most concrete possible way the horror of Brutus's actual deed in contrast to the idealism with which he undertakes it. Moreover, the blood that he smears on himself "is the symbol and mark of the blood and destruction which is to flow through the rest of the play" (524). The conspirators may drain the blood from Caesar's body, but they are unable to destroy his vengeful spirit.

Building on the insistence that poetic imagery and stage imagery complement each other in a play, Maurice Charney focuses on three "image themes" in *Julius Caesar*: storm, blood, and fire (42). Each of these themes is ambiguous, he urges, because their interpretation depends on whether one favors Caesar or the conspirators, though the play favors neither one. Charney traces the "blood theme" from its introduction in Brutus's conversation with Cassius (2.1.167, TLN 799) to Titinius's lament for Cassius in 5.3.60–62, TLN 2545–48. Following Kirschbaum, Charney emphasizes stage action, pointing out that blood imagery keeps Caesar's assassination before the audience by having Caesar's body on stage for most of 3.1 and 3.2, including the "fearful blood ritual" in which Brutus leads the conspirators (52). Blood and hunting dominate Antony's oration in such a way as to stress "butchery rather than the sacrifice Brutus hoped for" before the assassination (55). Cassius's death by the same sword that he used to kill Caesar "is the reciprocity of blood for blood" (59).

Two critics publishing simultaneously in *Shakespeare Studies* took their discussion of *Julius Caesar*'s imagery in the direction of Elizabethan religion. Naomi Conn Liebler emphasized the possible influence of Plutarch's *Life of Romulus* on *Julius Caesar* and on Shakespeare's way of imagining the feast of Lupercal in particular, since Plutarch's *Romulus* describes the Lupercal in greater detail than any of his other biographies. Where blood imagery is concerned, Liebler points out that "the cutting up of the sacrificial *pharmakos* [scapegoat], whose blood is then smeared upon the flesh of the priestly celebrants, is one of the central events in the rites of the Lupercalia," and she compares the ritual to Brutus's "insistence on the semblance of a ritual as a pattern for Caesar's assassination" (183). Elizabethans would have responded to the ritual aspects of Shakespeare's play, learned from Plutarch, because their own lives were full of "Lupercalia-like rites" (189). David Kaula's interpretation of religion in *Julius Caesar* addresses the reformation context in particular. Adoration of Caesar in the play "is something akin to Roman Catholic worship" (199), just as Cassius's satirical description of Caesar's weaknesses is akin to Protestant attacks on the Pope (200). Blood imagery makes Caesar "a redeemer who voluntarily sheds his blood for the spiritual sustenance of his people," and Decius's crafty description of Calpurnia's dream imagines Romans competing for "relics" of Caesar as Catholics in England sought relics of their martyrs to Elizabeth's regime (204–05). Following this train of thought, "we might even see a moderate form of Protestantism reflected in Brutus' self-conscious Stoic virtue" (206).

Postmodern criticism in the 1980s gave the study of imagery new life and new forms. Postmodern commentary on imagery of the body in *Julius Caesar* depends on a perceived disjunction between conscious intention and unconscious motivation—a disjunction that is frequently described in terms of a suspicious false consciousness, seen in *Julius Caesar*, for example, in a recurring pattern of self-deception. Gail Kern Paster addressed the unquestioned assumption of gender hierarchy in her comments on blood imagery in *Julius Caesar*, pointing out that Mikhail Bakhtin distinguishes "the grotesque, essentially medieval conception of an unfinished, self-transgressing open body of hyperactive orifices" from a "classical body" that is relatively complete, closed, and therefore perceived as more nearly perfect (285). Paster argues that this distinction is not only historical (medieval vs. early modern) but also gendered, with the "open" body being female and the "closed" body male. With this distinction in mind, she reads the body images of *Julius Caesar* as a complex attempt on the conspirators' part to make Caesar female (a vulnerable, bleeding body), countered by Antony's attempt to "recuperate Caesar's body for his own political uses by redefining Caesar's blood and Caesar's bleeding" (286). Paster draws on and acknowledges Charney's and Kaula's essays in particular, but her intent is not to trace the workings of Shakespeare's creative imagination but to find traces of unconscious patriarchal bias in the play's language, imagery, and action. Paster affirms Kaula's reading of Decius's reinterpretation of Calpurnia's dream, for example, as influenced by the medieval cult of the Holy Blood (294), and she points out that "Decius Brutus specifically allegorizes Caesar as a lactating figure" by using the verb "suck" to describe the action of Romans who gather for nourishment at Caesar's bloody fountain (295). This strikingly original interpretation of blood imagery in *Julius Caesar* has opened up new possibilities of understanding the play, both textually and historically.

Writing at the same time as Paster, Mark Rose took blood imagery in the direction of still another form of postmodern analysis, New Historicism. Caesar's assassination is "conspicuously ritualized," Rose points out, in the conspirators' smearing of Caesar's blood on themselves—a ceremony Brutus imagines being performed in future theaters (298–99). Caesar's bloody death thus becomes the paradoxical basis of his historic monumentality, which Shakespeare's play celebrates as "a kind of political Mass"—a point Rose compares to Kaula's analysis of Caesar as a political redeemer modeled on Christ (301). What Caesar redeems is Roman political order, which he initiates as the *de facto* first emperor and the founder of an imperial tradition that the Tudor monarchs frequently invoked as the basis of their own authority (302). "Drained out of the official religion," Rose observes, "magic and ceremony reappeared not only on the stage, but in the equally theatrical world of the court" (302). Though Rose seems unaware of Stephen Greenblatt's essay on exorcism, first published five years earlier, Rose's interpretation of the bleeding Caesar is fully compatible with Greenblatt's ideas, which became the basis of New Historicism's positing of a historical false consciousness about religion, art, and political power. The Elizabethan theater was crucial, Greenblatt argues, in England's transition from a sacred to a secular culture. Shakespeare's plays evoke sacred signs but consistently secularize them in a form "drained" of "institutional and doctrinal significance," so that "the official position is *emptied out*, even as it is loyally confirmed" (125–26). What had once been spiritually literal became merely literary, as the culture took "a drastic swerve from the sacred to the secular—in the theater" (126). Both Rose and Greenblatt use the image of "draining" to describe late Elizabethan secularization: both see the theater as crucial to the process; both see the process as unavoidably political, given the theatricality of the court.

In a complex argument that effectively combines feminism and New Historicism, Coppèlia Kahn addresses the blood imagery of *Julius Caesar* in the context of republican competitiveness, which Shakespeare calls "emulation," in *Julius Caesar* (2.3.12, TLN 1141) and in other plays. False consciousness appears in the idealism that hides republican emulation from those engaged in it, especially Brutus (86). But parallel false consciousness also appears in the conception of the Roman Republic as "a distinctively masculine sphere in which debate and action, the exercise of reason and freedom, make men truly virile" (83). Moreover, Kahn compares imagined Roman false consciousness to contemporary Elizabethan emulation at court (92–93). Roman *virtus* [manly excellence] thus defines republican virility as against female submissiveness, and Kahn interprets the contrast in much the same way as Paster. Portia's self-wounding is the oppositional counterpart to the conspirators' wounding of Caesar: the first is a woman's attempt to imitate a man's constancy (101), and the second "resoundingly feminizes Caesar" (104), after Decius successfully construes Calpurnia's predictive dream of the assassination as a nurturing image, which "recalls the legend of Romulus and Remus who, suckled by the she-wolf, were thus enabled to found the Roman state" (103). By attending carefully to both Roman and Elizabethan texts, Kahn freshly illuminates suspicion of power in *Julius Caesar*, where competitive Roman patricians and Elizabethan aristocrats are both concerned.

Closely related to imagery in *Julius Caesar* is Shakespeare's use of language that hovers somewhere between the symbolic, the literal, the psychological, and the supernatural, without being exclusively identifiable as any of them. This language is particularly striking on the night before the assassination of Caesar, when Casca meets Cicero and Cassius in succession (1.3). Though Cicero was an ambivalent stoic (sometimes even identified as anti-stoic), he was one of ancient Rome's most influential purveyors of stoicism, while Cassius is a self-proclaimed Epicurean (5.1.76, TLN 2416), and each speaks in this scene consistently with his philosophical profession, yet the scene is about more than philosophy. Both Cicero and Cassius respond without concern to the fearsome storm on the eve of Caesar's assassination, but the play does not make clear that their dismissive interpretation of the weather is definitive or even coherent. Moreover, the ambiguity of language throughout the scene suggests an interpenetration of inner and outer reality that makes the boundary between them impossible to discern.

In the eight and a half lines assigned to him in his sole appearance in the play, Cicero perfectly models a generalized Roman stoicism, remaining unperturbed by the severe weather, though it terrifies Casca, who personifies it in such a way as to make clear his belief that it is supernatural. The winds are so "scolding," the ocean so "ambitious," the clouds so "threat'ning" that the gods must be at odds with one another or inclined to destroy the world because it is "too saucy" (1.3.3–13, TLN 435–45). Cicero's sardonic reply indicates how little the storm affects him and how little he regards Casca for submitting to his fears: "Why, saw you anything more wonderful?" (1.3.14, TLN 446). Reacting strenuously to Cicero's implicit skepticism, Casca cites more amazing wonders he has seen, some of them taken by Shakespeare from Plutarch, who confirms Casca's view of them: "destiny may easier be foreseen, than avoided, considering the strange and wonderful signs that were said to be seen before Caesar's death" (Appendix A1, p. 198). Casca concludes with an emphatic statement of his (and Plutarch's) point that "prodigies" must not be dismissed as merely natural events (1.3.28–32, TLN 460–64). Cicero remains unimpressed by either the weather or Casca's interpretation of it, agreeing that "it is a strange disposèd time" but insisting that people often misconstrue things "Clean from the purpose of the things themselves" (1.3.33–35, TLN 465–67). But then, as if changing the subject, Cicero in fact introduces the very subject whose presence has been heavy by its absence from Casca's fearful assertions: "Comes Caesar to the Capitol tomorrow?" (1.3.36, TLN 468). Cicero is not referring to the conspiracy, because he has not been informed of it, so his question is weighty with dramatic irony. Without knowing it, he has put his finger on the very issue he has been dismissing: the wonders in the streets of Rome are not mere projections of Casca's fear; they are portents of Caesar's death. Cicero himself has misconstrued things clean from the purpose of the things themselves, because his question is portentous without his knowing it. It is not clear that Cicero's skepticism prevails in this conversation, given the quiet irony that undercuts him in the end.

Cicero's exit is simultaneous with Cassius's entry, which Casca marks by the same fearful challenge that opens *Hamlet* on a troubled dark night: "Who's there?" Cassius replies even more insouciantly than Cicero, all but mocking Casca's fear, but Cassius is not openly skeptical like Cicero; on the contrary, Cassius asserts that "heaven" has sent the wonders of the night "To make them instruments of fear and warning / Unto some monstrous state" (1.3.70–71, TLN 509–10). As an Epicurean, Cassius does not believe the gods have anything to do with mortal affairs, if the gods exist at all, but he accommodates himself to Casca for strategic reasons. He professes credulity about the portentous weather as heaven's warning about Caesar's ambition in order to persuade Casca to join in the effort to check that ambition—in effect, to put himself on heaven's side. This is why Cassius answers Casca's fearful question, "Who ever knew the heavens menace so?" with an answer that seems to refer to Caesar: "Those that have known the earth so full of faults" (1.3.44–45, TLN 481–83). Cassius does not construe the portents as a threat to himself but only to an unnamed guilty man who is "Most like this dreadful night, / ... yet prodigious grown / And fearful, as these strange eruptions are" (1.3.73–78, TLN 511–17).

Cassius's indirection accomplishes two purposes: it suggests a connection between inner and outer turbulence, and it introduces an extended verbal ambiguity in his exchange with Casca that makes their talk about suicide also implicitly a talk about assassination. The first of these purposes has already been suggested in Casca's description of the troubled night as "scolding," "ambitious," and "threat'ning"—all terms that reflect Casca's fear while applying to the portentous storm itself and Caesar's ascendancy. This kind of double entendre reappears in Cassius's assertion that the night's wonders are "instruments of fear and warning" and his description of the unnamed man (i.e., Caesar) as "prodigious grown / And fearful [i.e., fearsome]." Is the "fear" he twice mentions political, meteorological, internal to himself, or all three? He seems to suggest, if only for Casca's benefit, that the frightening events of the night mirror the frightened state of those who witness them because "heaven" is trying to warn Romans that something terrible is about to happen. Casca thinks this impending event is Caesar's coronation by the senate (1.3.85–88, TLN 525–26), and Cassius agrees, yet he fails to reckon with the thought of everyone watching the play—that "heaven" might be warning against the assassination that

Cassius himself is planning. The scene in *Julius Caesar* simply suggests all these possibilities without indicating how to decide between them. As Geoffrey Miles puts it, "The storm is all the more terrifying because, though it seems meaningful, its meaning is obscure" (127).

Ambiguous language about the assassination arises in Cassius's bold response to Casca's comment about Caesar's being crowned the next day: "I know where I will wear this dagger then: / Cassius from bondage will deliver Cassius" (1.3.89–90, TLN 529–30). His allusion to the assassination is obvious to anyone who knows he is a conspirator, but Casca does not know (though he seems to suspect), and Cassius uses language hinting at suicide ("life ... / Never lacks power to dismiss itself" [1.3.96–97, TLN 536–37]) seemingly in order to sound out Casca about the assassination without committing himself openly, while Casca replies in the same suggestively ambiguous terms (1.3.100–02, TLN 542–43). Even when they shake hands, and Cassius says he has already gathered certain patricians to join him in an "honorable dangerous" enterprise (1.3.124, TLN 566), neither of them says what he means, and Cassius concludes with another ambiguous reference both to the assassination and to inner and outer reality: "the complexion of the element / Is fev'rous, like the work we have in hand, / Most bloody, fiery, and most terrible" (1.3.128–30, TLN 570–72). Shakespeare leaves no doubt that something frightening, uncanny, and mysterious is afoot in *Julius Caesar*, but none of the principals seems able to say clearly what it is, just as we, the play's auditors, do not know precisely what it means.

CRITICAL HISTORY

Without knowing it, the critic who most strongly influenced the first two centuries of response to Shakespeare's writing in general, and to *Julius Caesar* in particular, was a Roman patrician, Quintus Horatius Flaccus, who turned twenty-one in the year Julius Caesar was assassinated. Though Shakespeare could hardly have known it, Horace (the Roman critic's more familiar English name) joined Brutus and Cassius as a young officer after Julius Caesar's assassination and commanded a legion at the battle of Philippi in 42 BCE—the concluding event in Shakespeare's play. Eventually pardoned by Octavius for his opposition, Horace nonetheless withdrew from political life and became an influential literary figure after the senate declared Octavius "Augustus" in 27 BCE. Thus sidelined from military and political action, Horace unwittingly set the standard for the first two centuries of interpreting *Julius Caesar* by penning a verse epistle, *Ars Poetica*, early in the long political calm following Octavius's defeat of Antony. Centuries later, Italian Renaissance critics came to regard *Ars Poetica* as a direct Latin equivalent to Aristotle's *Poetics* (Weinberg 1.111–55), and the prestige of Italian criticism brought Horace to prominence in early seventeenth-century England. Shakespeare's contemporary, Ben Jonson, not only rendered Horace's poem in English (published in 1640), but also largely followed *Ars Poetica* in the brief comments he penned on his fellow actor and playwright—the first critical response to Shakespeare and the first of many to interpret Shakespeare through a Renaissance Horatian lens.

The key terms that later critics learned from Horace were "nature" and "art." For Horace, "art" meant Greek models, by which Roman poets could learn to improve their own Latin poetry. Jonson rendered Horace's advice in his English couplet: "Take you the Greek examples for your light / In hand, and turn them over, day and night" ("Horace, His Art of Poetrie," 396–97; 268–69 in the Latin original). Renaissance poets learned from Latin models more than Greek, however, so for them "art" meant principally Horace himself, Virgil, Plautus, Seneca, and Cicero. Accordingly, Jonson frequently imitates or alludes to Horace in his commendatory poem for the Shakespeare First Folio of 1623, "To the Memory of My Beloved, the Author, Mr. William Shakespeare," and Jonson's praise is interlaced with admonitions to readers that Shakespeare was not artful enough, because he did not study classical models enough, "For a good poet's made as well as born" (64). Jonson pays Shakespeare a backhanded compliment in the commendatory poem when he remarks that though Shakespeare had "small Latin and less Greek" (31), the greatest Greek and Latin poets would gladly return from the dead to hear Shakespeare's plays. The qualifying clause is what has stuck in readers' memories, as Jonson surely meant it to.

Jonson was the first swallow in the spring of neoclassical criticism of Shakespeare on Horatian principles. For two centuries after Jonson, critics positioned themselves on a continuum according to their preference for nature or art in evaluating Shakespeare's writing. Those who praised him as a poet of nature tended to single out his characters in particular, finding that their "naturalness" compensated for the playwright's putative lack of classical "art" in other aspects of writing plays. Most critics, however, agreed with Jonson that Shakespeare's reliance on nature rather than art was a mistake. Especially influential in this vein was Thomas Rymer, whose censure of *Julius Caesar* is included in his *Short View of Tragedy* (1693). Rymer was a formidable critic not only for the narrow certitude of his theory but even more for his vituperative style. Horace had repeated the classical commonplace that tragic decorum required a high style and exclusive attention to noble character, and Rymer heaped scorn on Shakespeare for violating this decorum, especially for treating "the noblest Romans" with indignity. "But there is no other cloth in his wardrobe. Everyone must be content to wear a fool's coat who comes to be dressed by him" (156). By denying decorous nobility even to Shakespeare's patricians, Rymer went further than other neoclassical critics, who objected merely that Shakespeare indecorously mingles patricians and plebeians in the same play. "For indeed that language which Shakespeare puts in the mouth of Brutus would not suit or be convenient unless from some son of the shambles or some natural off-spring of the butchery" (151). Rymer's view of art was so extreme and so narrow that it denied any art to Shakespeare, blithely affirming that he drew only on nature and his own imagination, which "was still running after his masters, the cobblers, and parish clerks, and Old Testament strollers" (156).

Rymer's critical indignation had a large moral component, which he derived (or at any rate justified) from Horace's admonition that the best fictions mix "doctrine" (*utile*) with "delight" (*dulci*) (*Ars Poetica* 516; 360). Rymer was the first to infer that "doctrine" specifically required "poetic justice," that is, a presumed vindication of divine providence in a tragic plot by allotting a benign fortune to moral characters and a malign outcome to immoral ones. Rymer's authority solidified the topics of the Horatian debate concerning *Julius Caesar*, and high neoclassical criticism repeated those topics with variations in the eighteenth century. Critics who believed art should follow putatively Horatian and Aristotelian rules found Shakespeare's departure from the rules a problem in *Julius Caesar*. In this category are difficulties with the decorum of character (imagining plebeians in the same play with patricians; failing to make patricians speak and act like patricians), violations of the three unities, especially the failure to unify action and time, and the failure of "poetic justice." If the play ended with the death of Caesar, it would be very nearly continuous in time over the course of not much more than twenty-four hours, and it would not entail "extraneous" action leading to Brutus's eventual defeat. Shakespeare's failure to meet the requirements of art was due, moreover, to his ignorance of classical models—his failure to study Greek and Latin as assiduously as his critics had and with precisely their sense of taste.

Not all neoclassical critics faulted Shakespeare's art, however, and the most thoughtful and incisive neoclassical defense of Shakespeare as "the poet of nature" was by Samuel Johnson, in the preface to his edition of Shakespeare (1765). Johnson uses the phrase to mean that Shakespeare "holds up to his readers a faithful mirror of manners and of life" (7.62). Johnson wittily and cogently demolishes arguments for the unities of time and place (7.76–80) and asserts that Shakespeare "has well enough preserved the unity of action," in that his plays have discernible beginnings and middles, "and the end of the play is the end of expectation" (7.75). This is not to say that Shakespeare was without faults, as Johnson shows by enumerating "faults sufficient to obscure and overwhelm any other merit" (7.71–74). Among them is the violation of poetic justice: "he makes no just distribution of good or evil, nor is always careful to show in the virtuous a disapprobation of the wicked; he carries his persons indifferently through right and wrong, and at the close dismisses them without further care, and leaves their examples to operate by chance" (7.71). As Johnson here echoes the familiar neoclassical complaint that Shakespeare lacked art, it is hardly surprising that "nature" and "natural" recur throughout Johnson's preface.

But Johnson's Horatian thinking about Shakespeare and "nature" goes beyond character to include what might be called "untrained originality." "The English nation, in the time of Shakespeare, was yet struggling to emerge from barbarity" (7.81), Johnson believed, so for Shakespeare "the greater part of his excellence was the product of his own genius" (7.87), since he lacked the example of art. Johnson was easily persuaded by the conventional neoclassical argument that Shakespeare was "natural" in the same way as Homer: "Perhaps it would not be easy to find any author except Homer who invented as much as Shakespeare, who so much advanced the studies which he cultivated, or effused so much novelty upon his age or country" (7.90). With "genius" as the explanation of Shakespeare's accomplishment,

Johnson's summary judgment about *Julius Caesar* in particular is easier to understand. Johnson was not moved by the play, and he therefore thought it exhibited less of Shakespeare's natural gifts than other tragedies did: "his adherence to the real story and to Roman manners seems to have impeded the natural vigor of his genius" (8.836). As the great poet of nature, in Johnson's estimation, Shakespeare did less well when it came to classical material, with its greater suitability to treatment as "art," in which Shakespeare was deficient.

The straitjacket that neoclassical critics had tied around themselves when they evaluated Shakespeare by means of Horace and Aristotle was at last thrown off by critics writing under the influence of Romanticism in the early nineteenth century. To be sure, neoclassical criticism is subtler and more various than Romantic critics made it out to be for their own polemical purposes, and their innovations sometimes seem continuous with it. For example, when Samuel Taylor Coleridge declared in the early nineteenth century "*Poeta nascitur, non fit*" (Ringler, "*Poeta*," 497), he evidently didn't realize that he was Latinizing an English formulation by Leonard Digges from as early as 1640 ("Poets are born, not made" [Vickers 1.27]), nor that Digges in turn was deliberately responding to Ben Jonson's claim that "a good poet's made as well as born" ("To the Memory" 64). The "organic form" championed by both the German critic A.W. von Schlegel and his English follower Coleridge can be seen as a carry-over from neoclassical criticism—an attempt to assert unity in Shakespeare's plays where the three neoclassical unities were manifestly inapplicable. Still, unlike Digges, Coleridge was not reacting against Jonson in his declaration about the poet. (Though he undoubtedly knew the Horatian allusion, he had something else entirely in mind.) When he defended organic unity, Coleridge was not repeating a commonplace, as neoclassical criticism had learned to do by the end of the eighteenth century; he was defending something new and persuasive that persisted in its own turn as a critical assumption until the mid-twentieth century. Moreover, the new character criticism was more than a variation on the Horatian decorum of character. In short, Romantic critics set off in a genuinely new direction, which made an impact on the understanding of *Julius Caesar* as well as other plays.

The new direction was marked by character criticism in particular, which became the favored means of understanding Shakespeare's plays until the early twentieth century. "The unity of character pervades the whole of his dramas," Coleridge asserted, closely linking character with "the unity of feeling" (Bate 129), in deliberate contrast to the neoclassical three unities which represent merely mechanical coherence, imposed from without, rather than "organic form" (128). "In all his [Shakespeare's] various characters," Coleridge observes, in his clearest linking of character and organic form, "we still feel ourselves communing with the same human nature, which is every where present as the vegetable sap in the branches, sprays, buds, blossoms, and fruits, their shapes, tastes, and odours" (159–60).

Though the Romantics' emphasis on character continued some neoclassical critics' admiration for Shakespeare's characters, the Romantics explained characterization differently and tied it to a new conception of unity in the plays. Their view was so influential that it is still evident in the New Variorum Edition of *Julius Caesar*, published in 1913, which devotes the first two-thirds of its critical summary to "The Character of Caesar" and "The Character of Brutus" (386–420). Schlegel pointed the way in this direction with his declaration that "Caesar is not the hero of the piece, but Brutus" (Bate 374), a point on which critics differed repeatedly. Coleridge was frankly puzzled by Brutus: "I do not at present see into Shakespeare's motive, his rationale, or in what point of view he meant Brutus's character to appear" (375). Hazlitt, however, thought Brutus's character drives the plot (377). Continuing discussion of character in the New Variorum Edition by no means settled the long-running debate: the extensive comments merely illustrate how the debate originated in the Romantic assumption that Shakespearean characterization is the most important thing about the plays.

This assumption achieved its most magisterial expression in A.C. Bradley's *Shakespearean Tragedy* (1904), the effective culmination of the Romantic tradition. Although Bradley attended to just four plays— *Hamlet*, *Othello*, *King Lear*, and *Macbeth*—he noted in passing that Shakespearean tragedy "is pre-eminently the story of one person, the 'hero,'" and "in *Julius Caesar* Brutus is the 'hero'" (16). Writing shortly after Bradley, M.W. MacCallum treated the three plays Shakespeare derived from Plutarch in the vein of Bradley's character criticism, though MacCallum struck a balance in the Romantic debate about the "hero" of *Julius Caesar*. On one hand, MacCallum agreed with those who thought the "spirit of Caesar" (2.1.168, TLN 800) is present from first to last (214), even when Julius Caesar himself is not, and this "spirit," which eventually prevails in Octavius, the future first emperor, is according to MacCallum, "the spirit of Empire, the spirit of practical greatness in the domains of war, policy, organisation" (241). Brutus, on the other hand, is both "the model republican, the paragon of private and civic virtue" (233) and "the spirit of loyalty to duty" (241). Like Caesar, Brutus imperfectly represents the ideal he stands for, and the gap between spirit and human embodiment accounts both for personal inconsistencies on Caesar's and Brutus's parts and for Brutus's ultimate failure, which symbolizes the eclipse of republicanism by imperialism.

Coming at the end of a critical tradition, MacCallum was easy to dismiss as old-fashioned and out of touch, as J.C. Maxwell made clear in his mid-century summary of writing about the Roman plays (6). MacCallum anticipated two major movements in twentieth-century criticism of *Julius Caesar*, however, and for that alone he deserves acknowledgment. For one thing, his perception of Caesar's place in history is consistent with a critical tradition concerning Shakespeare, history, and politics that gathered strength and endured well past the time of Maxwell's summary. MacCallum pointed to two passages in North's translation of Plutarch that supported a providentialist reading of Caesar's rise (215–16). (For more such passages in Plutarch, see Miller 181–82.) MacCallum was impressed with this reading, because he thought it explained Shakespeare's view of Julius Caesar as "the spirit of Empire." Even the weaknesses that Shakespeare invented for Caesar, MacCallum maintains, including Caesar's self-deception, are "spots in the sun." Shakespeare is not concerned with them but rather with "the plenary inspiration of Caesar's life, the inspiration that made him an instrument of Heaven and that was to bring peace and order to the world" (230).

MacCallum's notion that Shakespeare saw powerful and influential men as "instruments of Heaven" acquired increasing solidity in the first half of the twentieth century and received its greatest impetus from E.M.W. Tillyard's *Shakespeare's History Plays* (1944). Tillyard reacted against Romantic character criticism, turning instead to the history of ideas and the presumed assumptions of Shakespeare's audience. Still, Tillyard's continuity with MacCallum on some points is evident. Henry VII and his dynasty fostered a "Tudor myth," Tillyard argues, concerning their progenitor's accession and marriage to Elizabeth of York as "the providential and happy ending of an organic piece of history" (29). Tillyard considers the driving force behind this myth to be a sense of historical cause and effect that first appeared in the Tudor chronicler Polydore Vergil (35). Henry IV's violation of divinely appointed royal rulership in his overthrow of Richard II almost a century before Henry VII's accession was an originating cause that "shows the justice of God punishing and working out the effects of a crime, till prosperity is re-established in the Tudor monarchy" (36). A dynamic historical principle thus complemented a static image of hierarchy, which Tillyard describes with copious contemporary references in *The Elizabethan World Picture*, also published in 1944. The point of intersection for history and image was the idea of *order*, the title of Chapter Two in *The Elizabethan World Picture*, where Tillyard cites Ulysses's speech on "degree" in *Troilus and Cressida*, as J.E. Phillips had done earlier (5–6). Order manifests itself both in the smoothly running monarchy (including legitimate succession) and in the obedience, deference, and degree of cosmic and political hierarchy.

Though Tillyard had little to say about *Julius Caesar*, his ideas soon became dominant in Shakespearean criticism, and their impact on subsequent interpretation of *Julius Caesar* is evident. J. Leeds Barroll brought enormous erudition to the task of showing that Shakespeare's contemporaries inherited a tradition of seeing providence in Roman history in much the same way that they saw it in English history. Augustus's "beneficial unification" of Rome after the civil wars was thus directly analogous to "the Tudor myth itself" (Barroll 328). Ernest Schanzer took a different view of the play, but his view required him explicitly to reject the providentialist reading, thereby confirming its importance in contemporary criticism by default. Schanzer thought *Julius Caesar* was a "problem" play because it focuses on a moral problem—namely, the sacrifice of "personal loyalties" "to political ideals" (*Problem* 68). He therefore disagreed that "the spirit of Caesar in the sense of 'Caesarism,' the absolute rule of a single man, informs the second part of the play" (35), and he took issue with J.E. Phillips on this point in particular (36n1).

The providentialist reading of Julius Caesar reached its high-water mark in *Shakespeare's Pagan World* (1973) by J.L. Simmons, who argued that the plays derived from Plutarch "are more genuinely Roman than is usually recognized" because they antedate Christian revelation and therefore offer a genuinely "pagan world," devoid of the moral clarity that one finds in the English history plays (7). Acknowledging Barroll's essay for this view (8n21), Simmons traces it to the Augustinian idea of history, which informs Thomas North's Epistle Dedicatory to Queen Elizabeth in his translation of Plutarch. Simmons also acknowledges, however, that Augustine's view is not one of providential triumphalism, and Simmons's reading of *Julius Caesar* follows suit. Citing the same passages on providential Caesarism from North's translation of Plutarch that MacCallum had cited, Simmons argues that "practical politics and providence" alike "urge the necessity of one-man rule" (72). In other words, a strong man is necessary to prevent political chaos, but Simmons offers minimal assent to the strong man himself, emphasizing both Shakespeare's invented character weaknesses in Caesar and the play's sympathy to Brutus. "The play develops a conflict between the good of Caesar (political order, stability, and glory), flawed by his potential evil, and Brutus's ideal of a world in which no Caesar is necessary, flawed by the nature of man" (86). Simmons's complex and ironic analysis and his emphasis on Caesar's weaknesses tests the providential reading about as strongly as it could be tested and still hold together. With the rise of new historicism and cultural materialism in the decade after Simmons's book appeared, reaction against Tillyard in particular became so strong that providentialist interpretations virtually disappeared from the critical record.

At just about the same time that "imperialist" readings of *Julius Caesar* began to lose favor, "republican" readings acquired increasing credibility. MacCallum had suggested this possibility too, in his defense of Brutus as "the model republican, the paragon of private and civic virtue" (233), and a long stage tradition, outlined below, had understood Brutus in just the way MacCallum describes him. But the new political interest in republicanism focused on more than Brutus. Allan Bloom thought Shakespeare paradoxically traced the destruction of the Republic to the greatest of its exemplars, Julius Caesar, who understood that "the corruption of the people is the key to mastery of Rome" (80), and Richard Henze similarly blamed the Republic's failure in *Julius Caesar* on the plebeians' craving for an absolute ruler. A.W. Bellringer argued more analytically that *Julius Caesar* marked the transition from Republic to Empire, because the expansion of the Republic had made its formative virtues inapplicable in a new political context that was defined by an open-ended struggle for power among patrician generals who had no new territory to conquer.

Bellringer's point was developed in an influential book-length study by Paul Cantor, who acknowledged Bloom (211n20) in arguing that *Coriolanus* and *Antony and Cleopatra* represent, respectively, the Republic and the Empire, with *Julius Caesar* as the transition from one to the other. For Cantor, as for Bellringer, "the Republic is corrupted and eventually destroyed by its very success in conquering the world" (Cantor 16). John Kayser and Ronald Lettieri not only developed Cantor's idea but also defended it on the basis of Elizabethan interest in the Roman Republic as a mixed polity (200), thus complicating the "imperialist" interpretation of *Julius Caesar* as an Elizabethan apology for the emergence of divine right monarchy (detailed references in Parker 112). Jan Blits analyzed the first scene of *Julius Caesar* in Cantor's terms, and John Velz ("*Orator*") discussed the play's political rhetoric as a marker of the transition Cantor had described. Dennis Barthory took Cantor's insight in the direction of classical ethics, arguing that in both *Coriolanus* and *Julius Caesar* self-knowledge and political knowledge are complementary, as they are in Plato, so that characters' failure to know themselves dooms the Republic from the beginning. John Alvis and Barbara Parker also invoked classical ethics in their readings of *Julius Caesar*, with Alvis seeing the Republic in the same way Bloom had, as a perfectly mixed constitution destroyed by Caesar's corruption of the plebs, and Parker arguing that Plato's *Republic* informs Shakespeare's Roman Republic, with the triumph of mob rule in *Julius Caesar* marking "the passage of democracy into tyranny" (117).

With the advent of new historicism and cultural materialism, interest in the Republic produced the most positive evaluation to date of Shakespeare's Roman plebeians. Annabel Patterson identified Shakespeare himself as a plebeian who consistently favored the "popular voice," including its expression in *Julius Caesar*. Alan Sinfield dismissed Patterson as too conservative (17) and imagined a staging of *Julius Caesar* that would clarify how the plebeians were disfranchised by the arrest of the tribunes and then manipulated by patricians into supporting a patrician program. Christopher Holmes similarly defended the plebeians, re-imagining the mob's treatment of Cinna the poet as a ritual "rough riding" rather than literal murder.

The second point in which MacCallum anticipated twentieth-century critical developments concerning *Julius Caesar* was his recognizing that inconsistency in the characters of both Caesar and Brutus should be identified as self-deception. Noting Caesar's fear of supernatural signs, MacCallum acknowledges "a touch of self-deception as well as of superstition in Caesar, and this self-deception reappears in other more important matters," such as Caesar's repeated insistence that he is not afraid (220–21). As for Brutus, MacCallum thought he was "doubly duped, by his own subtlety and his own simplicity in league with his conscientiousness ... and such self-deception avenges itself as surely as any intentional crime" (255). Despite these canny insights, MacCallum was so impressed by Caesar's superiority as an imperial ideal that he played down his own observation and understated the extent to which Shakespeare had made Caesar and Brutus resemble one another.

Though MacCallum was a neo-Romantic critic, his recognition of self-deception resonates strongly with postmodern criticism, because self-deception is a key expression of what Paul Ricoeur calls "suspicion" in postmodern thinking (31–36). Formative in postmodernism, Ricoeur points out, are the ideas of Marx, Freud, and Nietzsche, who all recognized a disjunction between conscious intention and unconscious motivation, thereby challenging the emphasis on rational consciousness that had prevailed in western thinking since Descartes ("I think, therefore I am"). Following Engels, Marx called this disjunction "false consciousness," but all three of Ricoeur's "masters of suspicion" acknowledged it in various forms. Long before Ricoeur, MacCallum used Ricoeur's key word, "suspicion," in describing Caesar's self-deception: "if anything could make us suspicious, it would be his constant harping on his flawless valour" (221). Paradoxically, however, the most thoughtful expounders of self-deception in Shakespeare, Stanley Cavell and Harry Berger, have not addressed *Julius Caesar*, and the topic has been discussed since MacCallum principally in historical terms, as a product of Shakespeare's reflection on neo-stoicism and skepticism.

MacCallum's understatement of his own insight concerning self-deception was most importantly corrected in an article by Norman Rabkin, who was at the forefront of many postmodern developments in Shakespearean criticism. Rabkin pointed out close parallels between two consecutive scenes in *Julius Caesar* (2.1 and 2.2), with the argument that Shakespeare invented the parallels in order to emphasize similarities between Caesar and Brutus. Brutus's soliloquy in 2.1 shows "a capacity to be deceived by analogies of his own making" ("Structure" 244), and Caesar's insistence on his fearlessness in 2.2 "degenerates immediately from magnificence to bluster, culminating in inflated self-adulation ironic in the context" (245). A peculiar "balance of perception and self-righteous blindness" is apparent in both men (246), and the point of their "wishful self-deception" (249) is that "the spirit of Caesar" is avenged in the destruction of its mirror image, so that the play becomes, in effect, a revenge tragedy, in which Brutus's "crime against established order" (251) is punished. Rabkin thus preserved a vestige of the providential reading, even referring to "Nemesis" (251n11), while emphasizing an ironic reading of character in *Julius Caesar* that would have been impossible for MacCallum.

The most perceptive discussion of self-deception in *Julius Caesar* is by Geoffrey Miles, who is the play's most careful historical critic. Frankly acknowledging that "my greatest debt is to Simmons" (2n2), Miles sets Simmons's providentialism aside while illuminating Simmons's point that Shakespeare's Rome is a "world apart" by emphasizing the distinctive interdependence of individual identity and social identity—both emphatically "Roman." Miles proceeds by tracing two traditions of stoic constancy, one Ciceronian and the other Senecan, that he thinks are especially important in Shakespeare's Plutarchan plays. A "flaw" in both traditions, Miles maintains, "is the failure of self-knowledge" (138), which marks all the characters in *Julius Caesar*, but especially Brutus. Though Brutus appeals to republican idealism, he "seems unaware how far his decision to kill Caesar is motivated by personal and family pride" (131–32). In other words, he is self-deceived about his motives, and Miles draws an appropriate postmodern conclusion: "The play has an almost Freudian sense of how emotion can work all the more powerfully because it is repressed" (132).

PRODUCTION HISTORY

The earliest recorded performance of *Julius Caesar* is in the "straw-thatched" Globe playhouse, as seen by Thomas Platter on September 11, 1599 (Schanzer, "Platter," 466). Newly rebuilt in Shoreditch from timbers of the Theatre, which had originally been constructed north of the city in 1576 (Shapiro 1–7), the Globe was polygonal and open to the sky in the center. The thatched roof covered three vertical tiers of seats, a large thrust stage, a "tiring house" behind the stage, and a small second-storey acting area built above the tiring house. The actors wore elaborate costumes, perhaps with some recognition of Roman togas and short swords for *Julius Caesar*, but they performed without sets on the main stage bare of all except minimal properties—perhaps a movable statue of Pompey and a "seat" for Caesar. The "pulpit" from which Brutus and Antony deliver their orations was likely the upper acting area, with unscripted noise from the plebeians on stage covering the time required for the actors playing Brutus and Antony to ascend stairs backstage, so they could deliver their speeches and return to the main stage. The "hill" that Pindarus ascends, at Cassius's command, to survey the progress of battle at Philippi (5.3.20, TLN 2500) may simply have been a different part of the main stage, though it too could have been the upper acting area, with unscripted stage business again covering the actor's ascent and descent.

Julius Caesar requires no recourse to a curtained "discovery space" at the rear of the main stage, beneath the upper acting area. Brutus's "tent" is referred to several times, in connection with his quarrel with Cassius (4.2.46, 51, TLN 1961, 1967) and his sighting of Caesar's ghost (4.3.242, 245, 247, TLN 2247, 2251, 2255), but the "tent" was probably an imaginative space on the main stage, created simply by allusions to it, like the "Senate House" where Caesar is murdered. Caesar's ghost may have entered from under the stage, by way of a trap door, as the ghost of old Hamlet seems to do at least once in *Hamlet*. If so, then the area beneath the stage was a symbolic "hell," with "heavens" (several times referred to in *Julius Caesar*) likely represented by a blue ceiling above the main stage, with stylized stars, moon, and constellations painted on it. The gods never appear in *Julius Caesar*, though they are repeatedly alluded to and even appealed to. The play's emphasis is decidedly on the "middle earth," represented by the main stage, between heaven and hell.

With the restoration of both the monarchy and the theaters in 1660, acting editions of *Julius Caesar* were adapted to prevailing tastes, "some modernizing the vocabulary, clarifying the syntax, and preserving decorum of expression" in the neoclassical manner (Ripley 26). The performance text remained little changed from the Folio of 1623 until the publication of six quartos after 1682, almost certainly in response to the popularity of Thomas Betterton in the role of Brutus at the Drury Lane

Theatre (Bartlett), which was an indoor acting space, with a proscenium arch and artificial lighting. Also noticeable after the Restoration is an increasing Whig-liberal interpretation of Brutus as the *de facto* hero of the play in his opposition to tyranny. Two couplets were added, for example, to Brutus's dying speech:

> Now one last look, and then farewell to all,
> That wou'd with the unhappy Brutus fall.
> Scorning to view his Country's Misery,
> Thus *Brutus* always strikes for Liberty. (Ripley 29)

A few years later, in 1706, John Dennis wrote a prologue to be spoken by "the Ghost of Shakespeare," making the Whig emphasis clear by evoking putative Catholic tyranny, explicitly comparing Caesar to Philip II of Spain and implicitly recalling the recent (1688) repudiation of James II (Ripley 23–24).

The Whig reputation of *Julius Caesar* may account for a decided decline of English interest in the play in the second half of the eighteenth century, at the very time it was first performed in the American colonies. The American production at Philadelphia's Southwark Theatre in June, 1770, depicted the "noble struggles for Liberty by that renowned patriot Marcus Brutus ... shewing the necessity of his [Caesar's] death" (Ripley 100), and the tyrant Caesar would not have brought King Philip II or King James II to the mind of this audience as readily as King George III. Despite the compatible subject, few colonial productions of *Julius Caesar* seem to have been mounted, probably because competent male actors were hard to find, and because Lewis Hallam (who played Brutus in Philadelphia) preferred "one-man plays in which he could shine alone" (Ripley 101).

English interest in *Julius Caesar* revived with the production directed by John Philip Kemble in 1812, which strove for increasing classical severity in presentation (Ripley 50). Kemble arranged actors on stage in statuesque and often symmetrical groupings, and he took advantage of his elaborate indoor acting space to surround the actors with painted flats that evoked an ideal Rome as their setting. He cut the text more heavily than any previous director, emphasizing Brutus's stoic aspirations more strongly than his republicanism. Kemble eliminated the few remaining ambiguities from Shakespeare's Brutus, playing the role with severe restraint and resisting the impulse to evoke audience sentiment with displays of feeling (Ripley 67). So successful was his conception of the play that "throughout the next eighty years audiences saw no production which did not owe a direct and profound debt to the 1812 revival" (Ripley 73). Principal among these were William Charles Macready's productions at midcentury, notable for even greater historical realism in setting than Kemble had achieved and for a more lavish use of supernumeraries—as many as 107, according to Macready's prompt book (Ripley 79). Kemble's emphasis on historical realism was complemented in Macready's productions by Macready's own acting, especially in the part of Brutus. While retaining a façade of stoic control, he allowed himself a greater range of emotional expression, so the sense of self-suppression came through more strongly in his acting, and audiences were riveted by the contrast (Ripley 89–90). The Romantic emphasis on expressive feeling as the definition of character undoubtedly contributed to Macready's innovation.

The precedent set by Kemble for historical realism in the theater reached its climax in the productions of *Julius Caesar* by Herbert Beerbohm Tree, beginning in 1898. Tree shifted the emphasis in his production for the first time since the Restoration away from Brutus and toward Antony. This shift had the incidental effect of emphasizing Caesar's vengeful spirit and thus anticipating the imperial view of Caesar that MacCallum would shortly articulate. Tree cut the text more heavily than any of his predecessors, because the time required to change elaborate sets and to move large numbers of hired extras around the stage required the sacrifice of dialogue.

The twentieth century saw two important innovations in productions of *Julius Caesar*. The first of these, paradoxically, was a return to the Folio text, as directors deliberately turned away from the heavily cut scripts of Kemble and his successors. Important names in this development are William Poel and Harley Granville-Barker, who moved decisively away from nineteenth-century production values to emphasize what they thought of as an Elizabethan style, including open staging, ensemble acting, swift-moving action, and minimal background scenery, in addition to an uncut text. Poel influenced William Bridges-Adams's first uncut production of *Julius Caesar* since the Restoration, directed in 1919 at Stratford-upon-Avon (Ripley 197). By reducing scene changes and encouraging actors to speak briskly and to the point, without declamatory emphasis, Bridges-Adams was able to get through most of the Folio's scripts with few cuts in about three hours (Ripley 198). In 1926

Harcourt Williams directed a production of *Julius Caesar* at the Old Vic Theatre in London, with John Gielgud playing Antony as the "undeniable star," despite ensemble acting (Ripley 237).

The second important innovation in twentieth-century productions of *Julius Caesar* was the use of modern costumes in modern settings. Credit for this idea goes to Orson Welles and his remarkable *Julius Caesar* at the Mercury Theatre in New York in 1937. Welles swept aside the American counterpart to Kemble's tradition in the most popular production of the play in American history (157 performances). Welles professed to admire Elizabethan production values, but his admiration included neither the text, which he cut severely and rearranged so it could be played in less than two hours, nor costuming. His point was to evoke a setting so contemporary and familiar that "theatre-goers found themselves startled to hear the characters speak blank verse" (Ripley 227). In both costume and action, Caesar was imagined as a fascist dictator; Antony, a demagogue; and Brutus, a well-meaning but hapless intellectual, played by Welles himself (Ripley 230). Welles thus implicitly repudiated the imperial Caesar in his production at just about the time it was gaining traction in criticism of the play. The Mercury Theatre set was abstract, multi-leveled, and unchanged throughout the performance, departing completely from the huge realistic flats depicting ancient Rome in nineteenth-century productions. What Welles sacrificed in the set he more than made up for in the lighting, designed by Jean Rosenthal, who "defined space, narrowing and widening it at will, faded scenes in and out with cinematic freedom, picked out key faces and threw them into sharpened focus as a camera might, and created atmosphere with a speed and flexibility undreamt of by conventional scenery" (Ripley 226). Welles's production encouraged modern-dress productions of *Julius Caesar* in Cambridge in 1938 and London in 1939, and the BBC's first televised production of *Julius Caesar* in 1938 imitated Welles's fascist theme (Ripley 243).

John Gielgud's promise as Antony in the 1926 Old Vic production of *Julius Caesar* was more than fulfilled in the Cassius he played at the Shakespeare Memorial Theatre in Stratford-upon-Avon in 1950—the first major revival of the play after World War II. Jointly directed by Antony Quayle (who played Antony) and Michael Langham, the production used the Folio text almost uncut and borrowed heavily from Elizabethan revivalist presentation while using the huge stage of the

Memorial Theatre and elaborate Roman costuming to full advantage. Not surprisingly, Gielgud was invited to reprise his role as Cassius in the first major film production of *Julius Caesar*, directed by Joseph L. Mankiewicz in 1953, though the actor that everyone remembered from that film was Marlon Brando, who was nominated for an Oscar as best actor in his role of Antony. Mankiewicz's film was shot in black and white, using historically suggestive Roman costumes and large crowd scenes as adapted previously to film by Cecil B. DeMille from the nineteenth-century theater. John Hoyt's straight-arm salute to Caesar, when Hoyt's Decius enters Caesar's house, may be authentically Roman, but for most people in 1953 it must have suggested a Nazi salute, and it may be a tribute to Welles's use of the straight-arm salute to enhance his conception of Caesar as a fascist dictator. A second film of *Julius Caesar* was directed by Stuart Burge in color in 1970, with Gielgud again in the cast, this time as Caesar. Considerably shorter, at 76 minutes, than Mankiewicz's version, Burge's movie cast Charlton Heston as Antony and Jason Robards as Brutus. The full-bearded conspirators (Brutus excepted) may have been inspired by bearded radicals of the 1960s, but the costumes and realistic setting, as in the earlier film, were meant to be Roman.

The second production of *Julius Caesar* for television was again undertaken by the BBC, almost fifty years after the first. Departing entirely from the Welles-influenced modern-dress version of 1938, director Herbert Wise used color photography, Roman period costuming, and several elaborate sets, including debris, standing water, and stained pavement on the streets of Rome and live horses before the battle of Philippi. Virtually uncut at 161 minutes, Wise's film took full advantage of the medium, emphasizing close camera work, often depicting full faces and thereby emphasizing expression, eye contact, and glances both voluntary and involuntary. Soliloquies were shot as voice-overs, with the actor saying the words as if thinking them, so that every expression of the face is emphasized as the soliloquy progresses. Nothing on stage or in film had ever done the like for *Julius Caesar*.

Major theatrical productions of *Julius Caesar* since 1950 have offered various versions of the two twentieth-century innovations: Elizabethan revivalism and free-wheeling adaptation, the latter ultimately inspired by Welles. Michael Langham directed the play for the first time in a "functional Elizabethan setting" (Ripley 252) in Stratford, Ontario, in 1955, using the thrust stage designed by Tanya Moiseiwitsch, with the audience seated on three sides and entrances and exits made from every direction. For the first time, the fluidity of Elizabethan staging combined with the nineteenth-century splendor of historical Roman costuming and military insignia to produce a "complex texture undreamt of in proscenium settings, however flexible" (Ripley 252). Tyrone Guthrie, Peter Hall, and Peter Brook, on the other hand, turned to contemporary dramatists such as Artaud, Brecht, and Beckett for inspiration in adapting Shakespearean texts to their own visions. John Blatchley looked to Brook's *Lear* of 1962 in his conception of *Julius Caesar* in 1963, staged by the recently established Royal Shakespeare Company. Blatchley aimed to expose the hypocrisy of power by suggesting that "the ends do not justify the means" in politics (Ripley 262), and designer John Bury created a Brecht-like "alienation effect" by costuming actors in togas worn over modern military uniforms and designing an abstract set that suggested nothing historically Roman.

Highly conceptual productions of this kind, with abstract sets and deliberately anachronistic or merely suggestive (rather than literal) costuming, have become characteristic of "postmodern" staging, a term that suggests the deliberate rejection of classical correctness and historical accuracy that marked "modern" production values in the eighteenth and nineteenth centuries. Used in this sense, "postmodern" describes Orson Welles's modern-dress production of *Julius Caesar* in 1937, though the term is usually reserved for more recent developments. Sean Holmes's production of *Julius Caesar* in Stratford-upon-Avon's Shakespeare Memorial Theatre, the final production before it was closed for extensive remodeling in late 2006, thus combined a fairly complete text, ensemble acting, and Roman togas with a set that suggested ancient Rome rather than trying in any sense to reproduce it on stage. When Caesar was assassinated, he fell at the feet of a realistic statue of Pompey, but the orations of Brutus and Antony were delivered from a steep, almost ladder-like metal construction that was installed mid-stage for the purpose. Bearing no resemblance to either a marble Roman rostrum or the upper acting area of the Globe, this *ad hoc* podium advertised itself as intrusively artificial and thereby visually reminded the audience that they were witnessing a sixteenth-century play about a first-century BCE event in a twenty-first century setting.

SHAKESPEARE'S LIFE

BY DAVID BEVINGTON

The website of the Internet Shakespeare Editions (http://internetshakespeare. uvic.ca), in the section "Life & Times," has further information on many topics mentioned here: Shakespeare's education, his religion, the lives and work of his contemporaries, and the rival acting companies in London.

William Shakespeare was baptized on 26 April 1564, in Holy Trinity Church, Stratford-upon-Avon. He is traditionally assumed to have been born three days earlier, on 23 April, the feast day of St. George, England's patron saint. His father, John Shakespeare, prospering for years as a tanner, glover, and dealer in commodities such as wool and grain, rose to become city chamberlain or treasurer, alderman, and high bailiff, the town's highest municipal position. Beginning in 1577, John Shakespeare encountered financial difficulties, with the result that he was obliged to mortgage his wife's property and miss council meetings. Although some scholars argue that he was secretly a Catholic, absenting himself also from Anglican church services for that reason, the greater likelihood is that he stayed at home for fear of being processed for debt. His wife, Mary, did come from a family with ongoing Catholic connections, but most of the evidence suggests that Shakespeare's parents were respected members of the Established Church. John's civic duties involved him in carrying out practices of the Protestant Reformation. John and Mary baptized all their children at the Anglican Holy Trinity Church, and were buried there.

As civic official, John must have sent his son William to the King Edward VI grammar school close by their house on Henley Street. Student records from the period have perished, but information about the program of education is plentifully available. William would have studied Latin grammar and authors, including Ovid, Virgil, Plautus, Seneca, and others that left an indelible print on the plays he wrote in his early years.

Shakespeare did not, however, go to university. The reasons are presumably two: his father's financial difficulties, and, perhaps even more crucially, Shakespeare's own marriage at the age of eighteen to Anne Hathaway. Neither Oxford or Cambridge would ordinarily admit married students. Anne was eight years older than William. She was also three months pregnant when they were married in November 1582. A special license had to be obtained from the Bishop of Worcester to allow them to marry quickly, without the customary readings on three successive Sundays in church of the banns, or announcements of intent to marry. The couple's first child, Susanna, was born in late May 1583. Twins, named Hamnet and Judith, the last of their children, followed in February 1585. Thereafter, evidence is scarce as to Shakespeare's whereabouts or occupation for about seven years. Perhaps he taught school, or was apprenticed to his father, or joined some company of traveling actors. At any event, he turns up in London in 1592. In that year, he was subjected to a vitriolic printed attack by a fellow dramatist, Robert Greene, who seems to have been driven by professional envy to accuse Shakespeare of being an "upstart crow" who had beautified himself with the feathers of other writers for the stage, including Christopher Marlowe, George Peele, Thomas Nashe, and Greene himself.

Shakespeare was indeed well established as a playwright in London by the time of this incident in 1592. In that same year Thomas Nashe paid tribute to the huge success of the tragic death of Lord Talbot in a play, and the only play we know that includes Talbot is Shakespeare's *1 Henry VI*. We do not know for what acting company or companies Shakespeare wrote in the years before 1594, or just how he got started, but he seems to have been an actor as well as dramatist. Two other plays about the reign of Henry VI also belong to those early years, along with his triumphantly successful *Richard III*. These four English history plays, forming his first historical tetralogy, were instrumental in defining the genre of the English history play. Following shortly after the great defeat of the Spanish Armada in 1588, these plays celebrated England's ascent from a century of devastating civil wars to the accession in 1485 of the Tudor Henry VII, grandfather of Queen Elizabeth I. Shakespeare's early work also includes some fine ventures into comedy, including *A Comedy of Errors*, *The Two Gentlemen of Verona*, *Love's Labor's Lost*, and *The Taming of the Shrew*. He wrote only one tragedy at this time, *Titus Andronicus*, a revenge tragedy based on fictional early Roman history. Shakespeare also turned his hand to narrative poetry in these early years. *Venus and Adonis* in 1593 and *The Rape of Lucrece* in 1594, dedicated to the Earl of Southampton, seem to show Shakespeare's interest in becoming a published poet, though ultimately he chose drama as more fulfilling and lucrative. He probably wrote some of his sonnets in these years, perhaps to the Earl of Southampton, though they were not published until 1609 and then without Shakespeare's authorization.

Shakespeare joined the newly-formed Lord Chamberlain's Men, as an actor-sharer and playwright, in 1594, along with Richard Burbage, his leading man. This group quickly became the premier acting company in London, in stiff competition with Edward Alleyn and the Lord Admiral's Men. For the Lord Chamberlain's group, Shakespeare wrote his second and more artistically mature four-play series of English histories, including *Richard II*, the two *Henry IV* plays centered on the Prince who then becomes the monarch and victor at Agincourt in *Henry V* (1599). He also wrote another history play, *King John*, in these years. Concurrently Shakespeare achieved great success in romantic comedy, with *A Midsummer Night's Dream*, *The Merchant of Venice*, and *The Merry Wives of Windsor*. He hit the top of his form in romantic comedy in three plays of 1598–1600 with similar throw-away titles: *Much Ado About Nothing*, *As You Like It*, and *Twelfth Night, or What You Will*. Having fulfilled that amazing task, he set comedy aside until years later.

During these years Shakespeare lived in London, apart from his family in Stratford. He saw to it that they were handsomely housed and provided for; he bought New Place, one of the two finest houses in town. Presumably he went home to Stratford when he could. He was comfortably well off, owning as he did one share among ten in an acting company that enjoyed remarkable success artistically and financially. He suffered a terrible tragedy in 1596 when his only son and heir, Hamnet, died at the age of eleven. In that year, Shakespeare applied successfully for a coat of arms for his father, so that John, and William too, could each style himself as gentleman. John died in 1601, Shakespeare's mother in 1608.

Having set aside romantic comedy and the patriotic English history at the end of the 1590s, Shakespeare turned instead to problematic plays such as *All's Well That Ends Well*, *Measure for Measure*, and *Troilus and Cressida*, the last of which is ambivalently a tragedy (with the death of Hector), a history play about the Trojan War, and a bleak existential drama about a failed love relationship. He also took up writing tragedies in earnest. *Romeo and Juliet*, in 1594–96, is a justly famous play, but in its early acts it is more a comedy than a tragedy, and its central figures are not tragic protagonists of the stature of those he created in

1599 and afterwards: *Julius Caesar, Hamlet, Othello, King Lear, Macbeth, Timon of Athens, Antony and Cleopatra*, and *Coriolanus*, this last play written in about 1608. Whether Shakespeare was moved to write these great tragedies by sad personal experiences, or by a shifting of the national mood in 1603 with the death of Queen Elizabeth and the accession to the throne of James VI of Scotland to become James I of England (when the Lord Chamberlain's Men became the King's Men), or by a growing skepticism and philosophical pessimism on his part, is impossible to say; perhaps he felt invigorated artistically by the challenge of excelling in the relatively new (for him) genre of tragedy.

Equally hard to answer with any certainty is the question of why he then turned, in his late years as a dramatist, to a form of comedy usually called romance, or tragicomedy. The genre was made popular by his contemporaries Beaumont and Fletcher, and it is worth noting that the long indigenous tradition of English drama, comprising the cycles of mystery plays and the morality plays, was essentially tragicomic in form. The plays of this phase, from *Pericles* (c. 1606–08) to *Cymbeline, The Winter's Tale*, and *The Tempest* in about 1608–11, would seem to overlap somewhat the late tragedies in dates of composition. These romances are like the early romantic comedies in many ways: young heroines in disguise, plots of adventure and separation leading to tearfully joyful reunions, comic high-jinks, and so on. Yet these late romances are also as tinged with the tragic vision that the dramatist had portrayed so vividly: death threatens or actually occurs in these plays, the emotional struggles of the male protagonists are nearly tragic in their psychic dimensions, and the restored happiness of the endings is apt to seem miraculous.

Shakespeare seems to have retired from London to Stratford-upon-Avon some time around 1611; *The Tempest* may have been designed as his farewell to the theater and his career as dramatist, after which he appears to have collaborated with John Fletcher, his successor at the King's Men, in *Henry VIII* and *The Two Noble Kinsmen* (1613–14). His elder daughter, Susanna, had married the successful physician John Hall in 1607. In his last will and testament Shakespeare left various bequests to friends and colleagues, but to Anne, his wife, nothing other than his "second-best bed." Whether this betokens any estrangement between him and the wife, whom he had married under the necessity of her pregnancy and from whom he then lived apart during the two decades or so when he resided and worked in London, is a matter of hot debate. Divorce was impossible, whether contemplated or not. He did take good care of her and his family, and he did retire to Stratford. Anne lived on with Susanna and John Hall until she died in 1623. Shakespeare was buried on 25 April 1616, having died perhaps on 23 April, fifty-two years to the day after his birth if we accept the tradition that he was born on the Feast of St. George. He lies buried under the altar of Holy Trinity, next to his wife and other family members. A memorial bust, erected some time before 1623, is mounted on the chancel wall.

SHAKESPEARE'S THEATER

BY DAVID BEVINGTON

The website of the Internet Shakespeare Editions (http://internetshakespeare. uvic.ca) includes an extensive discussion of the theaters of Shakespeare's time, and the audiences that attended them: click on "Life & Times" and choose the menu item "Stage."

Where Shakespeare's plays of the early 1590s were performed we do not know. When he joined the newly-formed Lord Chamberlain's Men in 1594, with Richard Burbage as his leading man, most public performances of Shakespeare's plays would have been put on in a building called The Theatre, since, when it was erected in 1576 by Richard Burbage's father James Burbage, it was the only structure in London designed specifically for the performance of plays, and indeed the first such building in the history of English theater. Earlier, plays were staged by itinerant companies in inns and innyards, great houses, churchyards, public squares, and any other place that could be commandeered for dramatic presentation. In Shakespeare's time the professional companies still toured, but to a lesser extent, and several of them also derived part of their income from private performances at court.

The Theatre had been erected in Shoreditch (also called Moorfields), a short walking distance north of London's walls, in order to evade the too-often censorious regulations of the city's governing council. There, spectators might have chosen to see *Romeo and Juliet*, *A Midsummer Night's Dream*, *The Merchant of Venice*, *King John*, or *Richard II*. They would also have seen some earlier Shakespeare plays that he had brought with him (perhaps as the price needed to pay for a share in the company) when he joined the Lord Chamberlain's Men: plays such as *Richard III* and *The Taming of the Shrew*. When in the late 1590s the Puritan-leaning owner of the land on which the building stood, Giles Allen, refused to renew their lease because he wished "to pull down the same, and to convert the wood and timber thereof to some better use," the Lord Chamberlain's Men performed for a while in the nearby Curtain Theatre. Eventually, in 1599, they solved their problem with the landlord by moving lock, stock, and barrel across the River Thames to the shore opposite from London, just to the west of London Bridge, where audiences could reach the new theater—the Globe—by bridge or by water taxi, and where the players were still outside the authority of the city of London. At the time of this move, the River Thames was frozen over solid in an especially harsh winter, so that possibly they slid the timbers of their theater across on the ice.

At any event, the Globe Theatre that they erected in Southwark, not far from the location of today's reconstructed Globe, was in the main the same building they had acted in before. Because timbers were all hand-hewn and fitted, the best plan was to reassemble them as much as was feasible. No doubt the company decided on some modifications, especially in the acting area, based on their theatrical experience, but the house remained essentially as before.

No pictures exist today of the interiors of the Theatre, the Curtain, or the Globe. We do have Visscher's View of London (1616) and other representations showing the exteriors of some theatrical buildings, but for the important matter of the interior design we have only a drawing of the Swan Theatre, copied by a Dutchman, Arend van Buchell, from a lost original by the Dutch Johannes de Witt when he visited London in about 1596–98. In many respects, the Swan seems to have been typical of such buildings. As seen in the accompanying illustration, the building appears to be circular or polygonal, with a thatched roof (called *tectum* in the illustration's labels) over the galleries containing seats and another roof over the stage, but leaving the space for standing spectators open to the heavens. (In the modern Globe, similarly constructed, spectators intending to stand in the yard for a performance can purchase a plastic rain poncho to ward off England's frequent rain showers.) From other kinds of information about Elizabethan playhouses, we can estimate a diameter of about 70 feet for the interior space. A large rectangular stage labeled the *proscaenium* (literally, "that which stands before the scene"), approximately 43 feet wide and 27 feet deep, juts out from one portion of the wall into the yard or *planities siue arena* ("the plain place or arena"). The stage stands about 5½ feet above the surface of the yard. Two pillars support the roof over the stage, which in turn is surmounted by a hut. A flag is flying at the top, while a trumpeter at a door in the hut is presumably announcing the performance of a play. The spectators' seats are arrayed in three tiers of galleries. Stairway entrances (*ingressus*) are provided for spectators to gain access from the yard to the seats, labeled *orchestra* on the first level and nearest the stage, and *porticus* above.

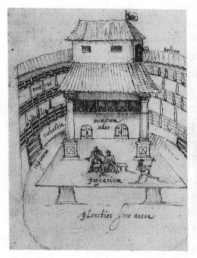

ABOVE, LEFT: This sketch of the Swan is the most complete we have of any theater of the time. The Swan was built in 1596; Shakespeare's company, The Chamberlain's Men, played there in the same year. RIGHT: This view of the first Globe by the Dutch engraver J.C. Visscher was printed in 1625, but must be taken from an earlier drawing, since the first Globe was burnt to the ground in 1613 at the first performance of Shakespeare's *Henry VIII*. There is substantial evidence that Visscher simplified the appearance of the theater by portraying it as octagonal: most scholars now believe that it had twenty sides, thus making it seem more circular than in this engraving.

The stage area is of greatest concern, and here the Swan drawing evidently does not show everything needed for performance in a theater such as the Globe. No trapdoor is provided, though one is needed in a number of Renaissance plays for appearances by ghostly or diabolical visitations from the infernal regions imagined to lie beneath the earth. The underside of the stage roof is not visible in this drawing, but from the plays themselves and other sources of information we gather that this underside above the actors' heads, known as the "heavens," displayed representations of the sun, moon, planets, and stars (as in today's London Globe). The back wall of the stage in the drawing, labeled *mimorum ades* or "housing for the actors," provides a visual barrier between the stage itself and what was commonly known as the "tiring house" or place where the actors could attire themselves and be ready for their entrances. The two doors shown in this wall confirm an arrangement evidently found in other theaters like the Globe, but the absence of any other means of access to the tiring house raises important questions. Many plays, by Shakespeare and others, seem to require some kind of "discovery space," located perhaps between the two doors, to accommodate a London shop, or a place where in *The Tempest* Prospero can pull back a curtain to "discover" Miranda and Ferdinand playing chess, or a place to which Falstaff, in the great tavern scene of *1 Henry IV*, can retire to avoid the Sheriff's visit and then be heard snoring offstage before he exits at scene's end into the tiring house. The modern Globe has such a discovery space.

Above the stage in the Swan drawing is what appears to be a gallery of six bays in which we can see seated figures watching the actors on the main stage, thereby surrounding those actors with spectators on all sides. But did theaters like the Swan or the Globe regularly seat spectators above the stage like this? Were such seats reserved for dignitaries and persons of wealth? Other documents refer to a "lords' room" in such theaters. The problem is complicated by the fact that many Elizabethan plays require some upper acting area for the play itself, as when Juliet, in Act II of *Romeo and Juliet*, appears "*above*" at her "*window*" to be heard by Romeo and then converses with him, or later, when Romeo and Juliet are seen together "*aloft*" at her "window" before Romeo descends, presumably by means of a rope ladder in full view of the audience, to go to banishment (3.5). Richard II appears "*on the walls*" of Flint Castle when he is surrounded by his enemies and is obliged to descend (behind the scenes) and then enter on the main stage to Bolingbroke (*Richard II*, 3.3). Instances are numerous. The gallery above the stage, shown in the Swan drawing, must have provided the necessary acting area "*above*." On those many occasions when the space was needed for action of this sort, seemingly the acting company would not seat spectators there. It is unclear how spectators sitting above would have seen action in the "discovery space" since it may have been beneath them.

On stage, in the drawing, a well-dressed lady, seated on a bench and accompanied perhaps by her lady-in-waiting, receives the addresses of a courtier or soldier with a long-handled weapon or staff of office. Even though the sketch is rough and imperfect, it does suggest the extent to which the plays of Shakespeare and his contemporaries were acted on this broad, open stage with a minimum of scenic effects. The actors would identify their fictional roles and their location by their dialogue, their costumes, and their gestures. On other occasions, when, for example, a throne was needed for a throne scene, extras could bring on such large objects and then remove them when they were no longer needed. Beds, as in the final scene of *Othello*, were apparently thrust on stage from the tiring house. The building itself was handsomely decorated and picturesque, so that the stage picture was by no means unimpressive, yet the visual effects were not designed to inform the audience about setting or time of the action. The play texts and the actors took care of that.

We have a verbal description of the Globe Theatre by Thomas Platter, a visitor to London in 1599, on the occasion of a performance of *Julius Caesar*. The description unfortunately says little about the stage, but it is otherwise very informative about the London playhouses:

> The playhouses are so constructed that they play on a raised platform, so that everyone has a good view. There are different galleries and places, however, where the seating is better and more comfortable and therefore more expensive. For whoever cares to stand below pays only one English penny, but if he wishes to sit, he enters by another door and pays another penny, while if he desires to sit in the most comfortable seats, which are cushioned, where he not only sees everything well but can also be seen, then he pays yet another English penny at another door. And during the performance food and drink are carried around the audience, so that for what one cares to pay one may also have refreshment.

Shakespeare's company may have included ten or so actor sharers, who owned the company jointly and distributed important roles among themselves. Richard Burbage was Shakespeare's leading man from 1594 until Shakespeare's retirement from the theater. Other actor sharers, such as John Heminges and Henry Condell, who would edit the First Folio collection of Shakespeare's plays in 1623, were his long-time professional associates. The quality of performance appears to have been high. Hired men generally took minor roles of messengers, soldiers, and servants. The women's parts were played by boys, who were trained by the major actors in a kind of apprenticeship and remained as actors of women's parts until their voices changed. Many went on in later years to be adult actors.

WILLIAM SHAKESPEARE AND *JULIUS CAESAR*:
A BRIEF CHRONOLOGY

(Some dates are approximate, notably those of Shakespeare's plays.)

100 BCE	Birth of Gaius Julius Caesar.
85	Birth of Marcus Junius Brutus and of Gaius Cassius Longinus (Cassius).
83	Birth of Marcus Antonius (Antony).
62	Birth of Gaius Octavius Thurinus (Octavius).
48	Caesar's defeat of Pompey at the battle of Pharsalus.
45	Caesar's defeat of Pompey's sons and his triumphal entry into Rome. Caesar's adoption of Octavius as his heir, renamed Gaius Julius Caesar Octavianus.
44	Caesar's assassination on 15 March ("Ides of March").
42	Defeat of Brutus and Cassius at the battle of Philippi, and their deaths by suicide.
31	Octavius's defeat of Antony at the battle of Actium.
30	Antony's death by suicide.
27	Octavius's title "Augustus" bestowed by the senate.
14 CE	Death of Augustus.
46–120	Life of Mestrius Plutarchus (Plutarch).
1509–47	Reign of Henry VIII.
1534	Act of Supremacy, declaring Henry VIII head of the Church of England.
1547–53	Reign of Edward VI.
1553–58	Reign of Mary I. Return to Catholicism.
1558–1603	Reign of Elizabeth I.
1563	Adoption of the Thirty-Nine Articles.
1564	William Shakespeare born April 23.
1569	Northern Catholic rebellion suppressed.
1576	James Burbage builds The Theatre.
1579	Sir Thomas North, *Plutarch's Lives*.
1582	Shakespeare's marriage to Anne Hathaway, November.
1583	Birth of Susanna, May 26.
1583–84	Plots against Elizabeth on behalf of Mary Queen of Scots.

1585	Births of Shakespeare's son Hamnet and his twin sister Judith, 2 February.
	Earl of Leicester sent to aid the Dutch against the Spanish.
1587	Execution of Mary Queen of Scots February 8.
1588	At some point, Shakespeare moves to London while his family remains in Stratford.
	War with Spain; the Spanish Armada fleet destroyed in July.
1588–94	Shakespeare writes the early comedies and histories and the early tragedy *Titus Andronicus*.
1592	Shakespeare attacked in print by Robert Greene.
1593	*Venus and Adonis*.
1593–1603	*The Sonnets*.
1594	Shakespeare joins the Lord Chamberlain's Men; *The Rape of Lucrece*.
1594–95	*A Midsummer Night's Dream, Richard II, Romeo and Juliet*.
1596–98	*The Merchant of Venice, Henry IV Parts 1 and 2*.
1597	Earl of Essex sent to Ireland to put down a rebellion led by the Earl of Tyrone.
1598–99	*Much Ado About Nothing, The Merry Wives of Windsor*.
1599	Shakespeare's company moves to the newly built Globe; *As You Like It, Henry V, Julius Caesar* (seen by Thomas Platter).
	Prohibition and public burning of satires.
1600–02	*Twelfth Night, Troilus and Cressida, Hamlet, All's Well That Ends Well*.
1601	Shakespeare's father dies.
	Essex's abortive rebellion and his execution.
	Thomas Dekker, *Satiromastix*; Ben Jonson, *Poetaster*; the "Poet's War."
1603	Shakespeare's company the Chamberlain's Men becomes the King's Men.
	Death of Elizabeth I; coronation of James I, March 24.
1603–04	*Measure for Measure, Othello*.
1604	James's confrontation of the Puritans at the Hampton Court Conference. Peace with Spain.
1605	The Gunpowder Plot foiled 5 November.

1605–06	*King Lear.*
1606–07	*Macbeth, Timon of Athens, Antony and Cleopatra, Pericles.*
1608	*Coriolanus.*
1609–11	*Cymbeline, The Winter's Tale, The Tempest.*
1613–14	*Henry VIII, The Two Noble Kinsmen.*
	Shakespeare in retirement, living in Stratford. Globe burns and is soon rebuilt.
1616	Death of Shakespeare, 23 April.
1623	First publication of *Julius Caesar* in the folio assembled by Shakespeare's fellow actors.

A NOTE ON THE TEXTS

Julius Caesar appeared in only one early version, and all subsequent texts are based on it. This is the version in the First Folio, printed seven years after Shakespeare's death by William and Isaac Jaggard as a profit-making venture undertaken by four investors named on the last page of the book. The publishers were assisted in their venture by John Heminge and Henry Condell, Shakespeare's fellow actors, who added their names to a brief and much-quoted preface, "To the great Variety of Readers." This Broadview text is taken directly from the facsimile of the First Folio that Charlton Hinman prepared and published with W.W. Norton in 1968.

Hinman's facsimile has been modernized in this edition according to the protocols for modernizing Shakespeare that have been laid down in the Guidelines for Editors of the Internet Shakespeare Edition, for which this text was originally prepared. The point of modernizing has been to reduce impediments to clarity and comprehension for a modern reader while remaining as faithful as possible to the Folio text. The principal alterations have been made in scene divisions, stage directions, spelling, punctuation, and lineation. For a complete description of the alterations, together with an explanation of them and a list of editions consulted, see the textual introduction to the ISE *Julius Caesar* at http://internetshakespeare.uvic.ca/Library/Texts/JC/intro/TextIntro/default/.

Scene divisions in this edition follow standard editorial practice since the eighteenth century. Customary practice in printed editions is to number lines of spoken verse and prose according to each scene, so that lines are designated by act, scene, and line number. In the present edition, lines are also numbered according to the Hinman Folio, which counts all typographical lines, including stage directions, from beginning to end. This is called "through-line numbering," and its abbreviation "TLN" is used in this edition's Introduction and footnotes. The line numbers of the Broadview text do not conform perfectly to Hinman's through-line numbering, but the difference is very slight, and the advantage of using TLN is precise reference to the Folio text in Hinman's edition, as well as to the online text on the website of the Internet Shakespeare Edition, from which the Broadview text is taken.

Cumulative TLNs are marked at the top of each page of the Broadview text.

The texts in the appendices have been lightly edited for this edition from the sixteenth- and seventeenth-century printed editions of Plutarch's *Lives* and Montaigne's *Essays*, respectively. Spelling and punctuation have been modernized, and brief notes added to assist the modern reader. The texts are based on scanned transcriptions of the original printed editions taken from the Internet.

CHARACTERS IN THE PLAY

While no list of characters appears in the First Folio, a list was added in 1709 by the play's first editor, Nicholas Rowe, and subsequent editors adopted it and added to it. The eighteenth-century practice of listing characters by order of presumed social rank (including all males before females) has since yielded to other organizational methods. The following list is organized by the perceived political prominence of characters in the play, together with their closest adherents in each case.

JULIUS CAESAR (Gaius Julius Caesar), born in 100 BCE to a patrician family, rose through military and political skill, daring, and luck during the turmoil of civil war that marked the late Roman republic. The alliance he formed with Crassus and Pompey in 60 enabled Caesar to become consul, but after he established his supremacy in the conquest of Gaul, the alliance failed, and he defeated Pompey at the battle of Pharsalus, in northern Greece, in 48. Pompey fled to Egypt, where he was killed, and where Caesar restored Cleopatra VII to power and conceived a son with her. After a triumphal return to Rome in 46, Caesar faced another war, this time with Pompey's sons, whom he defeated in Spain only with difficulty, again returning triumphantly to Rome in 45, when the play begins, conflating Caesar's second triumph with the feast of Lupercalia, 15 February 44. Shakespeare assigns Caesar only about a fourth as many lines as Brutus, and Shakespeare's unflattering portrait of the indomitable conqueror is in keeping with Plutarch's summary: "So he reaped no other fruit of all his reign and dominion, which he had so vehemently desired all his life, and pursued with such extreme danger, but a vain name only, and a superficial glory, that procured him the envy and hatred of his country" (Appendix A1, p. 204).

CALPURNIA (Calpurnia Pisonis, b. 75 BCE) was the third wife of Julius Caesar, whom he married to cement a political alliance with her father after divorcing his second wife, Pompeia. He was prepared to divorce Calpurnia as well, in order to pursue another political alliance by marrying Pompey's daughter, but Calpurnia remained devoted to him nonetheless, and according to Plutarch tried in vain to prevent Caesar' going to the Capitol on the day he was assassinated (Appendix A1, p. 198–99). One of only two named parts for women in *Julius Caesar*, her role was likely played by one of the Chamberlain's Men's leading boy actors in 1599.

MARK ANTONY (Marcus Antonius, b. 83 BCE) tied his fortunes closely to Caesar's, at one point becoming *flamen* or priest to Caesar in the latter's quest for divine status. Plutarch records Antony's offering Caesar a royal diadem during the Lupercalia on 15 February 44 (Appendix A1, p. 196). After Caesar's assassination, Antony showed considerable political adroitness, eventually forming a triumvirate with Octavius and Lepidus in 43. He was married to Fulvia, his third wife, in 47 or 46, and after Fulvia's death he married Octavia, Octavius's sister, in 40, but he also conceived three children with Cleopatra VII of Egypt. Shakespeare depicts Antony's liaison with Cleopatra and eventual defeat by Octavius in *Antony and Cleopatra*.

OCTAVIUS (born Gaius Octavius Thurinus, 63 BCE), grandson of Julius Caesar's sister, was adopted as heir by Caesar in 45 when Octavius was just seventeen years old. Managing his affairs, despite his youth, with remarkable skill and forcefulness after Caesar's assassination, Octavius eventually formed a triumvirate with Lepidus and Mark Antony, who married Octavius's sister, Octavia, to cement an alliance between them. Shakespeare depicts Octavius's defeat of his former ally in *Antony and Cleopatra*, which hints at the coming *pax Romana* established by Octavius when he became sole ruler of the late Roman republic and the first *de facto* emperor, with the title "Augustus" conferred on him by the senate in 27.

LEPIDUS (Marcus Aemilius Lepidus, b. c. 89 BCE) allied himself with Caesar in the civil wars and then with Antony after Caesar's assassination, eventually forming a triumvirate with Antony and Octavius in 43 BCE. Though he outranked his fellow triumvirs in inherited status, they outmaneuvered him politically, as Shakespeare shows in both *Julius Caesar* and *Antony and Cleopatra*.

BRUTUS (Marcus Junius Brutus) was born in 85 BCE, the proud scion of ancient defenders of the Roman republic, including Lucius Junius Brutus (alluded to in 1.2.158–61, 2.1.53–54, TLN 258–60, 672–73), in whose name Brutus issued coins in 55. He survived the instability of civil war in the late republic through canny financial dealing and astute political maneuvering with both Pompey, who had murdered Brutus's father, and with Pompey's rival, Caesar. Brutus divorced his first wife, Claudia, to marry Portia in 45 and joined the conspirators against Caesar in February 44. Failing to win popular support after Caesar's assassination, Brutus left Rome for Greece, seized the supplies Caesar had laid up for his Parthian campaign, and collected enormous sums from the treasuries of the eastern provinces, thus providing for an army with which to confront Antony and Octavius. The battle Shakespeare depicts at Philippi was in fact two battles in 42, with Brutus prevailing in the first against Octavius but suffering defeat and being deserted by his troops in the second. His part in *Julius Caesar* is by far the longest, about four times as long as the part for Caesar.

PORTIA (Porcia Catonis, b. c. 70 BCE), daughter of Marcus Porcius Cato and widow of Calpurnius Bibulus (Appendix A2, p. 211), married Brutus in 45 BCE, after he divorced his first wife. Plutarch describes her commitment to republican idealism, her pressing Brutus for details of the plot against Caesar, and her self-wounding. Portia died by her own hand in 43, after Brutus fled to Greece. Apart from Calpurnia's role, this is the only named part for a woman in the play, and it would have been taken by a leading boy actor in 1599.

LUCIUS and STRATO are depicted as servants of Brutus, though the latter has a Greek name (Straton) and is identified by Plutarch as a rhetorician who had taught Brutus (Appendix A2, p. 235). He appears for the first time late in the play, as if Brutus had met him in Greece, and he holds the sword on which Brutus dies. Shakespeare entirely invented the character of Lucius, though he had used the name in several other plays, as well as its Italian counterpart, Lucio.

CASSIUS (Gaius Cassius Longinus, b. before 85 BCE) supported Pompey in his contest with Caesar but made peace by seeking pardon from Caesar after Pompey was defeated at Pharsalus. Cassius competed with Brutus for a praetorship, which Caesar awarded to Brutus. Nevertheless, Cassius took a major part in the conspiracy with Brutus against Caesar and assisted Brutus in raising an army in the east to meet the triumvirs after Caesar's assassination. Believing he faced defeat in the first battle of Philippi in 42, Cassius killed himself. Though a minor figure in Roman history, Cassius has a large role in *Julius Caesar*, perhaps because of Plutarch's pungent summary of his character (Appendix A2, pp. 207–08), which helps to explain how Shakespeare imagines him.

CASCA (Publius Servilius Casca Longus, d. 42 BCE) is twice mentioned by Plutarch as the first conspirator to strike Caesar (Appendices A1, p. 201; A2, p. 214), but Casca's character is almost entirely made up by Shakespeare, who wrote a part for him almost as large as Caesar's.

DECIUS (Decimus Junius Brutus Albinus, b. c. 85 BCE) is described by Plutarch as so trusted by Caesar that Caesar made him his heir (Appendix A1, p. 199), though Decius joined the conspiracy and successfully persuaded Caesar to discount Calpurnia's fears, as Shakespeare writes. Humphreys notes that Decius's "participation is gross treachery, and carried through most unscrupulously" (127n).

CINNA (Lucius Cornelius Cinna) was Caesar's brother-in-law and had been pardoned by Caesar after Cinna joined a revolt led by Marcus Aemilius Lepidus, father of the triumvir, in 78 BCE. Prior to the assassination of Caesar, Cinna spoke publicly against Caesar but remained on the fringes of the conspiracy, just as Shakespeare depicts him, though he is the first to declare freedom after Caesar is struck down (3.1.78, TLN 1289).

METELLUS CIMBER was properly Lucius Tullius Cimber (d. 42 BCE), though both names appear in Plutarch. As a conspirator in *Julius Caesar*, he distracts Caesar by appealing for his banished brother's repeal, but Plutarch adds that Cimber threw Caesar's toga over his head to blind him and to signal the other conspirators to attack (Appendices A1, p. 201; A2, p. 214), a gesture which has been followed in some productions. Cimber's part in the play ends with the assassination.

TREBONIUS (Trebonius Gaius, d. 43 BCE) was a *tribunus plebes*, like Shakespeare's Flavius and Murellus, and he joined the conspirators against Caesar despite being made consul by Caesar in 45, the year before the assassination. Shakespeare follows Plutarch (Appendix A2, p. 214) in making Trebonius the conspirator who takes Antony aside before Caesar is attacked. He has a small part, with no lines following the assassination scene.

CAIUS LIGARIUS (Quintus Ligarius) was pardoned by Caesar for allying with Pompey, though Ligarius's hatred of tyranny inclined him to join the conspiracy anyway, despite being sick (Appendix A2, pp. 209–10). His brothers were killed after the assassination, but his own fate is unknown.

LUCILIUS and TITINIUS are Roman officers known only from Plutarch. Lucilius guards Brutus's tent during the night before the battle of Philippi and impersonates Brutus during the battle in order to draw enemy attention away from his commander (5.4.7–8, TLN 2610–11, Appendix A2, pp. 233–34). Shakespeare follows Plutarch in identifying Titinius as Cassius's officer, who kills himself when he sees Cassius dead (Appendix A2, pp. 231–32). Cassius earlier names an officer serving with Caesar in Spain as Titinius (1.2.127, TLN 225).

MESSALA (Marcus Valerius Messalla Corvinus) was born in 64 BCE, just two years before Octavius, whose fortunes he eventually followed. He fought with Cassius at Philippi, where he distinguished himself, then transferred his loyalty to Antony before finally allying with Octavius, for whom he proposed the title *pater patriae* in 2 BCE. Shakespeare imagines him as the messenger to Brutus concerning the death of Portia (4.3.188–89, TLN 2184–85), but Shakespeare follows Plutarch in depicting Messala's part in the battle of Philippi.

YOUNG CATO (Marcus Porcius Cato the younger, b. c. 73 BCE) was son of one of Caesar's proudest and most bitter enemies, as Shakespeare's Cato himself proclaims (5.4.4–6, TLN 2606–08). Cato the elder had committed suicide in 46 rather than accept Caesar's offer to pardon him for his support of Pompey. It is not surprising, therefore, that young Cato joins the conspirators after Caesar's assassination, and Shakespeare follows Plutarch (Appendix A2, p. 233) in depicting Cato's death at Philippi.

VARRUS and CLAUDIO are officers in Brutus's army whom he asks to sleep in his tent during the night before the battle of Philippi. Their names may be transposed from elsewhere in Plutarch (Varro and Claudius), but Shakespeare invented their roles; and as the variant spellings are consistent in all dialogue concerning them, it is not clear whether they are a mistake he would have corrected if a conscientious editor had pointed it out to him.

CLITUS, DARDANIUS, and VOLUMNIUS are soldiers in Brutus's army whom Brutus asks successively to assist him in his suicide, though all refuse and eventually flee, before Strato finally accedes to the request. Plutarch says Brutus puts the request to Volumnius "for the studies' sake which had brought them acquainted together" (Appendix A2, p. 235), a detail Shakespeare mentions in 5.5.26–27, TLN 2670–71.

CICERO (Marcus Tullius Cicero, b. 106 BCE) is perhaps the most famous and influential thinker and writer of ancient Rome, though Shakespeare gives him a very small part (just nine lines in one scene). He was murdered in the purge following Caesar's assassination, as Messala reports (4.3.179–80, TLN 2174). He did not join the conspiracy, though he publicly praised its outcome and condemned Antony as Caesar's successor.

PUBLIUS is a senator whom Shakespeare invented to play a minor but distinctive role. Knowing nothing of the conspiracy, he arrives at Caesar's house on the morning of March 15 simply to accompany Caesar to the senate (2.2.108–09, TLN 1103–05). Still knowing nothing, he prevents Artemidorus from warning Caesar (3.1.10, TLN 1214), and he registers shock and surprise when the deed is done (3.1.86–91, TLN 1297–1305). In short, he is an innocent bystander, caught up in affairs of which he has no knowledge. He is not to be confused with Publius Cimber, Metellus Cimber's fictional brother (3.1.57–73, TLN 1260–81).

POPILIUS LENA (Popilius Laena) is a senator, otherwise unknown, described by Plutarch (Appendix A2, p. 212) in a tense moment that Shakespeare mirrors closely. Popilius wishes Cassius well and strikes fear in the conspirators' hearts by talking quietly to Caesar just before the murder, until Brutus notices that neither Popilius nor Caesar registers any alarm (3.1.13–24, TLN 1217–30).

FLAVIUS and MURELLUS are *tribuni plebes*, loyal to Pompey and his sons and therefore indignant at the plebeians' celebration of Caesar's triumph as the play opens. The tribunes reappear silently in the next scene (1.2.2, TLN 86) and are later reported by Casca as "put to silence" (1.2.279, TLN 389–90) presumably by Caesar, as Plutarch reports (Appendices A1, p. 196; A3, p. 239). Murellus is called "Marullus" in Plutarch (Appendix A1, p. 196), and the eighteenth-century editor Theobald changed the name accordingly; but the Folio consistently uses "Murellus," and it is not a demonstrable mistake on Shakespeare's part.

A SOOTHSAYER (or prophetic seer) appears in Plutarch (Appendix A1, p. 198), as he does in Shakespeare, to warn Caesar about the Ides of March, and Caesar laughs off the warning when the day arrives, to which the Soothsayer offers a witty response (3.1.2, TLN 1205). Shakespeare invents his dialogue with Portia.

ARTEMIDORUS is identified by Plutarch as a "doctor of rhetoric in the Greek tongue" (Appendix A1, p. 200) who tried to warn Caesar of the conspiracy against him.

CINNA THE POET (Gaius Helvius Cinna) belonged to the circle of Alexandrian poets that included Catullus. Records of his poetry survive but not the poetry itself. The cruel manner of his death is recorded by Plutarch, as well as his prophetic dream and his friendship with Caesar (Appendix A1, p. 203).

Another POET who appears briefly, this time to protest the quarrel between Brutus and Cassius, is identified in North's translation of Plutarch as Marcus Phaonius (Favonius, b. c. 90 BCE) (Appendix A2, pp. 221–23), a cynic philosopher.

PINDARUS is identified by Plutarch as a Parthian freedman, captured in battle by Cassius and reserved for the purpose of assisting him in suicide, should the need arise (Appendix A2, p. 231), as it eventually does, both in Plutarch's account and in Shakespeare's.

The COBBLER is one of Shakespeare's most brilliantly inventive unnamed commoners, similar in many ways to the gravedigger who appears in Hamlet, written shortly after Julius Caesar. This is the only cobbler in all Shakespeare's writing, and the man's character reflects the derivation of the name for his craft: to cobble, or roughly patch up or put together, eventually applied principally to shoes (OED)—a duplicity of meaning that the cobbler deliberately exploits (1.1.10–11, TLN 14–15).

THE TRAGEDY OF JULIUS CAESAR

[1.1]¹

*Enter Flavius, Murellus,² and certain commoners over the stage.*³
FLAVIUS. Hence! Home, you idle creatures!⁴ Get you home!
  Is this a holiday? What, know you not,
  Being mechanical,⁵ you ought not walk
  Upon a laboring day, without the sign
  Of your profession?⁶ Speak, what trade art thou?   5
CARPENTER. Why, sir, a carpenter.⁷
MURELLUS. Where is thy leather apron and thy rule?⁸
  What dost thou with thy best apparel on?
  You, sir, what trade are you?
COBBLER. Truly, sir, in respect of⁹ a fine workman, I am but as   10
  you would say, a cobbler.¹⁰
MURELLUS. But what trade art thou? Answer me directly.¹¹

---

1 The play's first scene is continuous with its second, both occurring on the "feast of Lupercalia" (see Appendix A1, p. 195), 15 February 44 BCE, though Shakespeare has conflated the religious festival with Caesar's triumph which occurred the previous October. The arresting opening scene, with its powerful confrontation between tribunes and people and its background suggestion of one strong man replacing another, was prompted by just two sentences in North's Plutarch, which Shakespeare brilliantly expanded: "After that, there were set up images of Caesar in the city with diadems upon their heads, like kings. Those, the two tribunes, Flavius and Marullus, went and pulled down: and furthermore, meeting with them that first saluted Caesar as king, they committed them to prison" (Appendix A1, p. 196).
2 Most modern editions spell this name as North did—Marullus—though the First Folio spells it Murellus; see Characters in the Play, p. 73.
3 From the opposite direction of the tribunes.
4 Expressing reprobation or contempt.
5 Working class, common laborers.
6 Mark of your respective handicrafts, i.e., working clothes.
7 Timber framer or worker in heavy wood, in contrast to a "joiner" or fine workman.
8 (1) Measuring stick; (2) self-control, sense of propriety.
9 In comparison to.
10 (1) Patcher, mender, bungler; (2) maker and mender of shoes.
11 Without equivocation or misdirection.

COBBLER. A trade, sir, that I hope I may use, with a safe[1] conscience, which is indeed sir, a mender of bad soles.

15 FLAVIUS. What trade, thou knave?[2] Thou naughty knave, what
trade?

COBBLER. Nay, I beseech you, sir, be not out with me. Yet if you
be out,[3] sir, I can mend you.

MURELLUS. What mean'st thou by that? Mend me, thou saucy[4]
20 fellow?

COBBLER. Why, sir, cobble you.

FLAVIUS. Thou art a cobbler, art thou?

COBBLER. Truly sir, all that I live by is with the awl.[5] I meddle[6]
with no tradesman's matters,[7] nor women's matters;[8] but
25 withal[9] I am indeed, sir, a surgeon to old shoes: when they are
in great danger, I recover[10] them. As proper[11] men as ever trod
upon neat's leather,[12] have gone upon my handiwork.

FLAVIUS. But wherefore art not in thy shop today?
Why dost thou lead these men about the streets?

30 COBBLER. Truly sir, to wear out their shoes, to get myself into
more work. But indeed, sir, we make holiday to see Caesar, and
to rejoice in his triumph.[13]

MURELLUS. Wherefore rejoice? What conquest brings he home?
What tributaries[14] follow him to Rome,
35 To grace in captive bonds his chariot wheels?
You blocks! You stones! You worse than senseless things!
O you hard hearts! You cruel men of Rome!

---

1 Morally upright.
2 (1) Male commoner; (2) crafty rogue.
3 Removed from your equable or amicable state of mind, "put out"; have holes
in your shoes.
4 Insolent towards superiors, presumptuous.
5 Everything; a shoemaker's pointed tool for making holes in leather; penis.
6 (1) Concern or busy myself with; (2) have sexual intercourse with.
7 Craftsmen's politics.
8 Sexual matters.
9 (1) In addition, besides, moreover; (2) all things considered (3) with my awl.
10 (1) Repair, resole; (2) restore health or wholeness to a person.
11 Excellent, admirable.
12 Cowhide.
13 Triumphal entry into Rome.
14 Those who pay tribute.

POMPEY (TLN 44)

Properly named Gnaeus Pompeius, the historical figure whom Shakespeare consistently calls Pompey was defeated by Caesar at Pharsalus and murdered in Egypt in 48 BCE. Six years older than Caesar, Pompey enjoyed early military success in ridding the Mediterranean of pirates and subduing the East (Syria and Judaea) for Rome. Caesar negotiated a three-way agreement among Pompey, Crassus, and himself in 60 BCE, including Pompey's marriage to Caesar's daughter Julia (Pompey's third marriage). Julia died in 54 BCE and Crassus a year later, increasing rivalry and tension between Caesar and Pompey that eventually resulted in open warfare and Pompey's defeat. Plutarch accords Pompey a biography in his *Lives*; and, in plays other than *Julius Caesar* itself, Shakespeare alludes to Pompey about four times as often as to Caesar.

Bust of Pompey, copied from a Roman original about 70 BCE. Used by permission of the Museo Archeologico Nationale di Venezia.

Knew you not Pompey many a time and oft?
Have you climbed up to walls and battlements,
40   To towers and windows, yea, to chimney tops,
Your infants in your arms, and there have sat
The livelong day, with patient expectation,
To see great Pompey pass the streets of Rome?[1]
And when you saw his chariot but appear,
45   Have you not made an universal shout,
That Tiber[2] trembled underneath her banks
To hear the replication of your sounds,
Made in her concave[3] shores?
And do you now put on your best attire?
50   And do you now cull[4] out a holiday?
And do you now strew flowers in his way
That comes in triumph over Pompey's blood?[5]
Begone!
Run to your houses! Fall upon your knees!
55   Pray to the gods to intermit the plague
That needs must light[6] on this ingratitude!
FLAVIUS. Go, go, good countrymen, and for this fault
Assemble all the poor men of your sort;
Draw them to Tiber banks,[7] and weep your tears
60   Into the channel, till the lowest stream
Do kiss the most exalted shores of all.[8]

Exeunt all the Commoners.

See whe'er[9] their basest mettle[10] be not moved:
They vanish tongue-tied in their guiltiness.
Go you down that way towards the Capitol;

---

1 Pompey added "Magnus" to his name in 81 BCE.
2 The river that flows through Rome.
3 Hollow, as in hollowed out river banks.
4 Pick, choose arbitrarily.
5 (1) Pompey's own blood; (2) Pompey's blood relations, i.e., his sons.
6 Suspend the plague that must necessarily fall.
7 Tiber's banks.
8 Flavius urges the plebeians to make amends for their fault in celebrating Caesar by weeping in the Tiber until it reaches flood stage.
9 Whether.
10 Temperament (with play on "metal" understood according to alchemical hierarchy).

This way will I. Disrobe the images, 65
If you do find them decked with ceremonies.[1]
MURELLUS. May we do so?
You know it is the Feast of Lupercal.[2]
FLAVIUS. It is no matter. Let no images
Be hung with Caesar's trophies. I'll about, 70
And drive away the vulgar from the streets;
So do you too, where you perceive them thick.
These growing feathers, plucked from Caesar's wing,
Will make him fly an ordinary pitch,
Who else would soar above the view of men, 75
And keep us all in servile fearfulness.[3]   *Exeunt.*

[1.2][4]

Enter Caesar, Antony for the course,[5] Calpurnia, Portia, Decius, Cicero,
Brutus, Cassius, Casca, a Soothsayer; after them Murellus and Flavius.
CAESAR. Calpurnia.

CASCA.   Peace ho! Caesar speaks.

CAESAR.   Calpurnia!

CALPURNIA. Here, my Lord.

CAESAR. Stand you directly in Antonio's way
When he doth run his course. Antonio!

ANTONY. Caesar, my Lord? 5

CAESAR. Forget not in your speed, Antonio,
To touch Calpurnia, for our elders say,
The barren touchèd in this holy chase,
Shake off their sterile curse.[6]

ANTONY.   I shall remember.
When Caesar says, "Do this," it is performed. 10

---

1 External accessories of pomp.
2 15 February.
3 "Disabling Caesar like a falcon will prevent his rise to a high pitch (the highest point a falcon reaches before swooping on prey), so far out of sight of men
as to be a god" (Daniell, 161n.).
4 Caesar's triumph continues on the feast of Lupercalia.
5 Costumed to run.
6 Curse of sterility.

CAESAR. Set on, and leave no ceremony out. [*Sennet*][1]

SOOTHSAYER. Caesar!

CAESAR. Ha? Who calls?

CASCA. Bid every noise be still! Peace yet again!

15 CAESAR. Who is it in the press[2] that calls on me?
    I hear a tongue shriller than all the music
    Cry "Caesar." Speak! Caesar is turned to hear.

SOOTHSAYER. Beware the ides of March.[3]

CAESAR.   What man is that?

BRUTUS. A soothsayer bids you beware the ides of March.

20 CAESAR. Set him before me. Let me see his face.

CASSIUS. Fellow, come from the throng! Look upon Caesar.

CAESAR. What say'st thou to me now? Speak once again.

SOOTHSAYER. Beware the ides of March.

CAESAR. He is a dreamer. Let us leave him. Pass.

                Sennet.[4] *Exeunt* [*all but Brutus and Cassius*].

25 CASSIUS. Will you go see the order of the course?[5]

BRUTUS. Not I.

CASSIUS. I pray you, do.

BRUTUS. I am not gamesome.[6] I do lack some part
    Of that quick spirit that is in Antony.

30   Let me not hinder, Cassius, your desires.
    I'll leave you.

CASSIUS. Brutus, I do observe you now of late.
    I have not from your eyes that gentleness
    And show of love as I was wont to have.

35   You bear too stubborn and too strange a hand
    Over your friend that loves you.

BRUTUS.   Cassius,
    Be not deceived. If I have veiled my look,
    I turn the trouble of my countenance
    Merely upon myself. Vexed I am

---

1 Music signaling ceremonial entrance or exit.
2 Crowd.
3 15 March.
4 See 1.2.11, TLN 101n.
5 The ceremonial course run by Antony and others.
6 Merry, playful, sportive.

CASSIUS PERSUADES BRUTUS
(TLN 123–429)

Following Plutarch, Shakespeare depicts the friendship between
Cassius and Brutus as ambivalent, with ineradicable undertones of
rivalry. Plutarch remarks that "Cassius ... was Brutus's familiar friend,
but not so well given and conditioned as he" (Appendix A2, p. 205),
and notes that the two had contended for a praetorship, with Caesar
favoring Brutus (cf. 1.2.306, TLN 420), "therefore they strove one
against the other." It is clear by the end of this scene that Cassius's
affirmation of friendship is itself a gambit in his attempt to persuade
Brutus to join the conspiracy (1.2.301–15, TLN 415–29). Cassius's success is not evidence of his superiority to Brutus, because he recognizes
that the conspirators need Brutus if they are to succeed. Moreover,
Cassius consistently defers to Brutus, even when Cassius's judgment
is superior, as it nearly always is.

   In this long conversation Shakespeare imagines Brutus as a stoic
and Cassius as an Epicurean (see Appendix B, p. 224). The stoic Brutus
believes passions should be controlled because they are the only con-
trollable part of the human situation, which is otherwise determined
by inexorable destiny. This is why Brutus thinks that to be vexed with
passions is a detriment ("soil") to his behavior (1.2.39–42, TLN 131–34).
When he describes himself as "poor Brutus" (1.2.46, TLN 138), he is not
indulging in self-pity: rather, he is thinking of himself as deficient in
"conceptions only proper to myself" (1.2.41, TLN 133), that is, as coming
short of his own stoic ideal, which is why he is "at war" with himself.
The conflict he feels is not only between his admiration for and grati-
tude to Caesar and his concern about Caesar's bid for absolute power in
the republic; it is also between his irrepressibly strong feelings and his
belief that he should not give way to them. Self-division is a necessary
precondition for self-deception, but recognizing that one is divided
against oneself is not necessarily equivalent to self-knowledge. For
Shakespeare, division of the self was one of the oldest dramatic devices
for imagining moral conflict, familiar from personification allegory
in medieval and Renaissance morality plays in which self-deception
is also imagined in moral terms.

   Cassius uses Brutus's stoic idealism to persuade him to join the conspiracy. Though Cassius is no morality play Vice, his conversation with

(continued)

Brutus follows the contours of the Vice's temptation, which explains the similarities between this scene and Iago's conversations with Othello. When Cassius says he has noted Brutus's internal struggle but has kept his thoughts to himself (1.2.48–50, TLN 140–42), his declaration is disingenuous in a way that Brutus fails to notice, because Cassius is not keeping his thoughts to himself as he speaks: he is seeking to plumb the depths of Brutus's soul in order to sway Brutus to the side of the conspirators. Cassius's later facetiousness about conjuring a ghost (1.2.147, TLN 245) is true to his Epicureanism (5.1.76, TLN 2416), which was a materialist belief, denying any existence of the soul apart from the body. Having referred sarcastically to Caesar as a "god" (1.2.121, TLN 219), Cassius glibly invokes all the gods at once (1.2.148, TLN 247) because Epicureans did not believe that the gods, if they existed, had anything to do with human beings. Epicureanism also explains Cassius's defiance of the thunderstorm in 1.3.45–52, TLN 484–90, because he thinks that it is merely natural and not, as Casca fears, that it means anything. The appearance of Caesar's ghost later in the play can be taken either as an ironic challenge to Cassius's materialism or as confirmation of it, if the ghost is thought merely to be a hallucination produced by Brutus's sleeplessness and fatigue, as Brutus himself at first suspects (4.3.275.01, TLN 2289–90).

Sir John Gielgud as Cassius and James Mason as Brutus from the 1953 film of *Julius Caesar*, directed by Joseph L. Mankiewicz. Illustration used by permission of Getty Images.

Of late with passions of some difference,[1]   40
Conceptions only proper to myself,
Which give some soil,[2] perhaps, to my behaviors;
But let not therefore my good friends be grieved,
Among which number, Cassius, be you one,
Nor construe any further my neglect   45
Than that poor[3] Brutus with himself at war,
Forgets the shows of love to other men.

CASSIUS. Then Brutus, I have much mistook your passion,
By means whereof, this breast of mine hath buried
Thoughts of great value, worthy cogitations.   50
Tell me, good Brutus, can you see your face?

BRUTUS. No, Cassius, for the eye sees not itself
But by reflection, by some other things.

CASSIUS. 'Tis just.[4]
And it is very much lamented, Brutus,   55
That you have no such mirrors as will turn
Your hidden worthiness into your eye,
That you might see your shadow.[5] I have heard,
Where many of the best respect[6] in Rome,
Except immortal Caesar, speaking of Brutus   60
And groaning underneath this age's yoke,
Have wished that noble Brutus had his eyes.[7]

BRUTUS. Into what dangers would you lead me, Cassius,
That you would have me seek into myself
For that which is not in me?   65

CASSIUS. Therefore,[8] good Brutus, be prepared to hear;
And since you know you cannot see yourself
So well as by reflection, I, your glass,
Will modestly discover to yourself
That of yourself which you yet know not of.   70

---

1 Conflicting strong feelings.
2 Stain or discoloring mark.
3 Lacking or deficient in a proper or desired quality.
4 True, well said.
5 Reflection.
6 Highest regard or social rank.
7 Could see (what others of "best respect" can see).
8 For that, as to that.

And be not jealous on me, gentle Brutus.
Were I a common laughter,[1] or did use
To stale with ordinary oaths[2] my love
To every new protester;[3] if you know

75 That I do fawn on[4] men and hug them hard
And after scandal[5] them; or if you know
That I profess myself[6] in banqueting
To all the rout,[7] then hold me dangerous.

Flourish,[8] and shout.

BRUTUS. What means this shouting? I do fear the people
Choose Caesar for their king.

80 CASSIUS.   Ay, do you fear it?
Then must I think you would not have it so.
BRUTUS. I would not, Cassius, yet I love him well.
But wherefore do you hold me here so long?
What is it that you would impart to me?

85 If it be aught toward the general good,
Set honor in one eye and death i'th'other,
And I will look on both indifferently.[9]
For let the gods so speed[10] me, as I love
The name of honor more than I fear death.

90 CASSIUS. I know that virtue to be in you, Brutus,
As well as I do know your outward favor.[11]
Well, honor is the subject of my story.
I cannot tell what you and other men
Think of this life, but for my single self,

95 I had as lief not be,[12] as live to be

---

1 Subject or matter for laughter, laughing-stock.
2 Or if I were accustomed to foul with commonplace oaths.
3 One who makes a protestation or solemn affirmation.
4 Affect a servile fondness toward.
5 Spread scandal concerning, defame.
6 Declare (my friendship) openly in carousing.
7 Rabble.
8 Trumpet fanfare.
9 (1) Without concern, impassively; (2) impartially.
10 Prosper.
11 Countenance, face.
12 Just as soon not live.

In awe of such a thing as I myself.[1]
I was born free as Caesar, so were you;
We both have fed as well; and we can both
Endure the winter's cold as well as he.
For once, upon a raw and gusty day,   100
The troubled Tiber, chafing with her shores,
Caesar said to me, "Dar'st thou, Cassius, now
Leap in with me into this angry flood
And swim to yonder point?"[2] Upon the word,
Accoutrèd[3] as I was, I plungèd in   105
And bade him follow. So indeed he did.
The torrent roared, and we did buffet[4] it
With lusty sinews,[5] throwing it aside,
And stemming[6] it with hearts of controversy.[7]
But ere we could arrive the point[8] proposed,   110
Caesar cried, "Help me, Cassius, or I sink."
I, as Aeneas, our great ancestor,
Did from the flames of Troy upon his shoulder
The old Anchises[9] bear, so, from the waves of Tiber
Did I the tirèd Caesar. And this man   115
Is now become a god, and Cassius is
A wretched creature[10] and must bend his body[11]
If Caesar carelessly but nod on him.
He had a fever when he was in Spain,

---

1 An ordinary mortal like me.
2 Cassius's story is an example of Shakespeare's inventiveness, both to emphasize Caesar's vulnerability and to suggest Cassius's rhetorical facility. Though
no such account occurs in Plutarch, he records an event in Egypt when Caesar
saved his own life by strong swimming, even holding books in one hand over
his head to preserve them (Appendix A1, p. 193).
3 Attired, equipped.
4 Beat back, contend with.
5 Vigorous strength.
6 Making headway against.
7 Filled with contention, rivalry.
8 Arrive at the point.
9 An elderly Trojan prince who was rescued by his son Aeneas when Troy fell
to the Greeks. The journey of Aeneas from Troy, which led to the founding of
Rome, is recounted in Virgil's *Aeneid*.
10 Instrument or puppet.
11 Bow.

120 And when the fit was on him, I did mark
How he did shake. 'Tis true, this god did shake.
His coward lips[1] did from their color fly,
And that same eye, whose bend doth awe[2] the world,
Did lose his luster.[3] I did hear him groan.
125 Ay, and that tongue of his, that bade the Romans
Mark him and write his speeches in their books,
"Alas," it cried, "Give me some drink, Titinius,"
As a sick girl. Ye gods, it doth amaze me
A man of such a feeble temper[4] should
130 So get the start of[5] the majestic world
And bear the palm[6] alone.   *Shout. Flourish.*

BRUTUS. Another general shout?
I do believe that these applauses are
For some new honors that are heaped on Caesar.
135 CASSIUS. Why man, he doth bestride[7] the narrow world
Like a colossus,[8] and we petty men
Walk under his huge legs, and peep about
To find ourselves dishonorable graves.
Men at some time[9] are masters of their fates.
140 The fault, dear Brutus, is not in our stars,[10]
But in ourselves that we are underlings.
"Brutus" and "Caesar." What should be in that "Caesar"?
Why should that name be sounded[11] more than yours?
Write them together: yours is as fair a name.
145 Sound them: it doth become the mouth as well.
Weigh them: it is as heavy. Conjure[12] with 'em:

---

1 Lips like cowards.
2 Gaze does terrify.
3 Its luster.
4 (1) Mental balance or composure; (2) bodily habit, constitution, condition;
(3) mental constitution, habitual disposition.
5 Ahead of.
6 Of victory (continuing the metaphor from *get the start of*).
7 Straddle.
8 Huge statue.
9 Sometimes, occasionally.
10 Controlling destiny.
11 Resound.
12 Cast spells.

"Brutus" will start[1] a spirit as soon as "Caesar."
Now in the names of all the gods at once,
Upon what meat[2] doth this our Caesar feed
That he is grown so great?[3] Age, thou art shamed!   150
Rome, thou hast lost the breed[4] of noble bloods![5]
When went there by an age since the great flood,
But it was famed with[6] more than with one man?
When could they say, till now, that talked of Rome,
That her wide walks[7] encompassed but one man?   155
Now is it Rome indeed, and room enough
When there is in it but one only man.
Oh, you and I have heard our fathers say
There was a Brutus once[8] that would have brooked
Th'eternal[9] devil to keep his state in Rome   160
As easily as a king.
BRUTUS. That you do love me, I am nothing jealous.[10]
What you would work me to,[11] I have some aim.[12]
How I have thought of this and of these times
I shall recount hereafter. For this present,[13]   165
I would not, so with love I might entreat you,
Be any further moved. What you have said,
I will consider; what you have to say,
I will with patience hear,[14] and find a time

---

1 Raise.
2 Upon what food.
3 (1) Stout, corpulent; (2) famous, renowned.
4 (1) Lineage, strain; (2) engendering, creating.
5 (1) Kindred, family; (2) offspring.
6 Renowned for.
7 (1) Place set apart for walking; (2) tract of land.
8 Lucius Junius Brutus, ancestor of Shakespeare's Brutus.
9 Everlasting.
10 Not in the least doubtful or mistrustful.
11 Convert or bring me to.
12 (1) Conjecture, guess; (2) intention, purpose. The phrase means "I have both a good guess and an intention regarding your purpose in talking to me."
13 Right now.
14 Brutus habitually asserts stoic self-control, trying to regain equanimity in the face of Cassius's eloquent and powerful indignation.

170 Both meet to[1] hear and answer such high things.[2]
Till then, my noble friend, chew upon[3] this:
Brutus had rather be a villager
Than to repute himself a son of Rome
Under these hard conditions as this time
175 Is like to lay upon us.
CASSIUS. I am glad that my weak words
Have struck but thus much show of fire[4] from Brutus.

Enter Caesar and his train.[5]
BRUTUS. The games are done, and Caesar is returning.
CASSIUS. As they pass by, pluck Casca by the sleeve,
180 And he will, after his sour fashion, tell you
What hath proceeded worthy note[6] today.
BRUTUS. I will do so. But look you, Cassius,
The angry spot doth glow on Caesar's brow,[7]
And all the rest look like a chidden[8] train:
185 Calpurnia's cheek is pale, and Cicero
Looks with such ferret and such fiery eyes[9]
As we have seen him in the Capitol,
Being crossed in conference[10] by some senators.
CASSIUS. Casca will tell us what the matter is.
190 CAESAR. Antonio!
ANTONY. Caesar?
CAESAR. Let me have men about me that are fat,
Sleek-headed[11] men, and such as sleep o'nights.
Yond Cassius has a lean and hungry look.
195 He thinks too much. Such men are dangerous.

---

1 Appropriate both to.
2 Serious matters.
3 (1) Meditate carefully about; (2) devise or plan deliberately concerning.
4 The image comes from striking two pieces of flint together to produce a spark and thereby start a fire.
5 Those accompanying him.
6 Worth noting.
7 Caesar is flushed with anger.
8 Scolded (from "chide").
9 Eyes narrowed in angry disapproval.
10 Opposed in debate.
11 Well-groomed.

ANTONY. Fear him not Caesar, he's not dangerous.
He is a noble Roman, and well given.[1]
CAESAR. Would he were fatter! But I fear him not.
Yet if my name were liable to fear,
I do not know the man I should avoid   200
So soon as that spare[2] Cassius. He reads much,
He is a great observer, and he looks
Quite through the deeds of men. He loves no plays,
As thou dost, Antony; he hears no music;
Seldom he smiles, and smiles in such a sort   205
As if he mocked himself and scorned his spirit
That could be moved to smile at anything.
Such men as he be never at heart's ease
Whiles they behold a greater than themselves,
And therefore are they very dangerous.   210
I rather tell thee what is to be feared
Than what I fear, for always I am Caesar.
Come on my right hand, for this ear is deaf,[3]
And tell me truly, what thou think'st of him.[4]
        Sennet. Exeunt Caesar and [all] his train [but Casca].
CASCA. You pulled me by the cloak.[5] Would you speak with me?   215
BRUTUS. Ay, Casca. Tell us what hath chanced today,
    That Caesar looks so sad.[6]
CASCA. Why, you were with him, were you not?
BRUTUS. I should not then ask Casca what had chanced.
CASCA. Why, there was a crown offered him; and being offered   220
    him, he put it by[7] with the back of his hand, thus, and then the
    people fell a-shouting.

---

1 Well disposed. As Brutus later underestimates Antony, so Antony now
underestimates Cassius, establishing parallel mistakes in the two camps. Both
Antony and Brutus unwittingly misdirect their ally's attention in a manner suggesting that the speaker knows better.
2 "Carrion-lean" (Appendix A1, p. 197).
3 Caesar earlier described himself as "turned to hear" (1.2,17, TLN 106, the
play's first indication of his vulnerability.
4 Caesar's admonition with the added "truly" may betray a hint of anxiety.
5 Cassius urged Brutus to do this, and Brutus agreed to. The sequence of direction and action is a revealing indication of Cassius's influence on Brutus.
6 Serious, sober.
7 Set it aside.

BRUTUS. What was the second noise for?

CASCA. Why, for that too.

225 CASSIUS. They shouted thrice.[1] What was the last cry for?

CASCA. Why, for that too.

BRUTUS. Was the crown offered him thrice?

CASCA. Ay, marry,[2] was't, and he put it by thrice, every time gen-
tler[3] than other; and at every putting by, mine honest neigh-
230 bors[4] shouted.

CASSIUS. Who offered him the crown?

CASCA. Why, Antony.

BRUTUS. Tell us the manner[5] of it, gentle[6] Casca.

CASCA. I can as well be hanged as tell the manner of it.[7] It was
235 mere foolery. I did not mark it. I saw Mark Antony offered
him a crown; yet 'twas not a crown, neither; 'twas one of these
coronets.[8] And as I told you, he put it by once; but for all that,
to my thinking, he would fain[9] have had it. Then he offered it to
him again; then he put it by again. But to my thinking, he was
240 very loath[10] to lay his fingers off it. And then he offered it the
third time; he put it the third time by. And still as[11] he refused
it, the rabblement[12] hooted, and clapped their chapped hands,
and threw up their sweaty nightcaps, and uttered[13] such a deal
of stinking breath, because Caesar refused the crown, that it
245 had almost choked Caesar, for he swooned,[14] and fell down at it.
And for mine own part, I durst[15] not laugh, for fear of opening
my lips and receiving the bad air.

---

1 Three times.

2 Indeed (an oath derived from Mary, mother of Jesus).

3 Less firmly.

4 Worthy fellow citizens (with patronizing or even contemptuous implication).

5 The way an action is performed.

6 (1) Well-born, noble (acknowledging Casca's patrician status); (2) generous,
polite (with possible irony).

7 Casca may mean (1) moral conduct; (2) measure, moderation; (3) reason,
cause.

8 Inferior crowns.

9 Gladly, willingly.

10 Disinclined, reluctant.

11 Whenever.

12 Mob.

13 (1) Vocalized; (2) gave forth, emitted.

14 Fainted.

15 Dared.

CASSIUS. But soft,[1] I pray you: what, did Caesar swoon?

CASCA. He fell down in the marketplace and foamed at mouth,
and was speechless.   250

BRUTUS. 'Tis very like.[2] He hath the falling sickness.[3]

CASSIUS. No, Caesar hath it not, but you and I,
And honest Casca: we have the falling sickness.[4]

CASCA. I know not what you mean by that, but I am sure Caesar
fell down. If the tag-rag people[5] did not clap him, and hiss him,   255
according as he pleased, and displeased them, as they use to
do[6] the players in the theater, I am no true man.

BRUTUS. What said he, when he came unto himself?

CASCA. Marry, before he fell down, when he perceived the common herd was glad he refused the crown, he plucked me ope[7]   260
his doublet,[8] and offered them his throat to cut. And I had
been[9] a man of any occupation,[10] if I would not have taken
him at a word, I would I might go to hell among the rogues,
and so he fell. When he came to himself again, he said, if he
had done or said anything amiss, he desired their worships[11] to   265
think it was his infirmity.[12] Three or four wenches where I stood,
cried, "Alas, good soul," and forgave him with all their hearts.
But there's no heed to be taken of them. If Caesar had stabbed
their mothers, they would have done no less.

BRUTUS. And after that, he came thus sad[13] away.   270

CASCA. Ay.

CASSIUS. Did Cicero say anything?

CASCA. Ay, he spoke Greek.

CASSIUS. To what effect?

---

1 Wait a minute!
2 That's likely.
3 Epilepsy.
4 We fall down before almighty Caesar.
5 Another derisory term for plebeians, suggesting patched and mended clothing.
6 Customarily do.
7 Pulled aside (to expose his bare throat).
8 Close-fitting garment, worn next to the skin.
9 If I had been.
10 (1) Craftsman, laborer; (2) man inclined to unthinking action.
11 Persons of note (honorific address).
12 Illness.
13 Morose.

275 CASCA. Nay, and[1] I tell you that, I'll ne'er look you i'th'face again. But those that understood him, smiled at one another and shook their heads. But for mine own part, it was Greek to me. I could tell you more news too: Murellus and Flavius, for pulling scarves[2] off Caesar's images, are put to silence. Fare you well.

280 There was more foolery yet, if I could remember it.

CASSIUS. Will you sup[3] with me tonight, Casca?

CASCA. No, I am promised forth.

CASSIUS. Will you dine with me tomorrow?

CASCA. Ay, if I be alive, and your mind hold, and your dinner

285 worth the eating.

CASSIUS. Good, I will expect you.

CASCA. Do so. Farewell both.   *Exit.*

BRUTUS. What a blunt[4] fellow is this grown to be! He was quick mettle[5] when he went to school.

290 CASSIUS. So is he now, in execution
Of any bold, or noble enterprise,
However he puts on this tardy form.[6]
This rudeness is a sauce to his good wit,[7]
Which gives men stomach[8] to digest his words
With better appetite.

295 BRUTUS.   And so it is.
For this time I will leave you:
Tomorrow, if you please to speak with me,
I will come home to you, or if you will,
Come home to me, and I will wait for you.

300 CASSIUS. I will do so. Till then, think of the world.

Exit Brutus.

Well, Brutus, thou art noble,[9] yet I see

---

1 If.
2 Decorations.
3 Eat supper.
4 Rude, unpolished.
5 Of a lively temperament.
6 Even though he adopts an appearance of dullness.
7 Ideas.
8 Appetite, inclination.
9 (1) A patrician; (2) morally upright; (3) an Elizabethan gold coin.

Thy honorable mettle[1] may be wrought
From that it is disposed. Therefore it is meet
That noble minds keep ever with their likes,[2]
For who so firm that cannot be seduced?   305
Caesar doth bear me hard,[3] but he loves Brutus.
If I were Brutus now, and he were Cassius,
He should not humor[4] me. I will this night
In several hands[5] in at his windows throw,
As if they came from several citizens,   310
Writings, all tending to the great opinion
That Rome holds of his name, wherein obscurely[6]
Caesar's ambition shall be glancèd at.
And after this, let Caesar seat him sure,[7]
For we will shake him, or worse days endure.   *Exit.* 315

[1.3][8]

Thunder and lightning. Enter Casca and Cicero.
CICERO. Good even,[9] Casca. Brought you Caesar home?[10]
   Why are you breathless, and why stare you so?
CASCA. Are not you moved, when all the sway[11] of earth
   Shakes like a thing unfirm?[12] O Cicero,
   I have seen tempests when the scolding[13] winds   5
   Have rived[14] the knotty[15] oaks, and I have seen

---

1 Temperament (with a pun on "metal" as in 1.1.62, TLN 69).
2 That noble minds should keep company with others like themselves.
3 Bears me ill will, dislikes me.
4 Gratify or indulge.
5 Styles of handwriting.
6 Indirectly.
7 Himself securely.
8 Shakespeare compresses time here: while the feast of Lupercalia and the ides of March are a month apart, in the play they seem separated by only one night.
9 Good evening.
10 Did you accompany Caesar to his house (after the Lupercalian festival)?
11 (1) Swinging motion; (2) force moving an object; (3) bias in a certain direction; (4) prevailing influence; (5) power of rule or command.
12 (1) Unsteady; (2) weak.
13 (1) Brawling; (2) reproving.
14 Split.
15 Gnarled, full of knots.

Th'ambitious ocean swell, and rage, and foam,
To be exalted with[1] the threatening clouds,
But never till tonight, never till now,
10   Did I go through a tempest dropping fire.
Either there is a civil strife in heaven,
Or else the world, too saucy with the gods,
Incenses them to send destruction.

CICERO. Why, saw you any thing more wonderful?[2]

15 CASCA. A common slave, you know him well by sight,
Held up his left hand, which did flame and burn
Like twenty torches joined; and yet his hand,
Not sensible of[3] fire, remained unscorched.
Besides—I ha'not since put up my sword—
20   Against[4] the Capitol I met a lion,
Who glazed[5] upon me and went surly by,
Without annoying[6] me. And there were drawn
Upon a heap[7] a hundred ghastly[8] women,
Transformèd with their fear, who swore they saw
25   Men all in fire walk up and down the streets.
And yesterday, the bird of night[9] did sit
Even at noonday upon the marketplace,
Hooting and shrieking. When these prodigies[10]
Do so conjointly meet, let not men say,
30   "These are their reasons, they are natural,"[11]
For I believe they are portentous[12] things
Unto the climate[13] that they point upon.[14]

---

1 Until it was as high as.
2 Did you see anything else to excite amazement?
3 Sensitive to, affected by.
4 Directly opposite.
5 Stared glassy-eyed.
6 Injuring.
7 Huddled together.
8 Pale with fear.
9 Owl.
10 Extraordinary things (with supernatural suggestion).
11 "These things have a perfectly natural explanation."
12 Ominous, divinely predictive.
13 Zone of the earth (astrological).
14 Pertain to.

CICERO. Indeed, it is a strange disposèd time.
  But men may construe things after their fashion[1]   *Important!*
  Clean from the purpose[2] of the things themselves.   35
  Comes Caesar to the Capitol tomorrow?
CASCA. He doth, for he did bid Antonio
  Send word to you he would be there tomorrow.
CICERO. Good night then, Casca. This disturbèd sky
  Is not to walk in.[3]
CASCA.   Farewell Cicero.   *Exit Cicero.* 40

Enter Cassius.
CASSIUS. Who's there?
CASCA.   A Roman.
CASSIUS.   Casca, by your voice.
CASCA. Your ear is good. Cassius, what night is this?
CASSIUS. A very pleasing night to honest men.
CASCA. Who ever knew the heavens menace so?
CASSIUS. Those that have known the earth so full of faults.   45
  For my part, I have walked about the streets,
  Submitting me[4] unto the perilous night,
  And thus unbracèd,[5] Casca, as you see,
  Have bared my bosom to the thunder-stone,[6]
  And when the cross blue lightning[7] seemed to open   50
  The breast of heaven, I did present myself
  Even in the aim[8] and very flash of it.[9]
CASCA. But wherefore did you so much tempt the heavens?
  It is the part of men to fear and tremble,
  When the most mighty gods by tokens[10] send   55

---

1 Interpret things according to their own feelings or nature.
2 Completely unrelated to.
3 Is not fit to walk under.
4 Submitting myself.
5 Unbuttoned (referring to the doublet).
6 Thunder-bolt, lightning.
7 (1) Forked lightning; (2) angry lightning.
8 At the very point where it was aimed.
9 Cassius's insouciance is consistent with his Epicureanism (5.1.76, TLN 2416); see Appendix B, p. 245 ff.
10 Signs.

Such dreadful heralds to astonish us.

CASSIUS. You are dull, Casca, and those sparks of life
That should be in a Roman you do want,[1]
Or else you use not. You look pale, and gaze,

60 And put on fear, and cast yourself in wonder,[2]
To see the strange impatience of the heavens.
But if you would consider the true cause
Why all these fires, why all these gliding ghosts,
Why birds and beasts from quality and kind,[3]

65 Why old men, fools, and children calculate,[4]
Why all these things change from their ordinance,[5]
Their natures and preformèd[6] faculties
To monstrous[7] quality—why, you shall find[8]
That heaven hath infused them with these spirits

70 To make them instruments of fear and warning
Unto some monstrous state.[9]
Now could I, Casca, name to thee a man,
Most like this dreadful night,
That thunders, lightens, opens graves,[10] and roars,

75 As doth the lion in the Capitol,
A man no mightier than thyself or me
In personal action, yet prodigious[11] grown
And fearful, as these strange eruptions[12] are.

CASCA. 'Tis Caesar that you mean. Is it not, Cassius?

80 CASSIUS. Let it be who it is, for Romans now
Have thews[13] and limbs like to their ancestors.

---

1 You lack.
2 Cassius accuses Casca of theatrical posturing.
3 Parallel terms meaning character or disposition.
4 Cast (a horoscope); i.e., even the simplest minds can read the signs.
5 What providence has ordained for them.
6 Predetermined.
7 Unnatural, deformed.
8 "Why" is an interjection.
9 (1) Condition; (2) political entity (i.e., Rome).
10 Because ghosts are abroad.
11 Extraordinary (with supernatural implication).
12 Burstings forth.
13 Muscles.

But woe the while,[1] our fathers' minds are dead,
And we are governed with our mothers' spirits
Our yoke[2] and sufferance[3] show us womanish.

CASCA. Indeed, they say, the senators tomorrow   85
Mean to establish Caesar as a king,
And he shall wear his crown by sea and land
In every place, save here in Italy.

CASSIUS. I know where I will wear this dagger then:
Cassius from bondage will deliver Cassius.   90
Therein,[4] ye gods, you make the weak most strong,
Therein, ye gods, you tyrants do defeat.
Nor stony tower, nor walls of beaten brass,
Nor airless dungeon, nor strong links of iron
Can be retentive to[5] the strength of spirit,   95
But life, being weary of these worldly bars,[6]
Never lacks power to dismiss itself.
If I know this, know all the world besides,[7]
That part of tyranny that I do bear
I can shake off at pleasure.   *Thunder still.*[8]

CASCA.   So can I: 100
So every bondman[9] in his own hand bears
The power to cancel his captivity.

CASSIUS. And why should Caesar be a tyrant then?
Poor man, I know he would not be a wolf,
But that he sees the Romans are but sheep;   105
He were no lion,[10] were not Romans hinds.[11]
Those that with haste will make a mighty fire
Begin it with weak straws. What trash is Rome,

---

1 Alas.
2 Apparatus for coupling oxen to the plow (metonymy for servitude).
3 Patience, forbearance.
4 By suicide (with possible hint at the assassination of Caesar).
5 Retain (deliberate rhetorical periphrasis).
6 (1) That which retains mortal life; (2) barriers to political freedom.
7 Let everyone else know what I know.
8 Continually.
9 Person legally bound in servitude, such as a serf or slave.
10 Would be no lion.
11 (1) Deer; (2) servants.

What rubbish and what offal,[1] when it serves
110 For the base[2] matter to illuminate
So vile a thing as Caesar! But, O grief,
Where hast thou led me? I perhaps speak this
Before a willing bondman; then I know
My answer must be made.[3] But I am armed,
115 And dangers are to me indifferent.[4]

CASCA. You speak to Casca, and to such a man
That is no fleering[5] tell-tale. Hold, my hand.[6]
Be factious[7] for redress of all these griefs,
And I will set this foot of mine as far
As who goes farthest.[8]

120 CASSIUS.   There's a bargain made.
Now know you, Casca, I have moved already
Some certain of the noblest-minded[9] Romans
To undergo with me an enterprise
Of honorable dangerous[10] consequence,
125 And I do know by this,[11] they stay for me
In Pompey's porch.[12] For now, this fearful night,
There is no stir or walking in the streets,
And the complexion of the element[13]
In favor's[14] like the work we have in hand:
130 Most bloody, fiery, and most terrible.

Enter Cinna.

---

1 Residue, waste (from off-fall).
2 Low.
3 I will be held accountable.
4 Unimportant, immaterial.
5 Flattering, mocking, sneering.
6 Wait, let's shake on it.
7 Committed to a faction or party.
8 I.e., if you are committed to a group to oppose the wrongs we have spoken of, I will go with you all the way.
9 Contrast "base," 1.3.110, TLN 551.
10 But dangerous.
11 By this time.
12 Sheltering colonnade for the theater; see Appendix A2, p. 211.
13 Appearance or disposition of the sky.
14 Countenance, appearance.

CASCA. Stand close[1] awhile, for here comes one in haste.
CASSIUS. 'Tis Cinna; I do know him by his gait;
    He is a friend. Cinna, where haste you so?
CINNA. To find out you. Who's that, Metellus Cimber?
CASSIUS. No, it is Casca, one incorporate   135
    To[2] our attempts. Am I not stayed for,[3] Cinna?
CINNA. I am glad on't. What a fearful night is this?
    There's two or three of us have seen strange sights.
CASSIUS. Am I not stayed for? Tell me.
CINNA. Yes, you are. O Cassius, if you could   140
    But win the noble Brutus to our party—
CASSIUS. Be you content.[4] Good Cinna, take this paper,
    And look you lay it in the praetor's chair,[5]
    Where Brutus may but find it.[6] And throw this
    In at his window. Set this up with wax   145
    Upon old Brutus' statue. All this done,
    Repair[7] to Pompey's porch, where you shall find us.
    Is Decius Brutus and Trebonius there?
CINNA. All but Metellus Cimber, and he's gone
    To seek you at your house. Well, I will hie,[8]   150
    And so bestow these papers as you bade me.
CASSIUS. That done, repair to Pompey's theater.[9]   *Exit Cinna.*
    Come, Casca, you and I will yet, ere day,[10]
    See Brutus at his house. Three parts of him
    Is ours already, and the man entire[11]   155
    Upon the next encounter yields him ours.[12]
CASCA. Oh, he sits high in all the people's hearts,

---

1 Out of the way, concealed.
2 Committed to.
3 Awaited, expected.
4 Never mind.
5 Brutus's official seat as praetor.
6 Only Brutus can find it.
7 Make your way.
8 Hurry, go quickly.
9 Theater to which "Pompey's porch" was attached, and where the Senate will be meeting.
10 Before daybreak.
11 Whole man.
12 Yields himself to us, joins our side.

And that which would appear offense in us,
His countenance, like richest alchemy,
160   Will change to virtue and to worthiness.
CASSIUS. Him and his worth and our great need of him
   You have right well conceited.[1] Let us go,
   For it is after midnight, and ere day,
   We will awake him and be sure of him.   *Exeunt.*

[2.1]

Enter Brutus in his orchard.
BRUTUS. What, Lucius, ho!
   I cannot, by the progress of the stars,
   Give guess how near to day— Lucius, I say!
   I would it were my fault to sleep so soundly.
5   When, Lucius, when? Awake, I say! What, Lucius!

Enter Lucius.
LUCIUS. Called you, my lord?
BRUTUS. Get me a taper[2] in my study, Lucius.
   When it is lighted, come and call me here.
LUCIUS. I will, my Lord.   *Exit.*
10   BRUTUS. It must be by his death, and for my part,
   I know no personal cause to spurn at[3] him,
   But for the general.[4] He would be crowned.
   How that might change his nature, there's the question.
   It is the bright day that brings forth the adder,
15   And that craves[5] wary walking.[6] Crown him that,[7]
   And then I grant we put a sting in him

---

1 Conceived, imagined.
2 Wax candle.
3 Kick at.
4 Common good, general benefit of all.
5 Requires.
6 I.e., as a warm day brings a snake out to sun itself, requiring one to walk carefully, so crowning Caesar will bring out the danger in him, requiring careful political moves.
7 "That" is understood as a pronoun referring to "king" with "adder" implied.

BRUTUS'S ORCHARD (TLN 615)

The setting is based on a sentence in Plutarch, contrasting Brutus's public calm with his private agitation: "But when night came that he was in his own house, then he was clean changed" (Appendix A2, p. 211). No indication of the garden occurs in the dialogue, but it is clearly a private space, open to the same night sky as in the previous scene, and immediately adjacent to Brutus's house. The stage direction has been taken as evidence that the Folio copy was authorial, because "orchard" is atmospheric, with no possibility of realistic rendering on an open stage in a day-lit theater such as the Globe, where *Julius Caesar* was first performed.

Whether or not Shakespeare wrote the stage direction, the setting can be consistently imagined as the urban garden of a wealthy land-owner in the Elizabethan manner, enclosed with a wall and attached to the back of the house, as illustrated in John Norden's engraving of London in 1593. The building called "The Beare house" near the bottom is close to where the Globe would be built at the end of the 1590s, and Norden shows it surrounded by the kind of house and garden that Shakespeare imagines for Brutus. For other illustrations and discussion, see Picard, 68–83; for a discussion of gardens and orchards in Elizabethan and Jacobean plays, see Ichikawa.

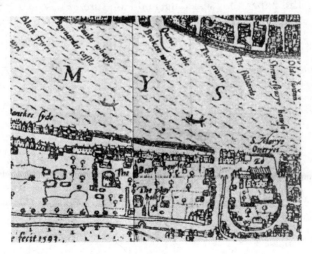

Detail from Norden's long view of London, 1593.

That at his will he may do danger[1] with.
Th'abuse of greatness is when it disjoins
Remorse from power, and to speak truth of Caesar,
20   I have not known when his affections swayed[2]
More than his reason. But 'tis a common proof
That lowliness[3] is young ambition's ladder,
Whereto the climber upward turns his face,
But when he once attains the upmost round,[4]
25   He then unto the ladder turns his back,
Looks in the clouds, scorning the base degrees[5]
By which he did ascend. So Caesar may.
Then lest he may, prevent.[6] And since the quarrel[7]
Will bear no color[8] for the thing he is,
30   Fashion[9] it thus: that what he is, augmented,
Would run to these and these extremities;[10]
And therefore think him as a serpent's egg,
Which hatched would, as his kind,[11] grow mischievous,[12]
And kill him in the shell.

Enter Lucius.
35   LUCIUS. The taper burneth in your closet,[13] sir.
Searching the window for a flint,[14] I found
This paper, thus sealed up, and I am sure
It did not lie there when I went to bed.

Gives him the letter.

---

1   Harm, damage.
2   Ruled, influenced.
3   Affected humility.
4   Rung.
5   (1) The ladder's lower rungs; (2) first moves in ambition's graduated scale; (3) plebeians.
6   I.e., therefore, since he may, someone must prevent him from doing so.
7   Argument or occasion of complaint.
8   Outward appearance, show, aspect.
9   (1) Contrive, manage; (2) modify, transform.
10   (1) Last points of an unfolding process; (2) severe political measures (tyranny).
11   According to its nature.
12   Harmful.
13   Private room, study.
14   To use in lighting the taper.

BRUTUS. Get you to bed again; it is not day.

Is not tomorrow, boy, the first of March?   40

LUCIUS. I know not, sir.

BRUTUS. Look in the calender, and bring me word.

LUCIUS. I will, sir.   *Exit.*

BRUTUS. The exhalations,[1] whizzing in the air,

Give so much light that I may read by them.   45

Opens the letter and reads.

"Brutus, thou sleep'st. Awake, and see thyself.

Shall Rome, etc. Speak, strike, redress!"[2]

"Brutus, thou sleep'st. Awake."

---

1 Meteors (thought to be vapor drawn from the earth by the sun).
2 Rectify (a wrong).

2.1.38.01–45: LETTERS TO BRUTUS (TLN 665–75)

The letters that Brutus reads were written on the orders of Cassius:

> I will this night
> In several hands in at his windows throw,
> As if they came from several citizens,
> Writings, all tending to the great opinion
> That Rome holds of his name, wherein obscurely
> Caesar's ambition shall be glancèd at. (1.2.308–13, TLN
> 422–27)

Cassius's intent in writing the letters is to motivate Brutus to join the conspiracy by flattering him and by suggesting widespread unhappiness with Caesar. In other words, Cassius designs the letters in such a way as to continue the pressure he has brought to bear on Brutus during their first conversation in the play.

The irony is that Brutus falls so completely for Cassius's ruse. Brutus believes that the letters indeed came from different sources, because they are written in "several hands"; he believes that the letters appeal

(continued)

Such instigations have been often dropped
50   Where I have took them up.[1]
"Shall Rome, etc." Thus must I piece it out:
Shall Rome stand under one man's awe? What Rome?[2]
My ancestors did from the streets of Rome
The Tarquin drive, when he was called a king.
55   "Speak, strike, redress!" Am I entreated
To speak and strike? O Rome, I make thee promise,[3]
If the redress will follow, thou receivest

---

1 Cassius has followed the plan he outlined in 1.2.308–13, TLN 422–427.
Brutus's falling for it is typical of victims of the Vice character in morality plays
(cf. Othello's response to Iago's temptations).
2 Which Rome is intended?
3 Rome, I promise you.

to him as a Roman patrician; he thinks of his ancestor, Lucius Junius
Brutus, though the letters do not mention him; he believes that he is
acting in complete rational independence, whereas he is really suc-
cumbing to pressure from Cassius. Brutus never for a moment suspects
that he is being manipulated, nor that Cassius is the one manipulating
him. Shakespeare would return to a similar device later in *Twelfth Night*,
where Malvolio is gulled by a fake letter in a scene that is hilariously
comical. The scene in Julius Caesar is not funny, but Brutus is gulled
no less completely than Malvolio.

In *Julius Caesar*, the scene involving the fake letters and Brutus's
response to them is still another way for Shakespeare to emphasize
Brutus's self-deception and the keenness of the competition between
Brutus and Cassius. Shakespeare follows Plutarch in making Cassius
an instigator who inflames Brutus's deep passions: "Cassius finding
Brutus's ambition stirred up the more by these seditious bills, did prick
him forward" (Appendix A1, p. 197). But Shakespeare makes clear that
Cassius needs Brutus for the conspiracy to succeed, and that Brutus is
the better man of the two, in his ability to lead, in his prestige, and in
his relative even-temperedness. Yet Brutus has so little self-knowledge
that Cassius is able to manipulate him, even playing on Brutus's belief
in his self-knowledge in order to do so.

Thy full petition at the hand of Brutus.

Enter Lucius.

LUCIUS. Sir, March is wasted[1] fifteen days.

Knock within.

BRUTUS. 'Tis good. Go to the gate, somebody knocks: 60

[*Exit Lucius.*]

 Since Cassius first did whet[2] me against Caesar,
 I have not slept.
 Between the acting of a dreadful thing
 And the first motion,[3] all the interim is
 Like a phantasma[4] or a hideous dream: 65
 The genius[5] and the mortal instruments[6]
 Are then in council,[7] and the state of man,
 Like to a little kingdom, suffers then
 The nature of an insurrection.

Enter Lucius.

LUCIUS. Sir, 'tis your brother[8] Cassius at the door, 70
 Who doth desire to see you.

BRUTUS.   Is he alone?

LUCIUS. No, sir. There are more with him.

BRUTUS.   Do you know them?

LUCIUS. No, sir. Their hats are plucked about their ears,
 And half their faces buried in their cloaks,
 That by no means I may discover them[9] 75

---

1 Spent. Thus has Shakespeare, in one night, moved time from 15 February to 15 March.
2 Sharpen (as a knife or sword).
3 Impulse, stimulus; i.e., between the doing of a dreadful thing and first impulse to do it.
4 Illusion, hallucination.
5 Spirit, soul.
6 The perishable parts of a human being which should serve as instruments of the immortal part.
7 Debate, discussion; i.e., the immortal part and the mortal parts are then in debate.
8 Brother-in-law.
9 Identify them (i.e., discover their identity).

By any mark of favor.[1]

BRUTUS.   Let 'em enter.   [*Exit Lucius.*]

They are the faction. O conspiracy,

Sham'st thou to show thy dangerous brow by night,

80   When evils are most free?[2] O then, by day

Where wilt thou find a cavern dark enough

To mask thy monstrous visage? Seek none, conspiracy!

Hide it in smiles and affability!

For if thou put thy native semblance on,

85   Not Erebus[3] itself were dim enough

To hide thee from prevention.

Enter the Conspirators, Cassius, Casca, Decius, Cinna, Metellus, and
Trebonius.

CASSIUS. I think we are too bold upon[4] your rest.

Good morrow,[5] Brutus. Do we trouble you?

90   BRUTUS. I have been up this hour, awake all night.

Know I these men that come along with you?

CASSIUS. Yes, every man of them, and no man here

But honors you, and every one doth wish

You had but that opinion of yourself

Which every noble Roman bears of you.

This is Trebonius.

95   BRUTUS.   He is welcome hither.

CASSIUS. This, Decius Brutus.

BRUTUS.   He is welcome too.

CASSIUS. This, Casca; this, Cinna; and this, Metellus Cimber.

BRUTUS. They are all welcome.

What watchful cares do interpose themselves

100   Betwixt your eyes and night?

CASSIUS. Shall I entreat a word?

They whisper.

DECIUS. Here lies the east. Doth not the day break here?

---

1 Facial feature.
2 Unhindered.
3 Classical hell.
4 Intrude too boldly.
5 Good morning.

CASCA. No.

CINNA. O pardon, sir, it doth; and yon gray lines
    That fret[1] the clouds are messengers of day.   105

CASCA. You shall confess that you are both deceived.[2]
    Here, as I point my sword, the sun arises,
    Which is a great way growing on[3] the south,
    Weighing[4] the youthful season of the year.
    Some two months hence,[5] up higher toward the north   110
    He first presents his fire, and the high east[6]
    Stands as the Capitol, directly here.

BRUTUS. Give me your hands all over,[7] one by one.

CASSIUS. And let us swear our resolution.

BRUTUS. No, not an oath. If not the face of men,[8]   115
    The sufferance[9] of our souls, the time's abuse[10]—
    If these be motives weak, break off betimes,[11]
    And every man hence, to his idle bed.[12]
    So let high-sighted[13] tyranny range on,[14]
    Till each man drop by lottery.[15] But if these,[16]   120
    As I am sure they do, bear fire enough
    To kindle cowards and to steel with valor
    The melting spirits of women, then, countrymen,
    What need we any spur but our own cause
    To prick us to redress?[17] What other bond   125
    Than secret Romans that have spoke the word

---

1 Adorn, interlace.
2 Mistaken.
3 Advancing toward (in its annual springtime movement).
4 Considering.
5 Earlier.
6 Due east.
7 Each one.
8 (1) The esteem of the public; (2) the dejected look of the people.
9 Suffering.
10 Corruption of the present era.
11 Immediately, before it is too late.
12 (1) Empty bed; (2) state requiring one to do nothing.
13 Having the sight directed aloft, supercilious.
14 Roam unchecked.
15 Be destroyed as if by chance, as the ranging tyrant arbitrarily chooses.
16 "These" refers to the three points listed in 2.1.115–16, TLN 745–46.
17 I.e., to compel us [as a spur] to right the wrong we have endured.

And will not palter?[1] And what other oath,
Than[2] honesty to honesty engaged,[3]
That this[4] shall be, or we will fall for it.
130　Swear[5] priests and cowards, and men cautelous,[6]
Old feeble carrions[7] and such suffering souls
That welcome wrongs. Unto bad causes swear
Such creatures as men doubt, but do not stain
The even virtue of our enterprise,
135　Nor th'insuppressive[8] mettle of our spirits,
To think that or[9] our cause or our performance
Did need an oath, when every drop of blood
That every Roman bears—and nobly bears—
Is guilty of a several bastardy,[10]
140　If he do break the smallest particle
Of any promise that hath passed from him.

CASSIUS. But what of Cicero? Shall we sound him?[11]
I think he will stand very strong with us.

CASCA. Let us not leave him out.

CINNA.　　　　　　　　　　No, by no means.

145　METELLUS. O let us have him, for his silver hairs
Will purchase us a good opinion
And buy men's voices to commend our deeds.
It shall be said his judgment ruled our hands.
Our youths and wildness shall no whit[12] appear,
150　But all be buried in his gravity.[13]

1　Equivocate, lie.
2　Than that of.
3　"Pledges of honor interchanged" (Dorsch, ed., 41n.)
4　"This" refers to the conspirators' united action; "that," to their trust and mutual loyalty, described in 2.1.128, TLN 758, on which their action is based.
5　Let swear.
6　(1) Deceitful, crafty; (2) cautious, wary.
7　Carcasses; i.e., people with no life in them worth the name.
8　Irrepressible, indomitable.
9　Either.
10 Individually guilty of an act that shows it is not true Roman blood.
11 Ask him about his view (of Caesar).
12 Not in the least.
13 Authority, seriousness (with unexpected wordplay on "grave" in *buried*).

BRUTUS. Oh, name him not; let us not break with[1] him,
　For he will never follow anything
　That other men begin.
CASSIUS. Then leave him out.
CASCA. 　　　　　　　　Indeed, he is not fit.
DECIUS. Shall no man else be touched but only Caesar? 　　155
CASSIUS. Decius, well urged. I think it is not meet
　Mark Antony, so well beloved of Caesar,
　Should outlive Caesar. We shall find of him

1　Disclose our secret to.

2.1.163–84: 　　BRUTUS REJECTS CASSIUS'S
　　RECOMMENDATION (TLN 795–816)

Cassius has no sooner suggested that Antony should be assassinated along with Caesar than Brutus immediately contradicts him, again indicating the tension between them; Brutus then proceeds to offer reasons for his view that not only are bad in themselves but also turn out to be mistakes in the long run. His analogy of Caesar and Antony to head and limbs, respectively (2.1.163–65, TLN 795–98), is ingenious but misleading, like his appeal to a natural analogy earlier in 2.1.14–15, TLN 630–31. The assassination is bound to be bloody, no matter how Brutus may try to disguise the fact, so the analogy is another example of Brutus's trying to hide the truth from himself, as well as from others. For Shakespeare and his audience, wrath and envy (2.1.165, TLN 797) were both deadly sins, and Brutus's argument that they should play no part in the assassination is an example of self-deceived special pleading, for the noble sentiment is impossible in fact, especially for a man who repeatedly exhibits both seething wrath and competitive envy without acknowledging them.

　Brutus idealizes the assassination as a sacred act by calling it a "sacrifice" (2.1.167, TLN 799), but his subsequent language betrays the grim reality he is trying to deny: "blood," "dismember," "bleed," "carve him," "carcass," "murderers." Asserting that the assassins aim at Caesar's

(continued)

A shrewd contriver.[1] And you know, his means,[2]

160 If he improve them,[3] may well stretch so far
As to annoy[4] us all: which to prevent,
Let Antony and Caesar fall together.
BRUTUS. Our course will seem too bloody, Caius Cassius,
To cut the head off and then hack the limbs,
165 Like wrath in death, and envy afterwards;

---

1 (1) Astute and able strategist (2) dangerous schemer.
2 · (1) Opportunities; (2) resources.
3 Employ them to advantage.
4 Damage, harass.

---

spirit, not his body (2.1.168–69, TLN 800–01), is another idealizing analogy that serves only to deceive Brutus himself. If the spirit of Caesar were indeed the conspirators' target, they would plan not an assassination but an opposing political movement. Caesar's spirit will in fact outlive his body, as Antony will promise (3.1.270–75, TLN 1498–1501), and as Brutus will discover at Philippi and will finally admit to himself (5.3.94–96, TLN 2583–85). When Brutus frankly acknowledges that Caesar must indeed bleed (2.1.171–72, TLN 803–04), he contradicts his idealizing in the previous lines, though his acknowledging it does nothing to deter him. His carefully balanced phrasing in 2.1.173–75, TLN 805–07 elegantly describes a dichotomy: "boldly" and "wrathfully" in two half lines, followed by a contrast between sacrifice (again) in 2.1.174, TLN 806 and feeding dogs in 2.1.175, TLN 807. The elegant language, however, inevitably reveals as much as it conceals. His argument that the conspirators' hearts should urge on their hands but then blame them for the deed is so deliberately self-deceived that the lines were cut from eighteenth-century acting editions to preserve Brutus's character, and they were not restored in performance until the early twentieth century. (Macbeth expresses a similar sentiment, though in different language: "The eye wink at the hand; yet let that be / Which the eye fears, when it is done, to see" (*Macbeth*, 1.4.52–53.)

Finally, Brutus decorously returns to the main point (2.1.182–84, TLN 815–16) with a repetition of his opening image (2.1.166, TLN 798), but the elegant symmetry of his speech cannot disguise the gruesome picture of a headless corpse.

For Antony is but a limb of Caesar.
Let's be sacrificers, but not butchers, Caius.
We all stand up against the spirit of Caesar,
And in the spirit of men there is no blood.
Oh, that we then could come by Caesar's spirit,   170
And not dismember Caesar! But, alas,
Caesar must bleed for it. And, gentle[1] friends,
Let's kill him boldly but not wrathfully;
Let's carve him as a dish fit for the gods,
Not hew him as a carcass fit for hounds.   175
And let our hearts, as subtle masters do,
Stir up their servants to an act of rage
And after seem to chide 'em. This shall make
Our purpose necessary and not envious;
Which so appearing to the common eyes,   180
We shall be called purgers, not murderers.
And for Mark Antony, think not of him,
For he can do no more than Caesar's arm,
When Caesar's head is off.
CASSIUS.   Yet I fear him,
For in the engrafted[2] love he bears to Caesar—   185
BRUTUS. Alas, good Cassius, do not think of him.
If he love Caesar, all that he can do
Is to himself: take thought, and die for Caesar.
And that were much he should,[3] for he is given
To sports, to wildness, and much company.   190
TREBONIUS. There is no fear[4] in him. Let him not die,
For he will live, and laugh at this hereafter.

                                                  Clock strikes.

BRUTUS. Peace! Count the clock.
CASSIUS.   The clock hath stricken[5] three.
TREBONIUS. 'Tis time to part.
CASSIUS.   But it is doubtful yet

---

1 (1) Noble; (2) honorable; (3) mild in disposition or behavior.
2 Grafted in, i.e., firmly implanted.
3 It would be a surprise if he did.
4 Nothing to be afraid of.
5 Struck.

195 Whether Caesar will come forth today or no.
For he is superstitious grown of late,
Quite from the main[1] opinion he held once
Of fantasy, of dreams, and ceremonies.[2]
It may be these apparent prodigies,

---

1 Contrary to the strong and basic.
2 Portents, omens.

2.1.192.01:   CLOCK STRIKES (TLN 826)

This is perhaps the play's most obvious and most famous anachronism (see also 3.1.98, TLN 1312). The mechanical clock was a medieval invention, unknown in ancient Rome. To simulate a clock striking at the Globe Theatre, someone presumably struck a bell backstage audibly enough to catch the conspirators' (and the audience's) attention.

Shakespeare also deliberately slows down the passage of time here. Cinna had noted the coming dawn almost a hundred lines earlier (2.1.104–05, TLN 734–35); yet now it is only 3 a.m. on March 15— long before dawn in Rome or London on that date, though the play would have been performed in the afternoon on a day-lit stage. The Elizabethan clock pictured here has a date on its face from just two years before the first performance of *Julius Caesar*. It marks the time with only an hour hand.

One-handed Elizabethan clock, Castletown, Sunderland, County Durham, UK.
Illustration from http://www.panaramio.com.

The unaccustomed terror of this night,   200
And the persuasion of his augurers[1]
May hold him from the Capitol today.
DECIUS. Never fear that. If he be so resolved
I can o'ersway him. For he loves to hear
That unicorns may be betrayed with trees,   205
And bears with glasses;[2] elephants, with holes;
Lions, with toils;[3] and men, with flatterers.
But when I tell him he hates flatterers,
He says he does, being then most flatterèd.
Let me work.   210
For I can give his humor the true bent,[4]
And I will bring him to the Capitol.
CASSIUS. Nay, we will all of us be there to fetch[5] him.
BRUTUS. By the eighth hour. Is that the uttermost?[6]
CINNA. Be that the uttermost, and fail not then.   215
METELLUS. Caius Ligarius[7] doth bear Caesar hard,[8]
Who rated him for speaking well of Pompey.
I wonder none of you have thought of him.
BRUTUS. Now, good Metellus, go along by him.[9]
He loves me well, and I have given him reasons.   220
Send him but hither, and I'll fashion[10] him.
CASSIUS. The morning comes upon's. We'll leave you, Brutus.
And friends, disperse yourselves, but all remember
What you have said, and show yourselves true Romans.
BRUTUS. Good gentlemen,[11] look fresh and merrily.   225
Let not our looks put on[12] our purposes,

---

1 Compelling influence (or settled conviction) of his soothsayers.
2 Mirrors.
3 Nets.
4 I can turn him in the way he is most disposed to go ("humor" = disposition).
5 (1) Go in quest of and convey back; (2) move to interest by some contrivance.
6 Very latest.
7 See above, Characters in the Play, p. 71.
8 Dislike Caesar.
9 Go visit him.
10 Modify, mold.
11 (1) Men of noble birth, patricians; (2) men of chivalrous instincts and fine feelings.
12 Show.

But bear it as our Roman actors do,
With untired[1] spirits and formal[2] constancy.
And so good morrow to you every one.

Exeunt [all but] Brutus.

230 Boy! Lucius! Fast asleep? It is no matter.
Enjoy the honey-heavy dew of slumber.
Thou hast no figures[3] nor no fantasies,
Which busy care draws in the brains of men.
Therefore thou sleep'st so sound.

Enter Portia.

PORTIA.   Brutus, my Lord.
235 BRUTUS. Portia! What mean you? Wherefore rise you now?
It is not for your health thus to commit
Your weak condition to the raw cold morning.
PORTIA. Nor for yours neither. You've ungently,[4] Brutus,
Stole from my bed, and yesternight at supper
240 You suddenly arose and walked about,
Musing and sighing, with your arms across,[5]
And when I asked you what the matter was,
You stared upon me, with ungentle looks.
I urged you further; then you scratched your head
245 And too impatiently stamped with your foot.
Yet I insisted; yet you[6] answered not,
But with an angry wafture[7] of your hand
Gave sign for me to leave you. So I did,
Fearing to strengthen that impatience
250 Which seemed too much enkindled, and withal
Hoping it was but an effect of humor,[8]
Which sometime hath his hour with every man.
It will not let you eat, nor talk, nor sleep;

---

1 (1) Not wearied; (2) not costumed (attired).
2 (1) Merely in outward appearance; (2) rigorously observant, precise.
3 Imaginary forms, phantasms.
4 Unkindly, roughly.
5 Conventional sign of inner turmoil.
6 Still I . . . still you.
7 Wave.
8 Mood.

And could it work so much upon your shape
As it hath much prevailed on your condition,   255
I should not know you[1] Brutus. Dear my Lord,
Make me acquainted with your cause of grief.
BRUTUS. I am not well in health, and that is all.
PORTIA. Brutus is wise, and were he not in health,
He would embrace the means to come by it.   260
BRUTUS. Why so I do. Good Portia, go to bed.
PORTIA. Is Brutus sick? And is it physical[2]
To walk unbracèd[3] and suck up the humors[4]
Of the dank morning? What, is Brutus sick,
And will he steal out of his wholesome bed   265
To dare the vile contagion of the night,
And tempt the rheumy[5] and unpurgèd air[6]
To add unto his sickness? No, my Brutus.
You have some sick offense[7] within your mind,
Which by the right and virtue of my place   270
I ought to know of. And upon my knees,[8]
I charm you,[9] by my once-commended beauty,
By all your vows of love, and that great vow[10]
Which did incorporate[11] and make us one,
That you unfold to me, your self, your half,   275
Why you are heavy,[12] and what men tonight
Have had resort[13] to you. For here have been
Some six or seven who did hide their faces
Even from darkness.
BRUTUS.   Kneel not, gentle Portia.

---

1 Recognize you as.
2 Beneficial to health.
3 Partially clothed.
4 Absorb the damp exhalations, vapors.
5 Damp, dank.
6 Air not cleaned by the sun's healthful influence.
7 Some harmful illness.
8 This is an implicit stage direction for the actor playing Portia.
9 I entreat you (in some potent name).
10 Marriage vow.
11 Combine into one body.
12 "Weighed down" with sorrow or grief.
13 Visited.

280 PORTIA. I should not need, if you were gentle Brutus.
　　　　Within the bond of marriage, tell me, Brutus,
　　　　Is it excepted, I should know no secrets
　　　　That appertain to you? Am I your self,
　　　　But as it were in sort, or limitation,
285　　To keep with you at meals, comfort your bed,
　　　　And talk to you sometimes? Dwell I but in the suburbs
　　　　Of your good pleasure? If it be no more,
　　　　Portia is Brutus' harlot, not his wife.
　　BRUTUS. You are my true and honorable wife,
290　　As dear to me as are the ruddy drops
　　　　That visit my sad heart.
　　PORTIA. If this were true, then should I know this secret.
　　　　I grant I am a woman, but withal
　　　　A woman that Lord Brutus took to wife.[1]
295　　I grant I am a woman, but withal
　　　　A woman well reputed, Cato's daughter.
　　　　Think you I am no stronger than my sex
　　　　Being so fathered, and so husbanded?
　　　　Tell me your counsels; I will not disclose 'em.
300　　I have made strong proof of my constancy,
　　　　Giving myself a voluntary wound
　　　　Here, in the thigh. Can I bear that with patience
　　　　And not my husband's secrets?
　　BRUTUS.　　　　　　　　　O ye gods!
　　　　Render me worthy of this noble wife.

　　　　　　　　　　　　　　　　　　　　　　Knock.

305　　Hark, hark, one knocks! Portia go in awhile,
　　　　And by and by thy bosom shall partake
　　　　The secrets of my heart.
　　　　All my engagements I will construe to thee,
　　　　All the charactery of my sad brows.[2]
310　　Leave me with haste.　　　　　　　　*Exit Portia.*

Enter Lucius and Ligarius.

1　Romans and Elizabethans alike held strongly patriarchal assumptions.
2　All that is written on my sad face.

Lucius, who's that knocks?

LUCIUS. Here is a sick man that would speak with you.

BRUTUS. Caius Ligarius, that Metellus spake of.
Boy, stand aside. Caius Ligarius, how?[1]

LIGARIUS. Vouchsafe[2] good morrow from a feeble tongue.[3]   315

BRUTUS. O what a time have you chose out, brave Caius,
To wear a kerchief.[4] Would you were not sick!

LIGARIUS. I am not sick, if Brutus have in hand
Any exploit worthy the name of honor.

BRUTUS. Such an exploit have I in hand Ligarius,   320
Had you a healthful ear to hear of it.

LIGARIUS. By all the gods that Romans bow before,
I here discard my sickness. Soul of Rome,
Brave son, derived from honorable loins,
Thou like an exorcist hast conjured up   325
My mortifièd spirit.[5] Now bid me run,
And I will strive with things impossible,
Yea, get the better of them. What's to do?

BRUTUS. A piece of work that will make sick men whole.

LIGARIUS. But are not some whole, that we must make sick?   330

BRUTUS. That must we also. What it is my Caius,
I shall unfold to thee as we are going
To whom it must be done.[6]

LIGARIUS.   Set on your foot,
And with a heart new-fired, I follow you
To do I know not what, but it sufficeth   335
That Brutus leads me on.   *Thunder.*

BRUTUS.   Follow me, then.   *Exeunt.*

---

1 (1) How is this possible? (2) How are you?
2 Please accept.
3 Ligarius is ill.
4 Cloth over the head (conventional stage signal for illness).
5 You have revived me.
6 I will explain what we are doing as we go to the house of the one to whom we are doing it.

[2.2]¹

Thunder and lightning. Enter Julius Caesar in his nightgown.²

CAESAR. Nor³ heaven nor earth have been at peace tonight.
　Thrice hath Calpurnia in her sleep cried out,
　"Help, ho, they murder Caesar!" Who's within?

Enter a servant.

SERVANT. My Lord.

5　CAESAR. Go bid the priests do present⁴ sacrifice,
　And bring me their opinions of success.⁵

SERVANT. I will, my lord.　　　　　　　　　　　　*Exit.*

Enter Calpurnia.

CALPURNIA. What mean you, Caesar? Think you to walk forth?
　You shall not stir out of your house today.

10　CAESAR. Caesar shall forth.⁶ The things that threatened me
　Ne'er looked but on my back. When they shall see
　The face of Caesar, they are vanishèd.

CALPURNIA. Caesar, I never stood on ceremonies,⁷
　Yet now they fright me. There is one within,

15　Besides the things that we have heard and seen,
　Recounts most horrid sights seen by the watch.⁸
　A lionness hath whelpèd⁹ in the streets,
　And graves have yawned¹⁰ and yielded up their dead;
　Fierce fiery warriors fight upon the clouds

20　In ranks, and squadrons, and right form of war,¹¹
　Which drizzled blood upon the Capitol.

1　The scene shifts to Caesar's home.
2　Dressing gown.
3　Neither.
4　Immediate.
5　Opinions about the beast's entrails, as predictors of fortune, good or bad.
6　Go forth.
7　Set store by (depended on) portents or omens.
8　Night watchmen.
9　Given birth.
10　Opened.
11　Regular formation for battle.

The noise of battle hurtled in[1] the air:
Horses do neigh, and dying men did groan,
And ghosts did shriek and squeal about the streets.
O Caesar, these things are beyond all use,[2]   25
And I do fear them.

---

1   Resounded crashingly through.
2   Extremely unusual.

2.2.10–12:   CAESAR'S FEAR (TLN 997–99)

Perhaps Shakespeare's most surprising invention in *Julius Caesar* is that
its title character is as challenged by barely suppressed fear as his principal antagonist, Brutus, is challenged by repressed anger and ambition.
One of Caesar's first declarations in the play is that he is not afraid of
Cassius (1.2.198–212, TLN 300–16), though his claim is so strident and
insistent that it clearly says the opposite of what Caesar intends. His
second declaration that he is fearless (2.2.10–12, TLN 997–99) is apparently intended to be majestic, but like the first it seems rather to proclaim the very thing it purports to deny, as Shakespeare emphasizes by
juxtaposing it with Caesar's order for a sacrifice. Consulting augurers
is supposed to reveal the future, and so much concern about the future
would seem unnecessary for one who is truly not afraid.
    Later, alone with his wife Calpurnia on the morning of the assassina-
tion, Caesar responds dismissively to her expressed fears for his safety
(2.2.32–37, TLN 1020–25). Again, however, Shakespeare juxtaposes
Caesar's brave talk with his inquiry about what the augurers found in
the sacrifice, and Caesar interprets the augurers' alarming report that the
beast had no heart with still another declaration of misplaced bravado
(2.2.41–48, TLN 1031–38). Calpurnia remonstrates with him reasonably,
easily persuading him not to go to the senate. Only Decius's ingenious
interpretation of Calpurnia's dream is enough to overcome Caesar's
fear by appealing to his vanity; indeed, Decius's boldest move is to state
the deepest truth about Caesar—that he is afraid (2.2.101, TLN 1094)—
thereby mixing the truth into his deception and making it all the stronger.
    Shakespeare thus matches the play's two most powerful patrician
rivals in their self-deception and lack of self-knowledge, as well as in

(continued)

CAESAR.   What can be avoided
    Whose end is purposed by the mighty gods?
    Yet Caesar shall go forth, for these predictions
    Are to the world in general as to Caesar.
30 CALPURNIA. When beggars die, there are no comets seen;
    The heavens themselves blaze forth[1] the death of princes

---

1 Skies (1) flame; (2) proclaim.

their being married to sensible and loving wives. Caesar's shaming of Calpurnia (who says nothing after 2.2.64, TLN 1057) is petty, faithless, and self-deceived (2.2.105–07, TLN 1098–99), since Caesar blames her for his own deepest feeling ("fears"), and she is right all along.

John Wilkes Booth (at left), actor and assassin of Abraham Lincoln, playing Antony, with his brothers Edwin (as Brutus) and Junius (as Julius Caesar) at the Winter Garden Theatre in New York, 1864. Illustration from http://www.artstor.org.

CAESAR. Cowards die many times before their deaths;
    The valiant never taste of death but once.
    Of all the wonders that I yet have heard,
    It seems to me most strange that men should fear,   35
    Seeing that death, a necessary end,
    Will come when it will come.

Enter a servant.

CAESAR.   What say the augurers?
SERVANT. They would not have you to stir forth today.
    Plucking the entrails of an offering forth,
    They could not find a heart within the beast.   40
CAESAR. The gods do this in shame of cowardice.
    Caesar should be a beast without a heart,
    If he should stay at home today for fear.
    No Caesar shall not. Danger knows full well
    That Caesar is more dangerous than he.   45
    We are two lions littered[1] in one day,
    And I the elder and more terrible;
    And Caesar shall go forth.
CALPURNIA.   Alas, my Lord,
    Your wisdom is consumed in confidence.[2]
    Do not go forth today. Call it my fear   50
    That keeps you in the house, and not your own.
    We'll send Mark Antony to the Senate House,
    And he shall say you are not well today.
    Let me upon my knee prevail in this.
CAESAR. Mark Antony shall say I am not well,   55
    And for thy humor,[3] I will stay at home.

Enter Decius.

    Here's Decius Brutus. He shall tell them so.
DECIUS. Caesar, all hail! Good morrow, worthy Caesar,
    I come to fetch you to the Senate House.

---

1 Born.
2 Overconfidence, presumption.
3 Mood.

60 CAESAR. And you are come in very happy[1] time
    To bear my greeting to the senators,
    And tell them that I will not come today—
    Cannot, is false; and that I dare not, falser:
    I will not come today. Tell them so, Decius.
    CALPURNIA. Say he is sick.
65 CAESAR.   Shall Caesar send a lie?
    Have I in conquest stretched mine arm so far
    To be afeard to tell gray-beards the truth?
    Decius, go tell them Caesar will not come.
    DECIUS. Most mighty Caesar, let me know some cause,
70   Lest I be laughed at when I tell them so.
    CAESAR. The cause is in my will; I will not come.
    That is enough to satisfy the Senate.
    But for your private satisfaction,
    Because I love you, I will let you know.
75   Calpurnia here, my wife, stays me at home.
    She dreamt tonight[2] she saw my statue,
    Which like a fountain with an hundred spouts
    Did run pure blood, and many lusty[3] Romans
    Came smiling and did bathe their hands in it.
80   And these does she apply for[4] warnings, and portents,
    And evils imminent; and on her knee
    Hath begged that I will stay at home today.
    DECIUS. This dream is all amiss interpreted:
    It was a vision fair and fortunate.
85   Your statue spouting blood in many pipes,
    In which so many smiling Romans bathed,
    Signifies that from you great Rome shall suck
    Reviving blood, and that great men shall press
    For tinctures,[5] stains,[6] relics,[7] and cognizance.[8]
90   This by Calpurnia's dream is signified.

---

1 Fortuitous, lucky.
2 Last night.
3 Merry, cheerful.
4 Interpret as.
5 (1) Heraldic term for colors in coats of arms; (2) alchemical term for spiritual principles infused into material things.
6 (1) Synonym for *tinctures*; (2) disgraces (ironic connotation).
7 Holy artifacts from a deceased saint.
8 Heraldic crest, coat of arms.

CAESAR. And this way have you well expounded it.

DECIUS. I have, when you have heard what I can say,
  And know it now: the Senate have concluded
  To give this day a crown to mighty Caesar.
  If you shall send them word you will not come, 95
  Their minds may change. Besides, it were a mock
  Apt to be rendered[1] for someone to say,
  "Break up the Senate till another time,
  When Caesar's wife shall meet with better dreams."
  If Caesar hide himself, shall they not whisper 100
  "Lo, Caesar is afraid"?
  Pardon me, Caesar, for my dear dear love
  To your proceeding[2] bids me tell you this,
  And reason to my love is liable.[3]

CAESAR. How foolish do your fears seem now, Calpurnia? 105
  I am ashamèd I did yield to them.
  Give me my robe,[4] for I will go.

Enter Brutus, Ligarius, Metellus, Casca, Trebonius, Cinna, and
Publius.

  And look where Publius is come to fetch me.

PUBLIUS. Good morrow, Caesar.

CAESAR.   Welcome, Publius.
  What, Brutus, are you stirred so early too? 110
  Good morrow, Casca. Caius Ligarius,
  Caesar was ne'er so much your enemy
  As that same ague[5] which hath made you lean.
  What is't o'clock?

BRUTUS.   Caesar, 'tis strucken eight.

CAESAR. I thank you for your pains and courtesy. 115

Enter Antony.

  See, Antony, that revels long o' nights,
  Is notwithstanding up. Good morrow, Antony.

ANTONY. So to most noble Caesar.

---

1 Likely to be reported.
2 Going onward and upward (to your coronation).
3 I.e., my sense of propriety is overruled by my love.
4 Outer garment.
5 Illness.

CAESAR.   Bid them prepare within.
I am to blame to be thus waited for.
120 Now, Cinna. Now, Metellus. What, Trebonius,
I have an hour's talk in store for you.
Remember that you call on me today.
Be near me, that I may remember you.
TREBONIUS. Caesar I will, [*aside*] and so near will I be,
125 That your best friends shall wish I had been further.
CAESAR. Good friends, go in, and taste some wine with me.
And we, like friends, will straight way go together.
BRUTUS. [*aside*] That every like is not the same,¹ O Caesar,
The heart of Brutus yearns² to think upon.   *Exeunt.*

[2.3]³

Enter Artemidorus [reading a paper].
ARTEMIDORUS.
   "Caesar, beware of Brutus; take heed of Cassius; come not
   near Casca; have an eye to Cinna; trust not Trebonius; mark
   well Metellus Cimber. Decius Brutus loves thee not. Thou
   hast wronged Caius Ligarius. There is but one mind in all
5 these men, and it is bent against Caesar. If thou be'est not
   immortal, look about you. Security gives way to conspiracy.⁴
   The mighty gods defend thee.
                                        Thy lover,⁵ Artemidorus."
   Here will I stand, till Caesar pass along,
10 And as a suitor⁶ will I give him this.
   My heart laments that virtue cannot live

---

1 That being like friends is not the same as being friends.
2 Grieves, is deeply moved.
3 The scene is based closely on an episode in Plutarch (Appendix A1, p. 200),
though Shakespeare invented the content of Artemidorus's warning. Having
been presented with omens, Caesar seems about to be presented with a human
admonition as well. The episode heightens tension and proves that Caesar has
friends, as well as enemies, but Artemidorus's last line (2.3.13, TLN 1143) adds to
the sense that destiny lies with the conspirators, not with Caesar, especially in
view of Artemidorus's ultimate failure.
4 I.e., freedom from suspicion leaves the way open for conspiracy.
5 Thy friend.
6 Petitioner.

Out of the teeth of emulation.[1]
If thou read this, O Caesar, thou mayst live;
If not, the Fates[2] with traitors do contrive.   *Exit.*

[2.4][3]

Enter Portia and Lucius.
PORTIA. I prithee, boy, run to the Senate House.
  Stay not to answer me, but get thee gone.
  Why dost thou stay?
LUCIUS.   To know my errand, madam.
PORTIA. I would have had thee there and here again
  Ere I can tell thee what thou shouldst do there.   5
  O constancy,[4] be strong upon my side!
  Set a huge mountain 'tween my heart and tongue.
  I have a man's mind, but a woman's might.
  How hard it is for women to keep counsel.[5]
  Art thou here yet?
LUCIUS.   Madam, what should I do?   10
  Run to the Capitol, and nothing else?
  And so return to you, and nothing else?
PORTIA. Yes, bring me word, boy, if thy lord look well,
  For he went sickly forth, and take good note
  What Caesar doth, what suitors press to him.   15
  Hark, boy, what noise is that?
LUCIUS. I hear none, madam.
PORTIA.   Prithee, listen well:
  I heard a bustling rumor,[6] like a fray,[7]
  And the wind brings it from the Capitol.

---

1 (1) Ambitious rivalry; (2) grudge against the superiority of others. The phrase means "beyond the bite of envious rivalry."
2 Three goddesses in Greek and Roman mythology who personified destiny.
3 Another domestic scene, this time back at Brutus's house, helps to build suspense in the lead-up to Caesar's assassination. Shakespeare invented Portia's extreme agitation, now that she has learned her husband's plan, and he shows it in her conversations with Lucius, the servant boy, and with the soothsayer who warned Caesar in the second scene (1.2.12–24, TLN 101–14).
4 (1) Steadfastness, fortitude; (2) determination (not to reveal the terrible secret).
5 Keep a secret.
6 Agitated din or noise.
7 Like a disturbance, fight.

20 LUCIUS. Sooth,[1] madam, I hear nothing.

Enter the Soothsayer.
PORTIA. Come hither, fellow. Which way hast thou been?
SOOTHSAYER. At mine own house, good lady.
PORTIA. What is't o'clock?
SOOTHSAYER.   About the ninth hour, lady.
PORTIA. Is Caesar yet gone to the Capitol?
25 SOOTHSAYER. Madam, not yet. I go to take my stand
      To see him pass on to the Capitol.
PORTIA. Thou hast some suit to Caesar, hast thou not?
SOOTHSAYER. That I have, lady, if it will please Caesar
      To be so good to Caesar as to hear me:
30   I shall beseech him to befriend himself.
PORTIA. Why, know'st thou any harm's intended towards him?
SOOTHSAYER. None that I know will be; much that I fear may
      chance.
      Good morrow to you. Here the street is narrow.
      The throng that follows Caesar at the heels
35   Of senators, of praetors, common suitors,[2]
      Will crowd a feeble man almost to death.
      I'll get me to a place more void,[3] and there
      Speak to great Caesar as he comes along.   *Exit.*
PORTIA. I must go in. Ay me! How weak a thing
40   The heart of woman is! O Brutus,
      The Heavens speed thee in thine enterprise.
      Sure the boy heard me. Brutus hath a suit
      That Caesar will not grant. O, I grow faint!
      Run Lucius, and commend me to my lord!
45   Say I am merry. Come to me again,
      And bring me word what he doth say to thee.
                                                Exeunt.

---

1 Truly.
2 See TLN 1139n.
3 More empty (less crowded).

[3.1]¹

Flourish.² Enter Caesar, Brutus, Cassius, Casca, Decius, Metellus,
Trebonius, Cinna, Antony, Lepidus, Artemidorus, Publius, [Popilius
Lena,] and the Soothsayer.

CAESAR. The ides of March are come.

SOOTHSAYER. Ay, Caesar, but not gone.

ARTEMIDORUS. Hail, Caesar! Read this schedule.³

DECIUS. Trebonius doth desire you to o'erread,
   At your best leisure, this his humble suit.⁴   5

ARTEMIDORUS. O Caesar, read mine first, for mine's a suit
   That touches Caesar nearer. Read it, great Caesar.

CAESAR. What touches us ourself shall be last served.⁵

ARTEMIDORUS. Delay not Caesar, read it instantly!

CAESAR. What, is the fellow mad?

PUBLIUS.   Sirrah,⁶ give place.⁷   10

CASSIUS. What, urge you your petitions in the street?
   Come to the Capitol.

                  [Caesar and his train move away.]

POPILIUS. I wish your enterprise today may thrive.

CASSIUS. What enterprise, Popilius?

POPILIUS.   Fare you well.

                  [Moves toward Caesar.]

BRUTUS. What said Popilius Lena?   15

CASSIUS. He wished today our enterprise might thrive:
   I fear our purpose is discoverèd.

BRUTUS. Look how he makes to Caesar: mark him.

CASSIUS. Casca, be sudden,⁸ for we fear prevention.

---

1 Caesar's assassination, which takes place in this scene, is the climax of the play's first half.
2 Trumpet fanfare.
3 Short note.
4 Petition.
5 (1) Attended to; (2) legally delivered of a writ, with dismissive wordplay on Artemidorus's suit as a legal process.
6 Diminutive of "sir" used to express contempt, reprimand, or assumption of authority on the part of the speaker.
7 (1) Get out of the way; (2) yield to your betters.
8 Act at once.

20   Brutus, what shall be done? If this be known,
      Cassius or Caesar never shall turn back,
      For I will slay myself.
    BRUTUS.   Cassius, be constant.
      Popilius Lena speaks not of our purposes,
      For look, he smiles, and Caesar doth not change.
25   CASSIUS. Trebonius knows his time, for look you, Brutus,
      He draws Mark Antony out of the way.

                           [*Exeunt Antony and Trebonius.*]

3.1:   **THE ASSASSINATION OF CAESAR**
                    (TLN 1200 FF.)

Caesar's death occurs just before the midpoint of the action, literally making the rest of the play anti-climactic, though Shakespeare relaxes none of the tension, and by placing the assassination so early he emphasizes the play's "undular" structure (Velz). From three domestic scenes (two at Brutus's house and one at Caesar's) full of quiet, furtive, and anxious dialogue, the action suddenly becomes public, ceremonial, and crowded. On the bare Globe stage, the scene would have started with Caesar walking from an imagined street, where the Soothsayer accosts him, to an imagined Capitol, with no change of scenery. In performance, the only distinction between the locations would have been Caesar's movement and probably his sitting down in a chair of state (3.1.34, TLN 1240). Otherwise, scene setting is done entirely through the characters' lines, as always in Shakespeare's plays.

A statue of Pompey (referred to in 3.1.115, 3.2.183, TLN 1330, 1725) also seems to be required near the place where Caesar falls. A statue of this sort could have been made of light lath and plaster, so that it could be easily moved on and off the stage. For other examples of statues in contemporary drama, see "image" in Dessen and Thomson. The illustration from a sixteenth-century book shows the same kind of anachronism as Shakespeare's play, including a medieval plumed helmet for Julius Caesar, whose assassination is depicted in a small illustration near the standing warrior.

Facing: Engraving of Julius Caesar by Virgil Solis (1514–62), from *The Illustrated Bartsch*, Vol. 19, Pt. 1. Illustration from http://www.artstor.org.

DECIUS. Where is Metellus Cimber? Let him go,
  And presently[1] prefer his suit[2] to Caesar.
BRUTUS. He is addressed.[3] Press near, and second him.
CINNA. Casca, you are the first that rears your hand.
CAESAR. Are we all ready? What is now amiss,   30

---

1 Immediately.
2 Present his petition.
3 Prepared.

That Caesar and his senate must redress?
METELLUS. Most high, most mighty, and most puissant[1]
    Caesar!
    Metellus Cimber throws before thy seat
    An humble heart.
35 CAESAR.   I must prevent[2] thee, Cimber.
    These couchings[3] and these lowly courtesies[4]
    Might fire the blood of ordinary men,
    And turn preordinance and first decree
    Into the lane of children. Be not fond[5]
40   To think that Caesar bears such rebel blood[6]
    That will be thawed from the true quality
    With that which melteth fools—I mean sweet words,
    Low-crookèd curtsies,[7] and base spaniel fawning.
    Thy brother[8] by decree is banishèd.
45   If thou doest bend, and pray, and fawn for him,
    I spurn thee[9] like a cur out of my way!
    Know, Caesar doth not wrong, nor without cause
    Will he be satisfied.
    METELLUS. Is there no voice more worthy than my own
50   To sound more sweetly in great Caesar's ear
    For the repealing of my banished brother?
    BRUTUS. I kiss thy hand, but not in flattery, Caesar,
    Desiring thee, that Publius Cimber may
    Have an immediate freedom of repeal.[10]
    CAESAR. What, Brutus?
55 CASSIUS.   Pardon, Caesar! Caesar, pardon!
    As low as to thy foot doth Cassius fall

---

1 Powerful.
2 Forestall.
3 Crouchings, prostrations.
4 (1) Humble civilities (courtesies); (2) low obeisances (curtsies; see also 3.1.43,
TLN 1250).
5 Foolish, silly.
6 Rebellious passion (i.e., wrongly swaying reason).
7 Deep-bent bowing.
8 Publius Cimber.
9 I kick thee.
10 Recall (from banishment).

To beg enfranchisement[1] for Publius Cimber.
CAESAR. I could be well moved, if I were as you.
  If I could pray to move, prayers would move me.[2]
  But I am constant as the northern star,[3]   60
  Of whose true fixed and resting[4] quality,
  There is no fellow in the firmament.
  The skies are painted with unnumbered sparks;
  They are all fire, and every one doth shine;
  But there's but one in all doth hold his place.   65
  So in the world: 'tis furnished well with men,
  And men are flesh and blood, and apprehensive;[5]
  Yet in the number I do know but one
  That unassailable holds on his rank[6]
  Unshaked of motion,[7] and that I am he,   70
  Let me a little show it, even in this:
  That I was constant Cimber should be banished,
  And constant do remain to keep him so.
CINNA. O Caesar—
CAESAR.   Hence! Wilt thou lift up Olympus?[8]
DECIUS. Great Caesar—
CAESAR.   Doth not Brutus bootless[9] kneel?   75
CASCA. Speak, hands, for me!
                         They stab Caesar.
CAESAR. *Et tu Brutè?*[10]—Then fall, Caesar!
                              Dies.

CINNA. Liberty! Freedom! Tyranny is dead!
  Run hence! Proclaim! Cry it about the streets!
CASSIUS. Some to the common pulpits and cry out!   80

---

1 Liberation (from the sentence of banishment).
2 If I could stoop as you do to pray others to change their minds, I would
change my mind too.
3 The pole star, most visible of the sphere of fixed stars as conceived by the
Ptolemaic cosmos.
4 Remaining stationary.
5 Intelligent, discerning.
6 Remains fixed in position.
7 Unmoving.
8 Dwelling place of the Greek gods.
9 Vainly, senselessly.
10 You also, Brutus?

Liberty, freedom, and enfranchisement!
BRUTUS. People and senators, be not affrighted.
Fly not! Stand still! Ambition's debt is paid.
CASCA. Go to the pulpit, Brutus.
DECIUS.   And Cassius too.
85 BRUTUS. Where's Publius?
CINNA. Here, quite confounded[1] with this mutiny.[2]
METELLUS. Stand fast together, lest some friend of Caesar's
   Should chance—
BRUTUS. Talk not of standing.[3] Publius, good cheer.
90 There is no harm intended to your person,
   Nor to no Roman else. So tell them, Publius.
CASSIUS. And leave us, Publius, lest that the people
   Rushing on us, should do your age some mischief.
BRUTUS. Do so, and let no man abide[4] this deed
95 But we the doers.

Enter Trebonius.
CASSIUS. Where is Antony?
TREBONIUS.   Fled to his house amazed.
   Men, wives, and children, stare, cry out, and run
   As it were doomsday.[5]
BRUTUS.   Fates, we will know your pleasures.
   That we shall die, we know. 'Tis but the time
100 And drawing days out that men stand upon.[6]
CASCA. Why, he that cuts off twenty years of life
   Cuts off so many years of fearing death.
BRUTUS. Grant that, and then is death a benefit.
   So are we Caesar's friends, that have abridged
105 His time of fearing death. Stoop, Romans, stoop,
   And let us bathe our hands in Caesar's blood

---

1 Confused, dismayed.
2 Discord, tumult.
3 Don't speak of organized resistance.
4 (1) Stay with (as opposed to *leave*); (2) endure the consequences of.
5 The biblical day of judgment, marking the end of time.
6 Depend upon, set store by. Brutus means that since we know we must die,
we depend on nothing but the daily passage of time until then.

Up to the elbows, and besmear our swords.
Then walk we forth, even to the marketplace,
And waving our red weapons o'er our heads,
Let's all cry, "Peace, freedom, and liberty!"   110
CASSIUS. Stoop then, and wash. How many ages hence
    Shall this our lofty scene be acted o'er,
    In states unborn and accents yet unknown!
BRUTUS. How many times shall Caesar bleed in sport,[1]
    That now on Pompey's basis[2] lies along,   115

---

1 Pastime, diversion (as perhaps in a play).
2 Pedestal of Pompey's statue.

3.1.98:   DOOMSDAY (TLN 1312)
             AND OTHER ANACHRONISMS

Like "angel" in 3.2.176 and 4.3.280, TLN 1718 and 2292, "doomsday" is
an explicitly Christian reference in *Julius Caesar*, which concludes with
events that took place several decades before the birth of Christ. Other
anachronisms include mechanical clocks (2.1.192.01–93, TLN 826–28),
an oath derived from the name of the Virgin Mary (1.2.228, TLN 332),
and hats habitually worn by noblemen (2.1.73, TLN 697). Shakespeare
did not include such anachronisms because he was especially ignorant,
but because no one in Elizabethan England had the finely developed
sense of historical and cultural differences that is familiar in our current age. As a consequence, history for Shakespeare was relatively
homogeneous, and imagining the Roman Republic and its history as
if it were Elizabethan London seemed perfectly natural and obvious.

As part of that homogeneous history, "doomsday" in *Julius Caesar*
establishes in one word the context in which frequent references to
Roman destiny are to be understood. Caesar's assassination is not the
end of the world, which would (for Shakespeare) be marked by the Last
Judgment (Doomsday), so the "tide of times" (3.1.257, TLN 1485) that
carries these heroic Romans to their triumphs and their deaths will go
on long after this event. A painting of Doomsday adorned the wall of
the Guild Chapel in Stratford, where Shakespeare grew up, exemplify-
ing the traditional importance of this apocalyptic event in the lives of

(continued)

No worthier than the dust!

CASSIUS. So oft as that shall be,
So often shall the knot of us[1] be called
The men that gave their country liberty.

DECIUS. What, shall we forth?

CASSIUS. Ay, every man away.
120 Brutus shall lead, and we will grace his heels
With the most boldest and best hearts of Rome.

Enter a servant.

---

1 Small band of persons.

---

ordinary Christians in the sixteenth century. The painting was covered with whitewash shortly before Shakespeare's birth, but everyone in Stratford as he was growing up would have been aware of the painting and even more aware of what it stood for.

Conjecturally restored wall painting of Doomsday, Stratford Guild Chapel. Courtesy of Shakespeare Birthplace Trust.

BRUTUS. Soft, who comes here? A friend of Antony's.
SERVANT. Thus, Brutus, did my master bid me kneel.
  Thus did Mark Antony bid me fall down,
  And being prostrate, thus he bade me say: 125
  "Brutus is noble, wise, valiant, and honest;
  Caesar was mighty, bold, royal, and loving.[1]
  Say I love Brutus, and I honor him;
  Say I feared Caesar, honored him, and loved him.
  If Brutus will vouchsafe that Antony 130
  May safely come to him, and be resolved
  How Caesar hath deserved to lie in death,
  Mark Antony shall not love Caesar dead
  So well as Brutus living, but will follow
  The fortunes and affairs of noble Brutus 135
  Thorough[2] the hazards of this untrod state,[3]
  With all true faith." So says my master Antony.
BRUTUS. Thy master is a wise and valiant Roman;
  I never thought him worse.
  Tell him, so please him come unto this place, 140
  He shall be satisfied, and by my honor
  Depart untouched.
SERVANT.   I'll fetch him presently.

                                     Exit servant.

BRUTUS. I know that we shall have him well to friend.[4]
CASSIUS. I wish we may, but yet have I a mind
  That fears him much, and my misgiving still 145
  Falls shrewdly[5] to the purpose.[6]

Enter Antony.
BRUTUS. But here comes Antony: Welcome, Mark Antony.
ANTONY. O mighty Caesar! Dost thou lie so low?

---

1 *Royal* means noble, generous (as ideally befits a monarch) and hints support-
ively at Caesar's ambition.
2 Through (two syllables are necessary for the meter).
3 New (unexplored) state of affairs.
4 As a friend.
5 (1) Sharply, severely; (2) grievously, intensely; (3) astutely, sagaciously.
6 My misgiving continues to be acutely relevant.

　　　　Are all thy conquests, glories, triumphs, spoils,
150　　Shrunk to this little measure? Fare thee well.
　　　　I know not, gentlemen, what you intend,
　　　　Who else must be let blood,[1] who else is rank;[2]
　　　　If I myself, there is no hour so fit
　　　　As Caesar's death's hour, nor no instrument
155　　Of half that worth as those your swords, made rich
　　　　With the most noble blood of all this world.
　　　　I do beseech ye, if you bear me hard,
　　　　Now, whilst your purpled hands do reek[3] and smoke,
　　　　Fulfill your pleasure.[4] Live[5] a thousand years,
160　　I shall not find myself so apt to die;
　　　　No place will please me so, no mean of death,[6]
　　　　As here by Caesar, and by you cut off,
　　　　The choice and master spirits of this age.
　　　　BRUTUS. O Antony! Beg not your death of us.
165　　Though now we must appear bloody and cruel,
　　　　As by our hands and this our present act
　　　　You see we do. Yet see you but our hands
　　　　And this, the bleeding business they have done.
　　　　Our hearts you see not; they are pitiful,[7]
170　　And pity to the general wrong of Rome—
　　　　As fire drives out fire, so pity, pity—
　　　　Hath done this deed on Caesar. For your part,
　　　　To you our swords have leaden[8] points, Mark Antony.
　　　　Our arms in strength of malice, and our hearts
175　　Of brothers' temper,[9] do receive you in,

1　Have blood taken (medical term).
2　(1) Abounding in, full of (blood); (2) proud, high-minded; (3) stout and strong.
3　Emit hot vapor (parallels "smoke").
4　Do what you want.
5　If I were to live.
6　No means to die.
7　Full of pity.
8　Our swords are ineffectual (because lead was too soft and heavy a metal for swords).
9　I.e., our strongly malicious weapons (toward Caesar) and our brotherly hearts (toward you).

With all kind love, good thoughts, and reverence.[1]
CASSIUS. Your voice[2] shall be as strong as any man's,
  In the disposing of new dignities.[3]
BRUTUS. Only be patient, till we have appeased
  The multitude, beside themselves with fear,   180
  And then we will deliver you[4] the cause
  Why I, that did love Caesar when I struck him,
  Have thus proceeded.
ANTONY.   I doubt not of your wisdom.
  Let each man render me his bloody hand.
  First, Marcus Brutus. will I shake with you;   185
  Next, Caius Cassius, do I take your hand;
  Now, Decius Brutus yours; now yours, Metellus;
  Yours, Cinna; and my valiant Casca, yours;
  Though last, not least in love, yours, good Trebonius.
  Gentlemen all. Alas, what shall I say?   190
  My credit[5] now stands on such slippery[6] ground,
  That one of two bad ways you must conceit me:[7]
  Either a coward, or a flatterer.
  That I did love thee, Caesar, oh, 'tis true!
  If then thy spirit look upon us now,   195
  Shall it not grieve thee dearer than thy death
  To see thy Antony making his peace,
  Shaking the bloody fingers of thy foes—
  Most noble—in the presence of thy corpse?
  Had I as many eyes as thou hast wounds,   200
  Weeping as fast as they stream forth thy blood,
  It would become me better, than to close
  In terms of friendship with[8] thine enemies.

---

1 Deep respect.
2 (1) Opinion; (2) vote.
3 Honors, offices.
4 Declare to you.
5 Credibility (with the conspirators), with perhaps a double meaning of trust
in the conspirators.
6 Precarious (with suggestion of the bloody floor on which he stands).
7 Believe me to be.
8 Make friends with, come to terms with.

Pardon me Julius! Here was't thou bayed,[1] brave hart,[2]
205 Here did'st thou fall, and here thy hunters stand
Signed in thy spoil[3] and crimsoned in thy Lethe.[4]
O world! Thou wast the forest to this hart,
And this indeed, O world, the heart of thee!
How like a deer, strucken by many princes,
210 Dost thou here lie!
CASSIUS. Mark Antony—
ANTONY.   Pardon me, Caius Cassius.
The enemies of Caesar shall say this;
Then in a friend it is cold modesty.[5]
CASSIUS. I blame you not for praising Caesar so,
215 But what compact mean you to have with us?
Will you be pricked[6] in number of our friends,
Or shall we on, and not depend on you?
ANTONY. Therefore I took your hands, but was indeed
Swayed from the point by looking down on Caesar.
220 Friends am I with you all, and love you all,
Upon this hope, that you shall give me reasons,
Why and wherein Caesar was dangerous.
BRUTUS. Or else were this[7] a savage spectacle.
Our reasons are so full of good regard
225 That were you, Antony, the son of Caesar,
You should be satisfied.
ANTONY.   That's all I seek,
And am moreover suitor that I may
Produce his body to the marketplace,
And in the pulpit, as becomes a friend,
230 Speak in the order of his funeral.[8]
BRUTUS. You shall, Mark Antony.
CASSIUS.   Brutus, a word with you:

---

1 Brought to bay, cornered by barking (or baying) dogs.
2 Stag.
3 Marked with the tokens of your slaughter.
4 Infernal river of forgetfulness in classical mythology.
5 Sober moderation.
6 Noted, marked down, originally with a literal pin-prick.
7 Or else this would be.
8 Ceremony of his funeral.

You know not what you do! Do not consent
That Antony speak in his funeral.
Know you how much the people may be moved
By that which he will utter?
BRUTUS.   By your pardon: 235
I will myself into the pulpit first,
And show the reason of our Caesar's death.
What Antony shall speak, I will protest[1]
He speaks by leave and by permission,
And that we are contented Caesar shall   240
Have all true rites and lawful ceremonies.
It shall advantage more than do us wrong.
CASSIUS. I know not what may fall. I like it not.
BRUTUS. Mark Antony, here, take you Caesar's body.
You shall not in your funeral speech blame us,   245
But speak all good you can devise of Caesar,
And say you do't[2] by our permission.
Else shall you not have any hand at all
About his funeral. And you shall speak
In the same pulpit whereto I am going,   250
After my speech is ended.
ANTONY.   Be it so.
I do desire no more.
BRUTUS. Prepare the body, then, and follow us.
                                        [*Exeunt all but*] Antony.
ANTONY. O pardon me, thou bleeding piece of earth,
That I am meek and gentle with these butchers!   255
Thou art the ruins of the noblest man
That ever livèd in the tide of times.[3]
Woe to the hand that shed this costly[4] blood!
Over thy wounds now do I prophesy,
Which like dumb mouths do ope their ruby lips,   260

---

1 Declare formally.
2 Do it (a contraction necessary for the meter).
3 Stream of history.
4 (1) Of great price or value; (2) involving loss or sacrifice (for Caesar, Antony,
and the conspirators).

To beg the voice and utterance[1] of my tongue:
A curse shall light upon the limbs[2] of men,
Domestic fury[3] and fierce civil strife
Shall cumber[4] all the parts of Italy;
265　Blood and destruction shall be so in use,
And dreadful objects so familiar,
That mothers shall but smile when they behold
Their infants quartered[5] with the hands of war,
All pity choked with custom of fell deeds;[6]
270　And Caesar's spirit ranging for revenge,
With Até[7] by his side come hot from hell,
Shall in these confines,[8] with a monarch's voice,
Cry havoc[9] and let slip[10] the dogs of war,
That this foul deed shall smell above the earth
275　With carrion men, groaning for burial.

Enter Octavius' servant.
You serve Octavius Caesar, do you not?
SERVANT. I do, Mark Antony.
ANTONY. Caesar did write for him to come to Rome.
SERVANT. He did receive his letters and is coming,
280　And bid me say to you by word of mouth—
O Caesar!
ANTONY. Thy heart is big. Get thee apart and weep.
Passion I see is catching, for mine eyes,
Seeing those beads of sorrow stand in thine,
285　Begin to water. Is thy master coming?
SERVANT. He lies tonight within seven leagues[11] of Rome.

1　(1) Vocal expression; (2) extreme degree, utmost extremity.
2　Any organs or parts of the body.
3　Civil war.
4　Overwhelm.
5　Cut into four pieces.
6　Familiarity of cruel deeds.
7　Greek goddess of ruin, here personifying vengeful bloodlust.
8　(1) Roman territory; (2) a bear-baiting arena (precursor to the Elizabethan playhouse) where dogs were "let slip" to torment a bear. See illustration at 2.1.01, TLN 615.
9　Order given for pillaging after a battle.
10　Unleash.
11　Approximately 21 miles or 33 kilometers.

ANTONY. Post back with speed, and tell him what hath chanced.
　Here is a mourning Rome, a dangerous Rome,
　No Rome of safety for Octavius yet.
　Hie[1] hence, and tell him so. Yet stay awhile;　　　　　　　290
　Thou shalt not back till I have borne this corpse
　Into the marketplace. There shall I try[2]
　In my oration how the people take
　The cruel issue of these bloody men,
　According to the which, thou shalt discourse　　　　　　295
　To young Octavius of the state of things.
　Lend me your hand.[3]

　　　　　　　　　　　　　　　　　　　　Exeunt.

[3.2]

Enter Brutus and goes into the pulpit, and Cassius with the plebeians.
PLEBEIANS. We will be satisfied![4] Let us be satisfied!
BRUTUS. Then follow me, and give me audience, friends.
　Cassius, go you into the other street,
　And part the numbers.[5]
　Those that will hear me speak, let 'em stay here;　　　　5
　Those that will follow Cassius, go with him;
　And public reasons shall be rendered[6]
　Of Caesar's death.
1 PLEBEIAN.　　　　　I will hear Brutus speak.
2 PLEBEIAN. I will hear Cassius and compare their reasons,
　When severally[7] we hear them renderèd.　　　　　　10
　　　　　　　[Exit Cassius, with some of the Plebeians.]
3 PLEBEIAN. The noble Brutus is ascended. Silence!
BRUTUS. Be patient till the last.

1　See 1.3.150n, TLN 597n.
2　Test.
3　Antony may solicit the Servant's help to carry Caesar's body off stage, though Antony enters alone with the body at 3.2.37 01, TLN 1569.
4　Hear a satisfactory explanation.
5　Divide the crowd.
6　(1) Reasons will be given publicly; (2) reasons will be given that affect the common good.
7　Separately, sequentially.

Romans, countrymen, and lovers![1] Hear me for my cause,[2] and
be silent, that you may hear. Believe me for mine honor, and
15   have respect to mine honor that you may believe. Censure[3] me
in your wisdom, and awake your senses[4] that you may the better judge. If there be any in this assembly, any dear friend of
Caesar's, to him I say, that Brutus' love to Caesar was no less
than his. If then that friend demand why Brutus rose against
20   Caesar, this is my answer: not that I loved Caesar less, but that

---

1 Friends.
2 (1) Motive, reason for action; (2) purpose, end; (3) matter of concern; (4) side
of a question espoused.
3 Judge.
4 Reason, intellectual powers.

3.2.13–43,   TWO FUNERAL ORATIONS
72–249:   (TLN 1543–77 AND 1610–1790)

One of Shakespeare's most remarkable accomplishments in *Julius
Caesar* was his composing of Brutus's and Antony's speeches. The only
hint Plutarch gives of Brutus's style is that "he counterfeited that brief
compendious manner of speech of the Lacedaemonians" (Appendix
A2, p. 206), which accounts for the laconic prose that Shakespeare gives
him, designed to offer the facts in a reasonable manner with minimal
rhetorical embellishment. Antony's speech, on the other hand, is a *tour
de force* of florid and emotive persuasion, for which Shakespeare had
only a suggestion in Plutarch: "He used a manner of phrase in this
speech, called Asiatic, which carried the best grace and estimation at
that time, and was much like to his manners and life: for it was full of
ostentation, foolish bravery, and vain ambition" (Appendix A3, p. 236).

  Nothing indicates that Brutus intended to make the crowd call
for him to replace Caesar (3.2.47–48, TLN 1581–83), but his failure to
anticipate their doing so is matched only by his failure to recognize
how dangerous their reaction might be to his republican ideal. He
thus hears their call without heeding it, as his immediate departure
makes clear, leaving the malleable plebeians in the hands of Antony
with an immensely powerful stage prop: Caesar's corpse. Antony seizes
the opportunity and works the crowd brilliantly, concluding with a

I loved Rome more. Had you rather Caesar were living and die all slaves, than that Caesar were dead to live all free men? As Caesar loved me, I weep for him; as he was fortunate, I rejoice at it; as he was valiant, I honor him; but as he was ambitious, I slew him. There is tears for his love; joy, for his fortune; 25 honor, for his valor; and death, for his ambition. Who is here so base that would be a bondman? If any, speak, for him have I offended. Who is here so rude[1] that would not be a Roman? If any, speak, for him have I offended. Who is here so vile that will not love his country? If any, speak, for him have I offended. 30 I pause for a reply.

---

1 Barbarous (denoting anyone outside Roman rule).

self-satisfied cynical comment to himself (3.2.249-50, TLN 1799–1800). His success is remarkable: in a stunning and sudden reversal of fortune, Antony has his enemies literally on the run by the time he concludes his speech (3.2.258-59, TLN 1809–10).

Herbert Beerbohm Tree playing Antony, 1898. Courtesy of Shakespeare Birthplace Trust.

ALL. None, Brutus, none.

BRUTUS. Then none have I offended. I have done no more to
Caesar than you shall do to Brutus. The question of his death
35 is enrolled[1] in the Capitol; his glory not extenuated,[2] wherein
he was worthy; nor his offenses enforced,[3] for which he suffered death.

Enter Mark Antony, with Caesar's body.

Here comes his body, mourned by Mark Antony, who, though
he had no hand in his death, shall receive the benefit of his
40 dying, a place in the commonwealth, as which of you shall not?
With this, I depart, that as I slew my best lover for the good of
Rome, I have the same dagger for myself, when it shall please
my country to need my death.

ALL. Live Brutus! Live! Live!

45 1 PLEBEIAN. Bring him with triumph home unto his house.

2 PLEBEIAN. Give him a statue with his ancestors.

3 PLEBEIAN. Let him be Caesar.

4 PLEBEIAN.   Caesar's better parts,
Shall be crowned in Brutus.

1 PLEBEIAN. We'll bring him to his house with shouts and
clamors.

50 BRUTUS. My countrymen!

2 PLEBEIAN. Peace! Silence! Brutus speaks.

1 PLEBEIAN. Peace, ho!

BRUTUS. Good countrymen, let me depart alone,
And for my sake, stay here with Antony.
55 Do grace[4] to Caesar's corpse, and grace his speech
Tending to Caesar's glories, which Mark Antony
By our permission is allowed to make.
I do entreat you, not a man depart,
Save I alone, till Antony have spoke.   *Exit.*

60 1 PLEBEIAN. Stay, ho! And let us hear Mark Antony.

3 PLEBEIAN. Let him go up into the public chair.

---

1 The reason for his death is recorded.
2 Diminished. disparaged.
3 Overstated, exaggerated.
4 Bestow honor on.

We'll hear him. Noble Antony, go up.

ANTONY. For Brutus' sake, I am beholding[1] to you.

4 PLEBEIAN. What does he say of Brutus?

3 PLEBEIAN. He says, for Brutus' sake   65
  He finds himself beholding to us all.

4 PLEBEIAN. 'Twere best he speak no harm of Brutus here!

1 PLEBEIAN. This Caesar was a tyrant.

3 PLEBEIAN.   Nay, that's certain:
  We are blest that Rome is rid of him.

2 PLEBEIAN. Peace! Let us hear what Antony can say.   70

ANTONY. You gentle Romans—

ALL.   Peace, ho! Let us hear him.

ANTONY. Friends! Romans! Countrymen! Lend me your ears.
  I come to bury Caesar, not to praise him.
  The evil that men do lives after them;
  The good is oft interrèd with their bones: 75
  So let it be with Caesar. The noble Brutus
  Hath told you Caesar was ambitious.
  If it were so, it was a grievous fault,
  And grievously hath Caesar answered[2] it.
  Here, under leave[3] of Brutus and the rest—   80
  For Brutus is an honorable man,
  So are they all, all honorable men—
  Come I to speak in Caesar's funeral.
  He was my friend: faithful and just to me.
  But Brutus says he was ambitious,   85
  And Brutus is an honorable man.
  He hath brought many captives home to Rome,
  Whose ransoms did the general coffers fill.
  Did this in Caesar seem ambitious?
  When that the poor have cried, Caesar hath wept;   90
  Ambition should be made of sterner stuff.
  Yet Brutus says he was ambitious,
  And Brutus is an honorable man.
  You all did see that on the Lupercal

---

1 Obliged, indebted.
2 Made amends, paid for.
3 By permission.

95 I thrice presented him a kingly crown,
Which he did thrice refuse. Was this ambition?
Yet Brutus says he was ambitious,
And sure he is an honorable man.
I speak not to disprove what Brutus spoke,
100 But here I am, to speak what I do know.
You all did love him once, not without cause.
What cause withholds you, then, to mourn for him?
O judgment! Thou art fled to brutish beasts,
And men have lost their reason! Bear with me;
105 My heart is in the coffin there with Caesar,
And I must pause till it come back to me.

1 PLEBEIAN. Methinks there is much reason in his sayings.

2 PLEBEIAN. If thou consider rightly of the matter,
Caesar has had great wrong.

3 PLEBEIAN.   Has he, masters?
110 I fear there will a worse come in his place.

4 PLEBEIAN. Marked ye his words? He would not take the
crown;
Therefore 'tis certain he was not ambitious.

1 PLEBEIAN. If it be found so, some will dear abide[1] it.

2 PLEBEIAN. Poor soul, his eyes are red as fire with weeping.

115 3 PLEBEIAN. There's not a nobler man in Rome than Antony.

4 PLEBEIAN. Now mark him, he begins again to speak.

ANTONY. But yesterday, the word of Caesar might
Have stood against the world. Now lies he there,
And none so poor to do him reverence.[2]
120 O masters! If I were disposed to stir
Your hearts and minds to mutiny and rage,
I should do Brutus wrong, and Cassius wrong,
Who you all know are honorable men.
I will not do them wrong; I rather choose
125 To wrong the dead, to wrong myself and you,
Than I will wrong such honorable men.
But here's a parchment with the seal of Caesar;

---

1 Sorely pay for.
2 I.e., "the meanest man is now too high to do reverence to Caesar" (Johnson).

I found it in his closet. 'Tis his will.
Let but the commons hear[1] this testament,
Which pardon me, I do not mean to read,   130
And they would go and kiss dead Caesar's wounds,
And dip their napkins in his sacred blood,
Yea, beg a hair of him for memory,
And dying, mention it within their wills,
Bequeathing it as a rich legacy   135
Unto their issue.
4 PLEBEIAN. We'll hear the will! Read it, Mark Antony!
ALL. The will! The will! We will hear Caesar's will!
ANTONY. Have patience, gentle friends. I must not read it.
    It is not meet you know how Caesar loved you.   140
    You are not wood, you are not stones, but men;
    And being men, hearing the will of Caesar,
    It will inflame you; it will make you mad.
    'Tis good you know not that you are his heirs,
    For if you should, oh, what would come of it?   145
4 PLEBEIAN. Read the will! We'll hear it, Antony!
    You shall[2] read us the will! Caesar's will!
ANTONY. Will you be patient? Will you stay awhile?
    I have o'ershot myself[3] to tell you of it,
    I fear I wrong the honorable men   150
    Whose daggers have stabbed Caesar. I do fear it.
4 PLEBEIAN. They were traitors! "Honorable men"?
ALL. The will! The testament!
2 PLEBEIAN. They were villains, murderers! The will! Read the
        will!
ANTONY. You will compel me then to read the will?   155
    Then make a ring about the corpse of Caesar,
    And let me show you him that made the will.
    Shall I descend? And will you give me leave?
ALL. Come down!
2 PLEBEIAN. Descend!
3 PLEBEIAN.   You shall have leave.

---

1 If you common people were only to hear.
2 Must (as in legal language).
3 Gone beyond what I intended (a metaphor from archery).

4 PLEBEIAN.   A ring!
   Stand round!

160 1 PLEBEIAN.   Stand from the hearse! Stand from the body!
   2 PLEBEIAN. Room for Antony! Most noble Antony!
   ANTONY. Nay, press not so upon me! Stand far'er[1] off.
   ALL. Stand back! Room! Bear back!
   ANTONY. If you have tears, prepare to shed them now.
165   You all do know this mantle;[2] I remember
      The first time ever Caesar put it on.
      'Twas on a summer's evening in his tent,
      That day he overcame the Nervii.
      Look, in this place ran Cassius' dagger through.
170   See what a rent the envious[3] Casca made.
      Through this, the well-belovèd Brutus stabbed,
      And as he plucked his cursèd steel away,
      Mark how the blood of Caesar followed it,
      As rushing out of doors to be resolved
175   If Brutus so unkindly[4] knocked or no;
      For Brutus, as you know, was Caesar's angel.[5]
      Judge, O you gods, how dearly Caesar loved him.
      This was the most unkindest[6] cut of all,
      For when the noble Caesar saw him stab,
180   Ingratitude, more strong than traitors' arms,
      Quite vanquished him; then burst his mighty heart,
      And in his mantle muffling up his face,
      Even at the base of Pompey's statue,
      Which all the while ran blood, great Caesar fell.
185   Oh, what a fall was there, my countrymen!
      Then I, and you, and all of us fell down,
      Whilst bloody treason flourished[7] over us.
      Oh, now you weep, and I perceive you feel

---

1   Farther (pronounced in one syllable for the meter).
2   Cloak.
3   (1) Jealous; (2) malicious.
4   (1) Cruelly; (2) unnaturally (taking "kind" to mean nature). I.e., to answer
whether Brutus knocked unkindly or not.
5   Minister of loving offices; favorite.
6   See 3.2.175n, TLN 1717n.
7   (1) Thrived, prospered; (2) made flourishes (as with a weapon).

The dint[1] of pity. These are gracious drops.
Kind souls, what weep you[2] when you but behold   190
Our Caesar's vesture[3] wounded? Look you here!
Here is himself, marred as you see with traitors.

1 PLEBEIAN. Oh, piteous spectacle!

2 PLEBEIAN.   O noble Caesar!

3 PLEBEIAN. Oh, woeful day!

4 PLEBEIAN.   Oh, traitors! Villains!

1 PLEBEIAN. Oh, most bloody sight!

2 PLEBEIAN.   We will be revenged!   195

ALL. Revenge! About![4] Seek! Burn! Fire! Kill! Slay!
Let not a traitor live!

ANTONY.   Stay, countrymen!

1 PLEBEIAN. Peace there! Hear the noble Antony!

2 PLEBEIAN. We'll hear him! We'll follow him! We'll die with
him.

ANTONY. Good friends! Sweet friends! Let me not stir you up   200
To such a sudden flood of mutiny.
They that have done this deed are honorable.
What private griefs they have, alas, I know not,
That made them do it. They are wise and honorable,
And will no doubt with reasons answer you.   205
I come not, friends, to steal away your hearts.
I am no orator, as Brutus is,
But, as you know me all, a plain blunt man
That love my friend, and that they know full well
That gave me public leave to speak of him: 210
For I have neither wit,[5] nor words, nor worth,
Action, nor utterance, nor the power of speech
To stir men's blood. I only speak right on.[6]
I tell you that which you yourselves do know;

---

1 Mark made by pressure.
2 (1) Why do you weep; (2) what? Do you weep (construing "what" as a sepa-
rate question or exclamation).
3 Clothing.
4 Go about it, get on with it.
5 Imaginative intelligence.
6 Directly, straightforwardly.

215 Show you sweet Caesar's wounds, poor poor dumb mouths,
And bid them speak for me. But were I Brutus,
And Brutus Antony, there were an Antony
Would ruffle up¹ your spirits and put a tongue
In every wound of Caesar that should move
220 The stones of Rome to rise and mutiny.

ALL. We'll mutiny!

1 PLEBEIAN.   We'll burn the house of Brutus!

3 PLEBEIAN. Away then! Come, seek the conspirators!

ANTONY. Yet hear me countrymen! Yet hear me speak!

ALL. Peace, ho! Hear Antony! Most noble Antony!

225 ANTONY. Why, friends, you go to do you know not what.
Wherein hath Caesar thus deserved your loves?
Alas you know not. I must tell you then:
You have forgot the will I told you of.

ALL. Most true! The will! Let's stay and hear the will!

230 ANTONY. Here is the will, and under Caesar's seal.
To every Roman citizen he gives,
To every several man, seventy-five drachmas.

2 PLEBEIAN. Most noble Caesar! We'll revenge his death!

3 PLEBEIAN. O royal Caesar!

ANTONY. Hear me with patience.

235 ALL.   Peace ho!

ANTONY. Moreover, he hath left you all his walks,
His private arbors, and new-planted orchards
On this side Tiber. He hath left them you
And to your heirs forever—common pleasures²
240 To walk abroad and recreate yourselves.
Here was a Caesar! When comes such another?

1 PLEBEIAN. Never, never! Come! Away! Away!
We'll burn his body in the holy place,
And with the brands fire the traitors' houses!
245 Take up the body!

2 PLEBEIAN. Go! Fetch fire!

3 PLEBEIAN. Pluck down benches!

---

1 Stir up (to indignation).
2 Pleasure grounds, recreational parks.

4 PLEBEIAN. Pluck down forms,[1] windows, anything!

                    Exit Plebeians [with the body].

ANTONY. Now let it work! Mischief,[2] thou art a-foot:

  Take thou what course thou wilt.   250

Enter servant.

  How now, fellow?

SERVANT. Sir, Octavius is already come to Rome.

ANTONY. Where is he?

SERVANT. He and Lepidus are at Caesar's house.

ANTONY. And thither will I straight to visit him.   255

  He comes upon a wish.[3] Fortune is merry,

  And in this mood will give us anything.

SERVANT. I heard him say Brutus and Cassius

  Are rid[4] like madmen through the gates of Rome.

ANTONY. Belike[5] they had some notice of the people 260

  How I had moved them. Bring me to Octavius.

                         Exeunt.

[3.3][6]

Enter Cinna the Poet, and after him the Plebeians.

CINNA. I dreamt tonight,[7] that I did feast with Caesar,

  And things unluckily charge my fantasy.[8]

  I have no will to wander forth of doors,

  Yet something leads me forth.

1 PLEBEIAN. What is your name?   5

2 PLEBEIAN. Whither are you going?

3 PLEBEIAN. Where do you dwell?

4 PLEBEIAN. Are you a married man or a bachelor?

---

1 (1) Benches; (2) window frames.
2 (1) Discord; (2) harm, evil.
3 As I had hoped.
4 Have rode.
5 In all likelihood, probably.
6 This brief scene, based closely on an episode reported by Plutarch (Appendix
A1, p. 203, and A2, p. 218), makes a telling point about mob violence.
7 See 2.2.275n, TLN 1069n.
8 Ominously oppress my imagination.

2 PLEBEIAN. Answer every man directly.[1]

10 1 PLEBEIAN. Ay, and briefly.

4 PLEBEIAN. Ay, and wisely.

3 PLEBEIAN. Ay, and truly, you were best.

CINNA. What is my name? Whither am I going? Where do I dwell? Am I a married man or a bachelor? Then to answer every

15 man, directly and briefly, wisely and truly: wisely I say, I am a bachelor.

2 PLEBEIAN. That's as much as to say, they are fools that marry. You'll bear me a bang[2] for that, I fear. Proceed directly!

CINNA. Directly I am going to Caesar's funeral.

20 1 PLEBEIAN. As a friend or an enemy?

CINNA. As a friend.

2 PLEBEIAN. That matter is answered directly.

4 PLEBEIAN. For your dwelling—briefly.

CINNA. Briefly, I dwell by the Capitol.

25 3 PLEBEIAN. Your name sir, truly.

CINNA. Truly, my name is Cinna.

1 PLEBEIAN. Tear him to pieces! He's a conspirator!

CINNA. I am Cinna the poet! I am Cinna the poet!

4 PLEBEIAN. Tear him for his bad verses! Tear him for his bad

30 verses!

CINNA. I am not Cinna the conspirator.

4 PLEBEIAN. It is no matter; his name's Cinna. Pluck but his name out of his heart, and turn him going.[3]

3 PLEBEIAN. Tear him! Tear him! Come! Brands ho! Firebrands

35 to Brutus! To Cassius! Burn all! Some to Decius' house, and some to Casca's! Some to Ligarius'! Away, go!

Exeunt all the plebeians.

---

1 Without equivocation or misdirection.
2 Receive a blow from me.
3 Send him packing (with ominous implication).

[4.1][1]

Enter Antony, Octavius, and Lepidus.

ANTONY. These many then shall die; their names are pricked.

OCTAVIUS. Your brother too must die. Consent you, Lepidus?

LEPIDUS. I do consent.

OCTAVIUS.   Prick him down, Antony.

LEPIDUS. Upon condition Publius shall not live,
  Who is your sister's son, Mark Antony.   5

ANTONY. He shall not live. Look, with a spot[2] I damn[3] him.
  But Lepidus, go you to Caesar's house,
  Fetch the will hither, and we shall determine
  How to cut off some charge in legacies.[4]

LEPIDUS. What, shall I find you here?   10

OCTAVIUS. Or here, or at the Capitol.   *Exit Lepidus.*

ANTONY. This is a slight, unmeritable[5] man,
  Meet to be sent on errands. Is it fit,
  The three-fold world divided, he should stand
  One of the three to share it?

OCTAVIUS.   So you thought him,   15
  And took his voice[6] who should be pricked to die
  In our black sentence and proscription.[7]

ANTONY. Octavius, I have seen more days than you,
  And though we lay these honors on this man
  To ease ourselves of divers sland'rous loads,[8]   20

---

1 From frenzied mob violence in a public place we move to cool decisions for judicial murder among select patricians in a quiet setting, but the result is the same in both cases: people die. Plutarch comments on the patricians' deliberations: "In my opinion there was never a more horrible, unnatural, and crueller change than this was" (Appendix A3, p. 242). The scene also reveals relations among the three men, who are trying to assert control of the republic (4.1.14–15, TLN 1868).

2 Mark, in this case with a pin-prick.

3 Condemn.

4 Reduce the amount bequeathed.

5 Insignificant, unable to claim merit.

6 (1) Recognized his right to speak; (2) took his recommendation.

7 Parallel ways to describe orders for executing their enemies .

8 Get rid of various accusations we might bear (by implying that Lepidus is responsible for them).

He shall but bear them, as the ass bears gold,
To groan and sweat under the business,
Either led or driven, as we point the way;
And having brought our treasure where we will,
25 Then take we down his load and turn him off
Like to the empty ass,[1] to shake his ears
And graze in commons.[2]

OCTAVIUS.   You may do your will,
But he's a tried and valiant soldier.

ANTONY. So is my horse, Octavius, and for that
30 I do appoint him store of provender.[3]
It is a creature that I teach to fight,
To wind,[4] to stop, to run directly on,
His corporal[5] motion governed by my spirit.
And in some taste[6] is Lepidus but so:
35 He must be taught, and trained, and bid go forth—
A barren-spirited fellow, one that feeds
On objects, arts, and imitations,
Which out of use, and staled by[7] other men,
Begin his fashion. Do not talk of him
40 But as a property.[8] And now, Octavius,
Listen[9] great things. Brutus and Cassius
Are levying powers;[10] we must straight make head.[11]
Therefore let our alliance be combined,[12]
Our best friends made,[13] our means stretched,[14]

---

1 Unloaded donkey.
2 (1) Land not privately owned but set aside for community use (properly "common"); (2) commoners, common people (perhaps glancing mean-spiritedly at the fact that Lepidus came from a nobler family than his fellow triumvirs).
3 Ample supply of horse feed.
4 Turn.
5 Bodily.
6 Sense.
7 Made stale by.
8 (1) Another's possession (i.e., not his own); (2) means to an economic end; (3) stage appurtenance.
9 Hear; attend to.
10 Raising armies.
11 Immediately press forward in opposition (to them).
12 Work together (implicitly acknowledging the rivalry).
13 Find strong allies.
14 Every resource be brought to bear.

And let us presently go sit in council   45
How covert matters may be best disclosed,[1]
And open perils surest answerèd.[2]
OCTAVIUS. Let us do so, for we are at the stake
And bayed about[3] with many enemies,
And some that smile have in their hearts, I fear,   50
Millions of mischiefs.[4]   *Exeunt.*

[4.2][5]

Drum. Enter Brutus, Lucilius, and the army. Titinius and Pindarus
meet them.
BRUTUS. Stand,[6] ho!
LUCILIUS. Give the word,[7] ho, and stand!
BRUTUS. What now, Lucilius, is Cassius near?
LUCILIUS. He is at hand, and Pindarus is come
    To do you salutation[8] from his master.   5
BRUTUS. He greets me well.[9] Your master, Pindarus,
    In his own change or by ill officers,[10]
    Hath given me some worthy[11] cause to wish
    Things done, undone; but if he be at hand
    I shall be satisfied.
PINDARUS.   I do not doubt   10
    But that my noble master will appear
    Such as he is, full of regard[12] and honor.
BRUTUS. He is not doubted. A word, Lucilius,

---

1 How things known only to ourselves may be best presented publicly.
2 Dealt with, responded to.
3 A metaphor from bear-baiting, in which a bear was chained to a stake to
fight off dogs who "bayed about" it, or barked fiercely as they attacked; see also
4.1.272–73, TLN 1500–01.
4 Evils.
5 Outside Brutus's tent in an army encampment.
6 Halt.
7 Pass the word.
8 Greet you.
9 His greetings are welcome.
10 Because he has changed himself or been influenced by poor officers.
11 Weighty, substantial.
12 High repute.

How he received you. Let me be resolved.[1]
15 LUCILIUS. With courtesy and with respect enough,
But not with such familiar instances,[2]
Nor with such free and friendly conference[3]
As he hath used of old.
BRUTUS.   Thou hast described
A hot friend cooling. Ever note, Lucilius,
20 When love begins to sicken and decay,
It useth an enforcèd ceremony.[4]
There are no tricks in plain and simple faith,
But hollow[5] men, like horses hot at hand,[6]
Make gallant show and promise of their mettle;
                                        Low march within.[7]
25 But when they should endure the bloody spur,
They fall their crests,[8] and like deceitful jades[9]
Sink in the trial.[10] Comes his army on?
LUCILIUS. They mean this night in Sardis to be quartered.
The greater part, the horse in general,[11]
Are come with Cassius.

Enter Cassius and his powers.[12]
30 BRUTUS.   Hark! he is arrived.
March gently[13] on to meet him.
CASSIUS. Stand, ho!
BRUTUS. Stand, ho! Speak the word along!
1 SOLDIER. Stand!
35 2 SOLDIER. Stand!
3 SOLDIER. Stand!

---

1 Certain, fully informed.
2 Friendly solicitations, loving and urgent entreaties.
3 Conversation.
4 Strained politeness.
5 Insincere, false.
6 Eager at the start.
7 Muffled drums beating a march within the tiring house, as if at a distance.
8 Lower their heads (in weariness and dispiritedness).
9 Inferior horses.
10 Fail when put to the test.
11 Mounted troops, cavalry.
12 Army.
13 In good order (i.e., without hostile signs).

CASSIUS. Most noble brother, you have done me wrong.

BRUTUS. Judge me, you gods! Wrong I mine enemies?
And if not so, how should I wrong a brother?

CASSIUS. Brutus, this sober form of yours hides wrongs,[1]   40
And when you do them—

BRUTUS.   Cassius, be content.[2]
Speak your griefs[3] softly. I do know you well.
Before the eyes of both our armies here,
Which should perceive nothing but love from us,
Let us not wrangle. Bid them move away;   45
Then in my tent, Cassius, enlarge your griefs,
And I will give you audience.[4]

CASSIUS.   Pindarus,
Bid our commanders lead their charges[5] off
A little from this ground.

BRUTUS. Lucilius, do you the like, and let no man   50
Come to our tent, till we have done our conference.
Let Lucius and Titinius guard our door.

Exeunt [all but] Brutus and Cassius.

[4.3][6]

CASSIUS. That you have wronged me doth appear in this:
You have condemned and noted Lucius Pella[7]
For taking bribes here of the Sardians,[8]

---

1 Upright demeanor conceals injuries.
2 Be calm or quiet.
3 Grievances.
4 I will listen to you.
5 Soldiers under their command or "charge."
6 This scene is continuous with the previous one (see 4.2.01–02, TLN 1908),
but editors since Pope have acknowledged an implicit change of location from
outside Brutus's tent to inside it (4.2.52, TLN 1967) by inserting a scene change.
On the Globe's fluid stage this change would not have been marked, especially
since Brutus and Cassius do not exit; however, Pope's printing innovation is
now almost 300 years old, and clarity of reference recommends it, since almost
all editions follow it. The guards Brutus posted outside his tent entrance inter-
cept the interruptive poet (4.3.124.01, TLN 2108).
7 "Brutus, upon complaint of the Sardians, did condemn and note Lucius Pella
for a defamed person " (Appendix A1, p. 222).
8 Citizens of Sardia.

Wherein my letters, praying on his side,
5   Because I knew the man, was slighted off[1]
BRUTUS. You wronged yourself to write in such a case.
CASSIUS. In such a time as this, it is not meet
   That every nice offense should bear his comment.[2]
BRUTUS. Let me tell you, Cassius, you yourself
10   Are much condemned to have an itching palm,[3]

---

1 Treated slightingly, disregarded.
2 It is not appropriate for every trivial misstep to be criticized.
3 You have a bad reputation for seeking corrupt financial advantage.

4.3:   QUARRELING PATRICIANS
                  (TLN 1970–2245)

The barely concealed competitive friction between Antony and
Octavius in the previous scene is immediately followed by open and
nearly violent conflict between Brutus and Cassius, who have been
in an uneasy contest with each other from the beginning of their alliance against Caesar. The succession of scenes suggests that Brutus
and Cassius have reached a later stage in their rivalry than the other
two, so the latest wave of patrician competition nears its peak as the
next wave gathers strength (Velz, "Undular").

The quarrel and reconciliation of Brutus and Cassius was one of the
most admired episodes in *Julius Caesar* in the eighteenth and nineteenth
centuries, because it was thought to display such nobility of spirit on
Brutus's part. While Shakespeare's Brutus is undoubtedly noble, as
Plutarch emphasizes (Appendix A2, p. 220), one of his most salient
qualities as a patrician is prideful self-ignorance, which appears in
his aggressive display of anger management as a way to maintain his
dominance over Cassius. Brutus and Cassius have left Rome, as noted
in 3.2.58–59, TLN 1810, and they are making camp with their armies
near Sardis (4.2.28, TLN 1940), capital of Lydia, now part of Turkey.
Contention for control of the republic has taken the contenders far
from Rome, where the republic originated, and the play will end without their returning to Rome or resolving their contention.

To sell and mart[1] your offices[2] for gold
To undeservers.

CASSIUS.   I, an itching palm?
You know that you are Brutus that speaks this,
Or by the gods, this speech were else your last!

BRUTUS. The name of Cassius honors this corruption,   15
And chastisement doth therefore hide his head.

CASSIUS. Chastisement!

BRUTUS. Remember March, the ides of March remember.

---

1 Market, traffic in.
2 Positions or posts to which certain duties are attached.

William Charles Macready playing Cassius in 1850. Illustration used by permission of
the Folger Shakespeare Library.

Did not great Julius bleed for justice' sake?
20 What villain touched his body that did stab
And not for justice?[1] What, shall one of us
That struck the foremost man of all this world
But for supporting robbers, shall we now
Contaminate our fingers with base bribes,
25 And sell the mighty space of our large honors[2]
For so much trash as may be graspèd thus?
I had rather be a dog and bay[3] the moon
Than such a Roman.
CASSIUS.   Brutus, bait[4] not me!
I'll not endure[5] it. You forget yourself
30 To hedge me in.[6] I am a soldier, I,
Older in practice, abler than yourself
To make conditions.
BRUTUS. Go to. You are not Cassius.
CASSIUS. I am.
35 BRUTUS. I say, you are not.
CASSIUS. Urge[7] me no more! I shall forget myself.
Have mind upon your health.[8] Tempt me[9] no farther.
BRUTUS. Away, slight[10] man.
CASSIUS. Is't possible?
BRUTUS.   Hear me, for I will speak.
40 Must I give way and room[11] to your rash choler?[12]
Shall I be frighted when a madman stares?
CASSIUS. O ye gods! Ye gods! Must I endure all this?

---

1 Which of us was so villainous as to stab for any cause but justice?
2 And sell the greatness of our honorable reputations and the high offices we
have power to confer.
3 Bark or howl at.
4 (1) Harass (as dogs "baited" a chained bear; (2) catch or trap by means of bait.
5 Put up with.
6 Crowd, challenge me.
7 Provoke.
8 Look out for your well-being (an obvious threat).
9 Put me to the test in a risky way.
10 Of no consequence.
11 Yield to and give scope to.
12 Foolish anger.

BRUTUS. All this? Ay, more. Fret[1] till your proud heart break.
    Go show your slaves how choleric you are,
    And make your bondmen tremble. Must I budge?[2]   45
    Must I observe[3] you? Must I stand and crouch
    Under your testy humor?[4] By the gods,
    You shall[5] digest the venom of your spleen,[6]
    Though it do split you. For from this day forth,
    I'll use you for my mirth, yea for my laughter,   50
    When you are waspish.[7]

CASSIUS.   Is it come to this?

BRUTUS. You say you are a better soldier.
    Let it appear so; make your vaunting true,
    And it shall please me well. For mine own part,
    I shall be glad to learn of[8] noble men.   55

CASSIUS. You wrong me every way. You wrong me, Brutus.
    I said an elder soldier, not a better.
    Did I say "better"?

BRUTUS.   If you did, I care not.

CASSIUS. When Caesar lived, he durst not[9] thus have moved me.

BRUTUS. Peace, peace! You durst not so have tempted him.   60

CASSIUS. I durst not?

BRUTUS. No.

CASSIUS. What? durst not tempt him?

BRUTUS.   For your life you durst not.

CASSIUS. Do not presume too much upon my love;
    I may do that I shall be sorry for.   65

BRUTUS. You have done that you should be sorry for.
    There is no terror, Cassius, in your threats,
    For I am armed so strong in honesty

---

1   Show annoyance.
2   Wince, flinch.
3   Humor, gratify.
4   Irritable temperament.
5   Must.
6   Poison of your ill temper.
7   Irascible, petulant.
8   (1) Learn from; (?) learn about.
9   Would not have dared.

That they pass by me as the idle wind,[1]
70   Which I respect not.[2] I did send to you
For certain sums of gold, which you denied me,
For I can raise no money by vile means.
By heaven, I had rather coin my heart[3]
And drop my blood[4] for drachmas than to wring
75   From the hard hands of peasants their vile trash
By any indirection. I did send
To you for gold to pay my legions,
Which you denied me. Was that done like Cassius?
Should I have answered Caius Cassius so?
80   When Marcus Brutus grows so covetous,
To lock such rascal counters[5] from his friends,
Be ready, gods: with all your thunderbolts
Dash[6] him to pieces.

CASSIUS.   I denied you not.

BRUTUS. You did.

CASSIUS.   I did not. He was but a fool
85   That brought my answer back. Brutus hath rived[7] my heart.
A friend should bear his friend's infirmities,
But Brutus makes mine greater then they are.

BRUTUS. I do not, till you practice them on me.

CASSIUS. You love me not.

BRUTUS.   I do not like your faults.
90 CASSIUS. A friendly eye could never see such faults.

BRUTUS. A flatterer's would not, though they do appear
As huge as high Olympus.

CASSIUS. Come, Antony, and young Octavius, come,
Revenge yourselves alone on Cassius,
95   For Cassius is aweary of the world,
Hated by one he loves, braved[8] by his brother,

---

1 Lightest breeze (i.e., insubstantial, inconsequential).
2 Pay no attention to.
3 Turn my heart into money.
4 Let my blood fall in drops.
5 Debased coins, trivial quantities.
6 Break violently.
7 See 1.3.6n, TLN 438n.
8 Defied.

Checked[1] like a bondman, all his faults observed,
Set in a notebook, learned, and conned by rote[2]
To cast into my teeth. Oh, I could weep
My spirit[3] from mine eyes. There is my dagger,   100
And here my naked breast; within, a heart
Dearer than Pluto's mine, richer than gold.
If that thou be'est a Roman, take it forth.
I that denied the gold will give my heart.
Strike as thou did'st at Caesar, for I know,   105
When thou did'st hate him worst, thou loved'st him better
Than ever thou loved'st Cassius.
BRUTUS.   Sheath your dagger.
Be angry when you will, it shall have scope;[4]
Do what you will, dishonor shall be humor.[5]
O Cassius, you are yokèd with a lamb   110
That carries anger as the flint bears fire,
Who much enforcèd, shows a hasty spark,
And straight is cold again.
CASSIUS.   Hath Cassius lived
To be but mirth and laughter to his Brutus,
When grief and blood ill-tempered[6] vexeth him?[7]   115
BRUTUS. When I spoke that, I was ill-tempered too.
CASSIUS. Do you confess so much? Give me your hand.
BRUTUS. And my heart too.
CASSIUS. O Brutus!
BRUTUS.   What's the matter?
CASSIUS. Have not you love enough to bear with me,   120
When that rash humor[8] which my mother gave me
Makes me forgetful?

---

1 Rebuked.
2 Learned by heart.
3 (1) Soul; (2) vital or animal spirits (the source of life).
4 Be angry whenever you want to; I won't try to stop you.
5 I.e., I'll regard your corruption or your flaring temper as something to be
humored.
6 Poorly mixed blood.
7 I.e., does Cassius's life amount to nothing more than to be the object of
Brutus's mockery when Cassius is troubled by grief and bad temper?
8 Disposition.

BRUTUS.　　　　　　　Yes, Cassius, and from henceforth,
When you are over-earnest with your Brutus,
He'll think your mother chides, and leave you so.[1]

Enter a Poet[, Lucilius, and Titinius].

125　POET. Let me go in to see the generals!
There is some grudge between 'em. 'Tis not meet
They be alone.

LUCILIUS.　　　　You shall not come to them!

POET. Nothing but death shall stay[2] me.

CASSIUS. How now? What's the matter?

130　POET. For shame, you generals! What do you mean?
Love, and be friends, as two such men should be,
For I have seen more years, I'm sure, than ye.

CASSIUS. Ha, ha! How vilely doth this cynic rhyme!

BRUTUS. Get you hence, sirrah! Saucy[3] fellow, hence!

135　CASSIUS. Bear with him, Brutus; 'tis his fashion.[4]

BRUTUS. I'll know his humor, when he knows his time.[5]
What should the wars do with these jigging[6] fools?
Companion,[7] hence.

CASSIUS.　　　　　　Away, away be gone.

Exit Poet.

BRUTUS. Lucilius and Titinius, bid the commanders
140　Prepare to lodge their companies[8] tonight.

CASSIUS. And come yourselves, and bring Messala with you
Immediately to us.　　　[*Exeunt Lucilius and Titinius.*]

BRUTUS.　　　　　Lucius, a bowl of wine.

CASSIUS. I did not think you could have been so angry.

BRUTUS. O Cassius, I am sick of many griefs.

145　CASSIUS. Of your philosophy you make no use,

1　Say no more about it.
2　Prevent.
3　See 1.1.19n, TLN 24n.
4　Manner.
5　I'll put up with his mood when he knows the right time to show it.
6　Moving jerkily (referring to the poet's bad verse).
7　Term of familiarity or contempt.
8　Billet their soldiers.

If you give place to accidental evils.[1]

BRUTUS. No man bears sorrow better. Portia is dead.

CASSIUS. Ha? Portia?

BRUTUS. She is dead.

CASSIUS. How scaped I killing, when I crossed you so?   150
    O insupportable and touching loss!
    Upon what sickness?

BRUTUS.   Impatient of my absence,
    And grief that young Octavius with Mark Antony
    Have made themselves so strong—for with her death[2]
    That tidings came—with this she fell distract,[3]   155
    And, her attendants absent, swallowed fire.[4]

CASSIUS. And died so?

BRUTUS.   Even so.

CASSIUS.   O ye immortal gods!

Enter Boy with wine and tapers.

BRUTUS. Speak no more of her. Give me a bowl of wine.
    In this I bury all unkindness, Cassius.   *Drinks.*

CASSIUS. My heart is thirsty for that noble pledge.   160
    Fill, Lucius, till the wine o'erswell the cup.
    I cannot drink too much of Brutus' love.   [*Drinks.*]
                                 [*Exit Lucius.*]

Enter Titinius and Messala.

BRUTUS. Come in, Titinius. Welcome, good Messala.
    Now sit we[5] close about this taper here,
    And call in question our necessities.[6]   165

CASSIUS. Portia, art thou gone?

BRUTUS.   No more, I pray you.
    Messala, I have here received letters

---

1 Cassius is referring to Brutus's stoicism. See Appendix B, p. 205 *et passim*.
2 News of her death.
3 Became distraught.
4 Portia has committed suicide by swallowing hot coals; see also Appendix A2, p. 236.
5 Let us sit.
6 Discuss what we need to do.

That young Octavius and Mark Antony
Come down upon us with a mighty power,[1]
170   Bending their expedition[2] toward Philippi.
MESSALA. Myself have letters of the self-same tenor.[3]
BRUTUS. With what addition?
MESSALA. That by proscription[4] and bills of outlawry
  Octavius, Antony, and Lepidus
175   Have put to death an hundred senators.
BRUTUS. Therein our letters do not well agree:
  Mine speak of seventy senators that died
  By their proscriptions, Cicero being one.
CASSIUS. Cicero one?
MESSALA.   Cicero is dead,
180   And by that order of proscription.
  Had you your letters from your wife, my Lord?
BRUTUS. No, Messala.
MESSALA. Nor nothing in your letters writ of her?
BRUTUS. Nothing, Messala.[5]
MESSALA.   That methinks is strange.
185 BRUTUS. Why ask you? Hear you aught of her in yours?
MESSALA. No, my lord.
BRUTUS. Now as you are a Roman, tell me true.
MESSALA. Then like a Roman, bear the truth I tell.
  For certain she is dead, and by strange manner.
190 BRUTUS. Why farewell Portia. We must die, Messala.
  With meditating that she must die once,[6]
  I have the patience to endure it now.
MESSALA. Even so great men great losses should endure.
CASSIUS. I have as much of this in art[7] as you,

---

1 See 4.1.42n, TLN 1898n.
2 (1) Speed (from "expedite"); (2) warlike enterprise.
3 Import, content. I.e., I have received letters to the same effect.
4 Sentence of death.
5 On Brutus's odd denial of what he knows, see Introduction, p. 20. For discussion of the apparent textual crux, see Jowett.
6 That she must die at some time.
7 (1) Skill; (2) artifice, pose (for others' benefit).

But yet my nature could not bear it so.[1]   195

BRUTUS. Well, to our work alive.[2] What do you think

   Of marching to Philippi presently?

CASSIUS. I do not think it good.[3]

BRUTUS.   Your reason?

CASSIUS.   This it is:

   'Tis better that the enemy seek us,

   So shall he waste his means, weary his soldiers,   200

   Doing himself offense,[4] whilst we, lying still,

   Are full of rest, defense, and nimbleness.

BRUTUS. Good reasons must of force[5] give place to better.

   The people 'twixt Philippi and this ground

   Do stand but in a forced affection,   205

   For they have grudged us contribution.[6]

   The enemy, marching along by them,

   By them[7] shall make a fuller number up,

   Come on refreshed, new-added,[8] and encouraged,

   From which advantage shall we cut him off,   210

   If at Philippi we do face him there,

   These people at our back.

CASSIUS.   Hear me, good brother—

BRUTUS. Under your pardon. You must note, beside,

   That we have tried the utmost of our friends,[9]

   Our legions are brim full, our cause is ripe.   215

   The enemy increaseth every day;

   We, at the height, are ready to decline.

   There is a tide in the affairs of men,

   Which taken at the flood leads on to fortune;

---

1 I.e., I understand the art of self-suppression as well as you, but by nature I could not bear what you are bearing.

2 Among the living (as opposed to the dead).

3 Despite their reconciliation, Brutus and Cassius clash again, as they have throughout the play. In this, their last disagreement, Cassius is again right but is overruled, as he has been in earlier instances.

4 Hurt, injury.

5 Necessarily.

6 Have reluctantly given us supplies.

7 Among them, through their territory/by their enlistment.

8 Reinforced.

9 Obtained all that we can from our allies.

220 Omitted, all the voyage of their life
　　Is bound in shallows and in miseries.
　　On such a full sea are we now afloat,
　　And we must take the current when it serves,
　　Or lose our ventures.[1]
CASSIUS.　　　　　　　Then with your will go on.
225 We'll along ourselves and meet them at Philippi.
BRUTUS. The deep of night is crept upon our talk,
　　And nature must obey necessity,[2]
　　Which we will niggard with a little rest.[3]
　　There is no more to say.
CASSIUS.　　　　　　No more, good night,
230 Early tomorrow will we rise, and hence.
BRUTUS. Lucius!

Enter Lucius.

　　　　　　　My gown.[4]　　　　　　　[*Exit Lucius.*]
　　　　　　　Farewell, good Messala.
　　Good night Titinius. Noble, noble Cassius,
　　Good night, and good repose.
CASSIUS. O my dear brother!
235 This was an ill beginning of the night.
　　Never come such division 'tween our souls;
　　Let it not, Brutus.

Enter Lucius with the gown.

BRUTUS.　　　　　　Everything is well.
CASSIUS. Good night, my lord.
BRUTUS.　　　　　　　Good night, good brother.
TITINIUS, MESSALA. Good night, Lord Brutus.
240 BRUTUS.　　　　　　　　　Farewell, everyone.
　　　　　　　Exeunt [*Cassius, Titinius, Messala*].
　　Give me the gown. Where is thy instrument?
LUCIUS. Here in the tent.

---

1 Commercial speculations, business risks.
2 Our nature (which is to sleep) must obey the need (for sleep).
3 Pay skimpily with a little sleep.
4 Dressing gown.

BRUTUS.   What? Thou speak'st drowsily!
  Poor knave,[1] I blame thee not; thou art o'er-watched.[2]
  Call Claudio and some other of my men.
  I'll have them sleep on cushions in my tent.   245
LUCIUS. Varrus and Claudio![3]

Enter Varrus and Claudio.

VARRUS.   Calls my Lord?
BRUTUS. I pray you, sirs, lie in my tent and sleep.
  It may be I shall raise you[4] by and by
  On business to my brother Cassius.
VARRUS. So please you, we will stand and watch your pleasure.[5]   250
BRUTUS. I will not have it so. Lie down, good sirs.
  It may be I shall otherwise bethink me.[6]
  Look, Lucius, here's the book I sought for so:
  I put it in the pocket of my gown.
LUCIUS. I was sure your lordship did not give it me.   255
BRUTUS. Bear with me, good boy. I am much forgetful.
  Canst thou hold up thy heavy eyes awhile,
  And touch thy instrument a strain or two?
LUCIUS. Ay, my lord, an't please you.
BRUTUS.   It does, my boy:
  I trouble thee too much, but thou art willing.   260
LUCIUS. It is my duty, sir.
BRUTUS. I should not urge thy duty past thy might;
  I know young bloods look for a time of rest.
LUCIUS. I have slept, my lord, already.
BRUTUS. It was well done, and thou shalt sleep again.   265
  I will not hold thee long. If I do live,
  I will be good to thee.

                            Music and a song.

---

1 Young male servant (spoken affectionately).
2 Overtired from remaining on duty ("watch"), with a suggestion that Brutus will watch over him.
3 See above, Characters in the Play, p. 72.
4 Wake you up.
5 Stay awake and await your commands.
6 Change my mind.

This is a sleepy tune. O murd'rous slumber,
Layest thou thy leaden mace upon my boy
270 That plays the music? Gentle knave, good night.
I will not do thee so much wrong to wake thee.
If thou dost nod, thou break'st thy instrument.
I'll take it from thee, and, good boy, good night.
Let me see, let me see. Is not the leaf turned down[1]
275 Where I left reading? Here it is I think.

Enter the Ghost of Caesar.
How ill this taper burns. Ha! Who comes here?
I think it is the weakness of mine eyes
That shapes this monstrous apparition.
It comes upon me! Art thou anything?
280 Art thou some god, some angel, or some devil
That mak'st my blood cold and my hair to stare?[2]
Speak to me what thou art!
GHOST. Thy evil spirit, Brutus.
BRUTUS.   Why com'st thou?
GHOST. To tell thee thou shalt see me at Philippi.
285 BRUTUS. Well; then I shall see thee again?
GHOST. Ay, at Philippi.
BRUTUS. Why, I will see thee at Philippi, then.
Now I have taken heart, thou vanishest.

                                        [*Exit Ghost.*]

Ill spirit, I would hold more talk with thee.
290 Boy! Lucius! Varrus! Claudio! Sirs! Awake!
Claudio!
LUCIUS. The strings, my lord, are false.[3]
BRUTUS. He thinks he still is at his instrument.
Lucius, awake!
295 LUCIUS. My lord?
BRUTUS. Did'st thou dream, Lucius, that thou so criedst out?
LUCIUS. My Lord, I do not know that I did cry.
BRUTUS. Yes that thou did'st. Did'st thou see anything?

---

1 Corner of the page folded over (to mark the place).
2 Stand up.
3 Out of tune.

LUCIUS. Nothing my Lord.

BRUTUS. Sleep again, Lucius. Sirrah Claudio!   300
  Fellow! Thou! Awake!

VARRUS.   My lord?

CLAUDIO.   My lord?

BRUTUS. Why did you so cry out, sirs, in your sleep?

VARRUS; CLAUDIO. Did we my Lord?

BRUTUS.   Ay. Saw you anything?

VARRUS. No, my lord. I saw nothing.

CLAUDIO.   Nor I my Lord.

BRUTUS. Go, and commend me to[1] my brother Cassius.   305
  Bid him set on his powers betimes before,[2]
  And we will follow.

VARRUS; CLAUDIO. It shall be done, my lord.

                                  Exeunt.

[5.1][3]

Enter Octavius, Antony, and their army.

OCTAVIUS. Now, Antony, our hopes are answerèd.
  You said the enemy would not come down
  But keep the hills and upper regions.
  It proves not so: their battles[4] are at hand.
  They mean to warn us[5] at Philippi here,   5

---

1 Greet for me.

2 Tell him to march away with his troops early in the morning, before me.

3 The approach of Antony and Octavius has been anticipated (4.3.168–70, TLN 2162–2164), and the last act begins with their arrival at Philippi (5.1.5, TLN 2333) to confront the combined forces of Brutus and Cassius. From the moment we see Antony and Octavius together for the second time, they are competing constantly with each other—a development Shakespeare has anticipated earlier in this play and will bring to fruition in *Antony and Cleopatra*. The first half climaxed in a violent and bloody assassination, which brought nothing to a conclusion, least of all the fierce competition for personal dominance that Caesar personified, and the second half climaxes in the violence of battle, which is also inconclusive. Though the battle at Philippi at least presents the two sides as evenly matched, it goes against the chief conspirators, so Caesar's supplanters are supplanted, and Caesar's spirit implicitly triumphs, as the play comes to a sudden stop, with the patrician competition unresolved.

4 Main forces (as opposed to scouts, skirmishers, or vanguard).

5 Challenge us.

    Answering before we do demand of them.[1]
ANTONY. Tut,[2] I am in their bosoms,[3] and I know
    Wherefore[4] they do it. They could be content
    To visit other places,[5] and come down[6]
10   With fearful[7] bravery,[8] thinking by this face[9]
    To fasten in our thoughts[10] that they have courage.
    But 'tis not so.[11]

Enter a Messenger.

MESSALA.   Prepare you, generals!
    The enemy comes on in gallant show.
    Their bloody sign of battle is hung out,
15   And something to be done[12] immediately.
ANTONY. Octavius, lead your battle[13] softly[14] on
    Upon the left hand of the even field.
OCTAVIUS. Upon the right hand, I; keep thou the left.
ANTONY. Why do you cross[15] me in this exigent?[16]
20 OCTAVIUS. I do not cross you, but I will do so.[17]   *March.*

Drum. Enter Brutus, Cassius, and their army[*: Lucilius, Titinius,*
Messala, and others].

---

1 Answering our question (i.e., our challenge) before we can ask it.
2 "An ejaculation (often reduplicated) expressing impatience or dissatisfaction with a statement, notion, or proceeding, or contemptuously dismissing it" (OED).
3 Intimately familiar with their thinking.
4 Why.
5 Come and meet us (said facetiously).
6 Attack.
7 Frightening.
8 (1) Courage; (2) gorgeous appearance.
9 Sight.
10 Make us believe.
11 Antony is boastfully overconfident (cf. headnote to 5.4, p. 182). Taken more broadly, however, his comment ironically applies to the patrician struggle as a whole, including his part in it.
12 Should or must be done.
13 Main force.
14 Warily, carefully.
15 Contradict.
16 Critical moment.
17 (1) I will do as I say; (2) I will cross you some day.

BRUTUS. They stand and would have parley.[1]

CASSIUS. Stand fast, Titinius, we must out[2] and talk.

OCTAVIUS. Mark Antony, shall we give sign of battle?

ANTONY. No, Caesar, we will answer on their charge.[3]

    Make forth![4] The generals would have some words.   25

OCTAVIUS. Stir not until the signal.[5]

BRUTUS. Words before blows. Is it so, countrymen?

OCTAVIUS. Not that we love words better, as you do.

BRUTUS. Good words are better then bad strokes, Octavius.

ANTONY. In your bad strokes, Brutus, you give good words.[6]   30

    Witness the hole you made in Caesar's heart,

    Crying, "Long live! Hail, Caesar!"

CASSIUS.   Antony,

    The posture of your blows are[7] yet unknown;

    But for[8] your words, they rob the Hybla[9] bees,

    And leave them honeyless.[10]

ANTONY.   Not stingless too?   35

BRUTUS. Oh yes, and soundless too.

    For you have stol'n their buzzing, Antony,

    And very wisely threat before you sting.

ANTONY. Villains![11] You did not so, when your vile[12] daggers

    Hacked one another in the sides of Caesar.   40

    You showed your teeth[13] like apes, and fawned[14] like hounds,[15]

    And bowed like bondmen, kissing Caesar's feet,

---

1 Conference before battle.

2 Must go out.

3 Respond to their initiative.

4 Let's go.

5 Octavius is addressing his soldiers, not Antony.

6 As you deliver cruel blows, Brutus, you use deceiving flattery.

7 How you will deal your blows (strike militarily) is.

8 As for.

9 Sicilian town, well known for its honey.

10 Cassius's point is that Antony spoke honeyed words to the conspirators after Caesar's assassination but behaved differently from his words.

11 An insult that still in the late sixteenth century retained its original social-class connotation of "low-born, base-minded rustic" (OED).

12 Morally despicable, base, depraved.

13 In a threatening grimace (like an animal).

14 Made physical gestures of deference and affection.

15 The Folio breaks this line at "apes" in order to make it fit the column.

Whilst damnèd Casca, like a cur, behind
Struck Caesar on the neck. Oh, you flatterers!

45 CASSIUS. Flatterers? Now, Brutus, thank yourself!
This tongue had not offended so today,
If Cassius might have ruled.[1]

OCTAVIUS. Come, come, the cause.[2] If arguing make us sweat,
The proof[3] of it will turn to redder drops.

50 Look, I draw a sword against conspirators!
When think you that the sword goes up[4] again?
Never till Caesar's three-and-thirty wounds
Be well avenged, or till another Caesar
Have added slaughter[5] to the sword of traitors.

55 BRUTUS. Caesar, thou canst not die by traitors' hands,
Unless thou bring'st them with thee.[6]

OCTAVIUS.   So I hope.
I was not born to die on Brutus' sword.

BRUTUS. Oh, if[7] thou wert the noblest of thy strain,[8]
Young man, thou couldst not die more honorable.[9]

60 CASSIUS. A peevish[10] schoolboy, worthless of such honor,
Joined with a masker and a reveler.

ANTONY. Old Cassius still.[11]

OCTAVIUS.   Come, Antony! Away!
Defiance, traitors, hurl we in your teeth!
If you dare fight today, come to the field;

65 If not, when you have stomachs![12]

Exeunt Octavius, Antony, and army.

---

1 Prevailed. Cassius reminds Brutus that Cassius wanted to have Antony killed with Caesar (2.1.156–62, TLN 788–94).
2 Let's get back to the point.
3 Trial.
4 Goes back into the scabbard.
5 Until I too be killed.
6 The only traitorous hands that can kill you are on your own side.
7 Even if.
8 Lineage, family.
9 Honorably (than to be killed by Brutus).
10 Foolish, irritable.
11 (1) Full of years (past your prime); (2) set in your ways (incapable of change).
12 Appetites for it; i.e., courage. The exchange of harsh words before battle is a device that goes back to classical epic poetry.

CASSIUS. Why, now blow wind! Swell billow![1] And swim bark![2]
    The storm is up, and all is on the hazard![3]
BRUTUS. Ho, Lucilius! Hark, a word with you.

                                        Lucilius stands forth.

LUCILIUS. My lord?

                        [*Brutus speaks apart with Lucilius.*]

CASSIUS. Messala.

                                [*Messala stands forth.*]

MESSALA.   What says my general?
CASSIUS.   Messala,   70
    This is my birthday, as this very day
    Was Cassius born. [Give me thy hand, Messala,
    Be thou my witness, that against my will,
    As Pompey was, am I compelled to set
    Upon one battle all our liberties.]   75
    You know that I held Epicurus strong
    And his opinion; now I change my mind,
    And partly credit things that do presage.[4]
    Coming from Sardis, on our former ensign[5]
    Two mighty eagles fell, and there they perched,   80
    Gorging and feeding from our soldiers' hands,
    Who to Philippi here consorted us.
    This morning are they fled away and gone,
    And in their steads do ravens, crows, and kites
    Fly o'er our heads and downward look on us   85
    As we were[6] sickly prey. Their shadows seem
    A canopy most fatal,[7] under which
    Our army lies ready to give up the ghost.[8]
MESSALA. Believe not so.

---

1 Let the waves rise.
2 Let the sailing vessel float.
3 At stake.
4 Portend. Cassius comes to doubt his Epicureanism, when he thinks omens are against him, because Epicureans believed that the gods did not interfere with human beings. See Appendix B, p. 245.
5 Foremost battle flag.
6 As if we were.
7 Sky most fateful or deadly.
8 Die.

CASSIUS.   I but believe it partly,

90   For I am fresh of spirit and resolved
To meet all perils very constantly.
BRUTUS. Even so,[1] Lucilius.
CASSIUS.   Now, most noble Brutus,
The gods today stand friendly, that we may,
Lovers[2] in peace, lead on our days to age.

95   But since the affairs of men rest still[3] uncertain,
Let's reason with the worst that may befall.
If we do lose this battle, then is this
The very last time we shall speak together.
What are you then determinèd to do?

100   BRUTUS. Even by the rule of that philosophy[4]
By which I did blame Cato for the death
Which he did give himself, I know not how,
But I do find it cowardly and vile,
For fear of what might fall,[5] so to prevent[6]

105   The time of life, arming myself with patience
To stay[7] the providence of some high powers
That govern us below.
CASSIUS.   Then, if we lose this battle,
You are contented to be led in triumph
Thorough[8] the streets of Rome?

110   BRUTUS. No Cassius, no. Think not, thou noble Roman,
That ever Brutus will go bound to Rome;
He bears too great a mind. But this same day
Must end that work the ides of March begun,
And whether we shall meet again I know not.

115   Therefore our everlasting farewell take.
Forever and forever, farewell Cassius!

---

1 Having finished his private conversation with Lucilius, Brutus now turns back to the assembled company.
2 Friends.
3 Remain always.
4 I.e., stoicism. See Appendix B, p. 245.
5 Befall, happen.
6 Cut short.
7 Wait for.
8 Through.

If we do meet again, why we shall smile;
If not, why then this parting was well made.
CASSIUS. Forever and forever, farewell Brutus!
If we do meet again, we'll smile indeed;   120
If not, 'tis true, this parting was well made.
BRUTUS. Why then, lead on. Oh, that a man might know
The end of this day's business ere it come!
But it sufficeth that the day will end,
And then the end is known. Come ho, away!   125

Exeunt.

[5.2][1]

Alarum.[2] Enter Brutus and Messala.
BRUTUS. Ride, ride, Messala! Ride, and give these bills
Unto the legions, on the other side.[3]

Loud alarum.

Let them set on at once, for I perceive
But cold[4] demeanor in Octavio's wing,
And sudden push gives them the overthrow.   5
Ride, ride, Messala! Let them[5] all come down.[6]

Exeunt.

[5.3][7]

Alarums. Enter Cassius and Titinius.
CASSIUS. O look, Titinius! Look! The villains fly![8]
Myself have to mine own turned enemy![9]

---

1 With no scene break in the Folio, the action moves straight from parley to battle near Philippi.
2 "Any noise—bells, trumpet blasts, or drum rolls—which would serve to indicate an enemy attack" (Long).
3 Of Brutus's own army.
4 Uncertain, timid.
5 Brutus's forces, to whom Messala is carrying the bills (written orders).
6 Attack.
7 The battle at Philippi continues, with a focus now on Cassius and his defeat.
8 Referring to his own fleeing soldiers.
9 My own men have become my enemy.

This ensign[1] here of mine was turning back;
I slew the coward and did take it[2] from him.

5 TITINIUS. O Cassius, Brutus gave the word too early,
Who having some advantage on Octavius,
Took it too eagerly. His soldiers fell to spoil,[3]
Whilst we by Antony are all enclosed.[4]

Enter Pindarus.

PINDARUS. Fly further off, my Lord! Fly further off!
10 Mark Antony is in your tents, my Lord!
Fly, therefore, noble Cassius! Fly far'er[5] off!

CASSIUS. This hill is far enough. Look, look, Titinius!
Are those my tents, where I perceive the fire?

TITINIUS. They are, my Lord.

CASSIUS.   Titinius, if thou lovest me,
15 Mount thou my horse, and hide thy spurs in him
Till he have brought thee up to yonder troops
And here again, that I may rest assured
Whether yond troops are friend or enemy.

TITINIUS. I will be here again even with a thought.[6]   *Exit.*

20 CASSIUS. Go, Pindarus, get higher on that hill!
My sight was ever thick.[7] Regard Titinius,
And tell me what thou not'st[8] about the field.

[*Pindarus goes up.*]

This day I breathèd first. Time is come round,
And where I did begin, there shall I end.
25 My life is run his compass.[9] Sirrah, what news?

PINDARUS. [*Above.*] O my Lord!

CASSIUS. What news?

---

1 The soldier carrying the ensign, or battle flag.
2 The standard (or ensign) carried by the soldier who is named for it.
3 Ceased fighting in order to plunder.
4 "Cassius found himself compassed in with the right wing of his enemies' army" (Plutarch). See Appendix A2, p. 230.
5 See 3.2.162n, TLN 1704n.
6 I will be there and back again as quickly as you can think it.
7 Weak.
8 What you see.
9 Has come full circle.

PINDARUS. Titinius is enclosèd round about
   With horsemen that make to him on the spur,[1]
   Yet he spurs on. Now they are almost on him!   30
   Now, Titinius! Now some light.[2] Oh, he lights too.
   He's ta'en![3]   *Shout.*
                And hark! They shout for joy.
CASSIUS. Come down. Behold no more.
   Oh, coward that I am to live so long,
   To see my best friend ta'en before my face.   35

Enter Pindarus [from above].
   Come hither, sirrah.
   In Parthia did I take thee prisoner,
   And then I swore thee,[4] saving of thy life,
   That whatsoever I did bid thee do,
   Thou should'st attempt it. Come now, keep thine oath,   40
   Now be a free man, and with this good sword
   That ran through Caesar's bowels, search[5] this bosom.
   Stand not to answer. Here, take thou the hilts,[6]
   And when my face is cover'd, as 'tis now,
   Guide thou the sword—
                           [Pindarus kills him.]
               Caesar, thou art revenged,   45
   Even with the sword that killed thee.
PINDARUS. So, I am free, yet would not so have been
   Durst I have done my will.[7] O Cassius,
   Far from this country Pindarus shall run,
   Where never Roman shall take note of[8] him.   *[Exit.]* 50

Enter Titinius and Messala.

---

1 Ride toward him at full gallop.
2 Alight, dismount.
3 Taken, captured.
4 Made you swear.
5 Penetrate.
6 Handle.
7 If I had dared to choose for myself.
8 Know about.

MESSALA. It is but change,[1] Titinius, for Octavius
    Is overthrown by noble Brutus' power,
    As Cassius' legions are by Antony.
TITINIUS. These tidings will well comfort[2] Cassius.
MESSALA. Where did you leave him?
55 TITINIUS.   All disconsolate,
    With Pindarus his bondman, on this hill.
MESSALA. Is not that he that lies upon the ground?
TITINIUS. He lies not like the living. Oh, my heart!
MESSALA. Is not that he?
TITINIUS.   No, this was he, Messala,
60   But Cassius is no more. O setting sun,
    As in thy red rays thou doest sink tonight,
    So in his red blood Cassius' day is set.
    The sun of Rome is set. Our day is gone;
    Clouds, dews, and dangers come; our deeds are done.
65   Mistrust of my success[3] hath done this deed.
MESSALA. Mistrust of good success hath done this deed.
    O hateful Error, Melancholy's child,[4]
    Why dost thou show to the apt[5] thoughts of men
    The things that are not? O Error, soon conceived,
70   Thou never com'st unto a happy birth,
    But kill'st the mother[6] that engendered thee.
TITINIUS. What, Pindarus! Where art thou, Pindarus?
MESSALA. Seek him, Titinius, whilst I go to meet
    The noble Brutus, thrusting this report
75   Into his ears. I may say "thrusting" it,
    For piercing steel and darts envenomed[7]
    Shall be as welcome to the ears of Brutus
    As tidings of this sight.
TITINIUS.   Hie[8] you, Messala,

---

1 Exchange of one thing for another.
2 Encourage, hearten.
3 Fear of my errand's result.
4 The product of depression or mental derangement.
5 Impressionable, quick to infer.
6 The mind that gives rise to error and is also destroyed by it.
7 Poisoned arrows.
8 See 1.3.150n, TLN 597n.

And I will seek for Pindarus the while.[1]

[*Exit Messala.*]

Why didst thou send me forth, brave Cassius?   80
Did I not meet thy friends, and did not they
Put on my brows this wreath of victory,
And bid me give it thee? Did'st thou not hear their shouts?
Alas, thou hast misconstrued everything.[2]
But hold thee, take this garland on thy brow.   85
Thy Brutus bid me give it thee, and I
Will do his bidding. Brutus, come apace,[3]
And see how I regarded Caius Cassius.
By your leave, gods. This is a Roman's part.[4]
Come Cassius' sword, and find Titinius' heart.   90

Dies.

Alarum. Retreat.[5] *Enter Brutus, Messala, young Cato,*[6] *Strato,*
Volumnius, and Lucilius.
BRUTUS. Where, where, Messala, doth his body lie?
MESSALA. Lo yonder, and Titinius mourning it.
BRUTUS. Titinius' face is upward.
CATO.   He is slain.
BRUTUS. O Julius Caesar, thou art mighty yet!
Thy spirit walks abroad and turns our swords   95
In our own proper[7] entrails.

Low Alarums.

CATO.   Brave Titinius!
Look, whe'er he have not crowned dead Cassius.
BRUTUS. Are yet two Romans living such as these?
The last of all the Romans, fare thee well!
It is impossible that ever Rome   100
Should breed thy fellow. Friends, I owe more tears
To this dead man than you shall see me pay.

---

1 Meanwhile.
2 Compare Cicero's comment on misconstruing at 1.3.34–35, TLN 466–67.
3 Quickly.
4 I.e., to commit suicide.
5 Military signal to retreat.
6 Portia's brother and Brutus's brother-in-law.
7 Very own.

I shall find time, Cassius, I shall find time.
Come therefore, and to Thasos send his body.
His funerals shall not be in our camp,
Lest it discomfort[1] us. Lucilius, come,
And come young Cato. Let us to the field.
Labio and Flavio set our battles[2] on.
'Tis three o'clock, and Romans, yet ere night,
We shall try fortune in a second fight.

Exeunt.

[5.4][3]

Alarum. Enter Brutus, Messala, young Cato, Lucilius, and Flavius.
BRUTUS. Yet, countrymen, oh yet, hold up your heads!
 [*Exit fighting, followed by Messala and Flavius.*]
CATO. What bastard doth not? Who will go with me?[4]
 I will proclaim my name about the field.
 I am the son of Marcus Cato, ho!
 A foe to tyrants, and my country's friend.
 I am the son of Marcus Cato, ho!

Enter soldiers and fight.
LUCILIUS. And I am Brutus, Marcus Brutus, I!
 Brutus, my country's friend! Know me for Brutus!
 [*Young Cato is killed.*]
 O young and noble Cato, art thou down?
 Why now thou diest as bravely as Titinius
 And mayst be honor'd, being Cato's son.

---

1 Discourage, dishearten.
2 Armies, as in 5.1.4, TLN 2332.
3 The action continues without interruption. Brutus has just announced a "second fight" (5.3.110, TLN 2600), which commences at once. This is, in effect, the second battle of Philippi that Plutarch says took place twenty days after the first. Plutarch notes that Brutus's deeds in the first battle "showed that he hoped not in vain to be conqueror" (Appendix A2, p. 232), and that a subsequent sea battle also ended victoriously for Brutus's navy, though the news failed to reach him in time to prevent the second land battle, without which Brutus would likely have emerged victorious simply by waiting, because Antony and Octavius were in desperate shape. Shakespeare's streamlining and compression of events at the end of the play produce a stronger sense of inevitable defeat for Brutus than in Plutarch's narrative.
4 Who will deny his pride of noble birth by not holding up his head?

SOLDIER. Yield, or thou diest!
LUCILIUS.   Only I yield to die.[1]
   There is so much that thou wilt kill me straight.
   Kill Brutus, and be honored in his death.[2]
SOLDIER. We must not. A noble prisoner!   15

Enter Antony.
SOLDIER. Room, ho![3] Tell Antony, Brutus is ta'en.
SOLDIER. I'll tell the news. Here comes the general.
   Brutus is ta'en! Brutus is ta'en, my lord!
ANTONY. Where is he?
LUCILIUS. Safe, Antony. Brutus is safe enough.   20
   I dare assure thee that no enemy
   Shall ever take alive the noble Brutus.
   The gods defend him from so great a shame!
   When you do find him, or alive or dead,
   He will be found like Brutus, like himself.   25
ANTONY. This is not Brutus, friend, but I assure you,
   A prize no less in worth. Keep this man safe;
   Give him all kindness. I had rather have
   Such men my friends than enemies. Go on,
   And see whe'er Brutus be alive or dead,   30
   And bring us word unto Octavius' tent
   How everything is chanced.
                                        Exeunt.

[5.5][4]

Enter Brutus, Dardanius, Clitus, Strato, and Volumnius.
BRUTUS. Come, poor remains of friends, rest on this rock.
CLITUS. Statilius showed the torchlight, but, my lord,
   He came not back. He is or ta'en or slain.
BRUTUS. Sit thee down, Clitus. Slaying is the word;
   It is a deed in fashion. Hark thee, Clitus.[5]   5

---

1 I yield only to die.
2 If you kill Brutus [i.e., me], it will be an honor to you.
3 Make way.
4 The battle at Philippi continues uninterrupted, as the play turns its final
focus on Brutus and his defeat.
5 Brutus inaudibly asks Clitus to kill him.

CLITUS. What I, my Lord? No, not for all the world!
BRUTUS. Peace[1] then, no words.
CLITUS.   I'll rather kill myself.
BRUTUS. Hark thee, Dardanius.
DARDANIUS.   Shall I do such a deed?
CLITUS. O Dardanius!
10 DARDANIUS. O Clitus!
CLITUS. What ill request did Brutus make to thee?
DARDANIUS. To kill him, Clitus. Look, he meditates.
CLITUS. Now is that noble vessel[2] full of grief,
    That it runs over even at his eyes.
15 BRUTUS. Come hither, good Volumnius. List a word.[3]
VOLUMNIUS. What says my lord?
BRUTUS.   Why this, Volumnius.
    The ghost of Caesar hath appeared to me
    Two several[4] times by night: at Sardis once,
    And this last night here in Philippi fields.[5]
    I know my hour is come.
20 VOLUMNIUS.   Not so, my lord.
BRUTUS. Nay, I am sure it is, Volumnius.
    Thou see'st the World, Volumnius, how it goes.
    Our enemies have beat us to the pit.[6]

                                    Low alarums.

    It is more worthy to leap in ourselves
25   Then tarry till they push us. Good Volumnius,
    Thou know'st that we two went to school together.
    Even for that, our love of old, I prithee,
    Hold thou my sword hilts[7] whilst I run on it.
VOLUMNIUS. That's not an office[8] for a friend, my lord.

                                    Alarum still.[9]

30 CLITUS. Fly! Fly, my Lord! There is no tarrying here!

---

1 Say nothing.
2 Container for liquids; in this case also a metaphor for person.
3 Listen.
4 Different.
5 Battlefield of Philippi.
6 As hunters drive a wild beast into a trap.
7 Handle, as in 5.3.43, TLN 2524.
8 Duty, appropriate function.
9 Fighting continues, with drums and trumpet calls.

BRUTUS. Farewell to you, and you, and you, Volumnius.[1]
   Strato, thou hast been all this while asleep.
   Farewell to thee too, Strato. Countrymen,
   My heart doth joy that yet in all my life
   I found no man but he was true to me.   35
   I shall have glory by this losing day
   More then Octavius and Mark Antony
   By this vile conquest shall attain unto.
   So fare you well at once,[2] for Brutus's tongue
   Hath almost ended his life's history.   40
   Night hangs upon mine eyes; my bones would rest,
   That have but labored to attain this hour.[3]

               Alarum. Cry within, "Fly! Fly! Fly!"

CLITUS. Fly, my Lord! Fly!
BRUTUS. Hence, I will follow.

          [Exeunt Clitus, Dardanius, and Volumnius.]

   I prithee, Strato, stay thou by thy lord.   45
   Thou art a fellow of a good respect;[4]
   Thy life hath had some smatch[5] of honor in it.
   Hold then my sword, and turn away thy face,
   While I do run upon it. Wilt thou, Strato?
STRATO. Give me your hand first. Fare you well, my lord.   50
BRUTUS. Farewell, good Strato.

               [Runs on his sword.]
       —Caesar, now be still.[6]
   I killed not thee with half so good a will.

                        Dies.
              Alarum. Retreat.

---

1 Brutus's extraordinary calm in the face of Clitus's alarm is Brutus's penultimate act of stoic self-control, just preceding his suicide. However, at 5.1.100–07,
TLN 2442–49 he indicated that a true stoic would not commit suicide even in
the face of certain defeat.
2 (1) All together; (2) immediately.
3 (1) that have labored arduously to get to this point; (2) that have labored
simply to find this (noble) rest; (3) that have labored for nothing but this hour
(of my death).
4 Rank or standing, as in 1.2.59, TLN 153.
5 Indication.
6 The ghost of a murdered person was supposed to be able to rest when the
murderer died.

Enter Antony, Octavius, Messala, Lucilius, and the army.

OCTAVIUS. What man is that?[1]

MESSALA. My master's man. Strato, where is thy master?

55 STRATO. Free from the bondage you are in, Messala.
    The conquerors can but make a fire of him,
    For Brutus only overcame himself,[2]
    And no man else hath honor by his death.

LUCILIUS. So Brutus should be found. I thank thee, Brutus,
60   That thou hast proved Lucilius' saying true.

OCTAVIUS. All that served Brutus, I will entertain[3] them.
    Fellow, wilt thou bestow thy time with me?

STRATO. Ay, if Messala will prefer me to you.

OCTAVIUS. Do so, good Messala.

MESSALA.   How died my master, Strato?

65 STRATO. I held the sword, and he did run on it.

MESSALA. Octavius, then take him to follow thee,
    That did the latest service to my master.

ANTONY. This was the noblest Roman of them all.
    All the conspirators save only he
70   Did that they did in envy of great Caesar;
    He only in a general honest thought
    And common good to all made one of them.
    His life was gentle,[4] and the elements
    So mixed[5] in him that nature might stand up,
75   And say to all the world, "This was a man!"

OCTAVIUS. According to his virtue, let us use him,
    With all respect and rites of burial.
    Within my tent his bones tonight shall lie,
    Most like a soldier, ordered honorably:[6]
80   So call the field[7] to rest, and let's away,
    To part[8] the glories of this happy day.

Exeunt omnes.

---

1 Referring to Strato.

2 I.e., no one defeated Brutus but himself.

3 Retain in service.

4 Noble.

5 According to Elizabethan science, the four elements were earth, air, fire, and water, corresponding to the four humors in the body.

6 I.e., the ceremony of respect for Brutus's body will be conducted honorably.

7 Battlefield.

8 (1) Share; (2) depart from.

APPENDIX A: PLUTARCH'S *LIVES*

[At some point in the 1590s, Shakespeare discovered Sir Thomas North's translation of Plutarch's *Lives of the Noble Grecians and Romans*, which had been published in 1579. The book transformed Shakespeare's conception of ancient Rome, as we can tell by comparing his early play, *Titus Andronicus*, with the three plays about Rome that he wrote after reading Plutarch: *Julius Caesar*, *Antony and Cleopatra*, and *Coriolanus*. Shakespeare's first Roman play has no clear historical source and a vague sense of ancient Rome, whereas those he wrote after reading Plutarch are deeply indebted to North's prose and evoke the Roman past in powerful and complex ways. While Shakespeare did not follow his newly discovered source slavishly, he paid attention to Plutarch's selection and arrangement of events, to the general assessment of the people Plutarch wrote about, and to particular points in Plutarch's description of character.

Reading North's translation today enables one to read the same words Shakespeare did, even though North's spelling, punctuation, syntax, and vocabulary are sometimes difficult. Because it came from his own time and place, Shakespeare would not have found North's prose as challenging as we do, and he was sometimes so impressed with it that it comes through directly in his own writing. At the same time, Shakespeare's way of imagining what happens reduces the confusion in North's narrative, and Shakespeare's selection, invention, and rearrangement of events heightens suspense, creates symmetry and thematic richness in the action, and renders character even more thoughtfully and more evocatively than his source does.

In these extracts from three of Plutarch's *Lives*, sections are numbered as they are in North's translation. The italicized summaries in square brackets are marginal glosses in North's edition. Spelling and punctuation are modernized, and notes are included to reduce some of the difficulties in syntax and vocabulary.]

1. FROM *LIFE OF CAESAR*

4. ... [*Caesar a follower of the common people.*] Now Caesar immediately won many men's good wills at Rome, through his eloquence in pleading of their causes, and the people loved him marvelously also,

because of the courteous manner he had to speak to every man, and to use them gently, being more ceremonious therein than was looked for in one of his years. Furthermore, he ever kept a good board, and fared well at his table, and was very liberal besides, the which indeed did advance him forward, and brought him in estimation with the people. His enemies, judging that this favor of the common people would soon quail, when he could no longer hold out that charge and expense, suffered him to run on, till by little and little he was grown to be of great strength and power.

5. ... [*Caesar's prodigality.*] Now for that he was very liberal in expenses, buying (as some thought) but a vain and short glory of the favor of the people, (where indeed he bought good cheap the greatest things that could be) some say, that before he bare[1] any office in the commonwealth, he was grown in debt, to the sum of thirteen hundred talents.

11. [*Caesar Praetor[2] of Spain.*] The government of the province of Spain being fallen unto Caesar, for that he was Praetor, his creditors came and cried out upon him, and were importunate of him to be paid. Caesar, being unable to satisfy them, was compelled to go unto Crassus, who was the richest man of all Rome, and that stood in need of Caesar's boldness and courage to withstand Pompey's greatness in the commonwealth.... Another time also when he was in Spain, reading the history of Alexander's acts, when he had read it, he was sorrowful a good while after, and then burst out in weeping. His friends seeing that, marveled what should be the cause of his sorrow. He answered them, "Do ye not think," said he, "that I have good cause to be heavy, when king Alexander, being no elder than myself is now, had in old time won so many nations and countries, and that I hitherunto have done nothing worthy of myself?"

13. ... [*Caesar reconcileth Pompey and Crassus together.*] Pompey and Crassus, two of the greatest personages of the city of Rome being at jar[3] together, Caesar made them friends, and by that means got unto himself the power of them both, for by color[4] of that gentle act and friendship of his, he subtly (unawares to them all) did greatly alter and

---

1 Bore (assumed responsibility for).
2 Praetors were magistrates annually elected to the Roman judiciary.
3 Odds.
4 Appearance.

change the state of the commonwealth. For it was not the private discord between Pompey and Caesar, as many men thought, that caused the civil war, but rather it was their agreement together, who joined all their powers first to overthrow the state of the Senate and nobility, and afterwards they fell at jar one with another.

14. ... [*Caesar married his daughter Julia to Pompey.*] Then Caesar, because he would be more assured of Pompey's power and friendship, he gave him his daughter Julia in marriage, which was made sure before unto[1] Servilius Caepio, and promised him in exchange Pompey's daughter, who was sure also unto Faustus, the son of Sulla. And shortly after also, Caesar self[2] did marry Calphurnia, the daughter of Piso, whom he caused to be made Consul, to succeed him the next year following.

15. [*Caesar a valiant soldier, and a skillful captain.*] All these things they say he did before the wars with the Gauls. But the time of the great armies and conquests he made afterwards, and of the war in the which he subdued all the Gauls (entering into another course of life far contrary unto the first) made him to be known for as valiant a soldier and as excellent a captain to lead men, as those that afore him had been counted the wisest and most valiant generals that ever were, and that by their valiant deeds had achieved great honor.... For in less than ten years' war in Gaul he took by force and assault above eight hundred towns, he conquered three hundred several nations, and having before him in battle thirty hundred thousand soldiers, at sundry[3] times, he slew ten hundred thousand of them, and took as many more prisoners.

16. [*The love and respect of Caesar's soldiers unto him.*] Furthermore, he was so entirely beloved of his soldiers, that to do him service (where otherwise they were no more than other men in any private quarrel) if Caesar's honor were touched, they were invincible, and would so desperately venture themselves and with such fury, that no man was able to abide them.

17. ... Now Caesar's self did breed this noble courage and life in them. First, for that he gave them bountifully, and did honor them also, showing thereby, that he did not heap up riches in the wars to maintain his life afterwards in wantonness and pleasure, but that he did keep it in

---

1 Who was already engaged to.
2 Himself.
3 Various.

store, honorably to reward their valiant service, and that by so much he thought himself rich, by how much he was liberal in rewarding of them that had deserved it. Furthermore, they did not wonder so much at his valiantness in putting himself at every instant in such manifest danger, and in taking so extreme pains as he did, knowing that it was his greedy desire of honor that set him on fire, and pricked[1] him forward to do it, but that he always continued all labor and hardness, more than his body could bear, that filled them all with admiration. For, concerning the constitution of his body, he was lean, white, and soft-skinned, and often subject to headache, and otherwhile[2] to the falling sickness[3] (the which took him the first time, as it is reported, in Cordoba, a city of Spain), but yet therefore yielded not to the disease of his body, to make it a cloak to cherish him withal, but contrarily, took the pains of war as a medicine to cure his sick body, fighting always with his disease, travelling continually, living soberly, and commonly lying abroad in the field. For the most nights he slept in his coach or litter, and thereby bestowed his rest, to make him always able to do something; and in the day-time he would travel up and down the country to see towns, castles, and strong places. He had always a secretary with him in the coach, who did still write as he went by the way, and a soldier behind him that carried his sword. He made such speed the first time he came from Rome, when he had his office, that in eight days he came to the River of Rhone. He was so excellent a rider of horse from his youth, that holding his hands behind him, he would gallop his horse upon the spur.

28. [*The discord betwixt Caesar and Pompey, and the cause of the civil wars.*] Now Caesar had of long time determined to destroy Pompey, and Pompey him also. For Crassus being killed amongst the Parthians, who only did see that one of them two must needs fall, nothing kept Caesar from being the greatest person, but because he destroyed not Pompey, that was the greater, neither did anything let[4] Pompey to withstand that it should not come to pass,[5] but because he did not first overcome Caesar, whom only he feared. For till then, Pompey had not long feared

---

1 Impelled.
2 Sometimes.
3 Epilepsy.
4 Prevent.
5 From bringing it about.

him, but always before set light by him,[1] thinking it an easy matter for him to put him down when he would, sith[2] he had brought him to that greatness he was come unto. But Caesar contrarily, having had that drift in his head from the beginning, like a wrestler that studieth for tricks to overthrow his adversary, he went far from Rome, to exercise himself in the wars of Gaul, where he did train his army, and presently[3] by his valiant deeds did increase his fame and honor. By these means became Caesar as famous as Pompey in his doings, and lacked no more to put his enterprise in execution, but some occasions of color,[4] which Pompey partly gave him, and partly also the time delivered him, but chiefly, the hard fortune and ill government at that time of the commonwealth at Rome.... [Caesar's competition with Pompey reached a crisis when the Senate ordered Caesar to disband his army.]

32. ... [*Caesar's doubtful thoughts at the river of Rubicon.*] When he was come unto the little river of Rubicon, which divided Gaul on this side the Alps from Italy, he stayed upon a sudden.[5] For, the nearer he came to execute his purpose, the more remorse he had in his conscience, to think what an enterprise he took in hand, and his thoughts also fell out more doubtful, when he entered into consideration of the desperateness of his attempt. So he fell into many thoughts with himself, and spake[6] never a word, waving[7] sometime one way, sometime another way, and oftentimes changed his determination, contrary to himself. So did he talk much also with his friends he had with him, amongst whom was Asinius Pollio, telling him what mischiefs[8] the beginning of this passage over that river would breed in the world, and how much their posterity and they that lived after them, would speak of it in time to come. But at length, casting from him with a noble courage all those perilous thoughts to come, and speaking these words, which valiant men commonly say, that attempt dangerous and desperate enterprises, "A man can be but once undone; come on," he passed over the river; and when he was come over, he ran with his coach and never stayed,

---

1 Considered him lightly.
2 Since.
3 Soon.
4 Excuses.
5 Suddenly halted.
6 Spoke.
7 Wavering.
8 Troubles.

so that before daylight he was within the city of Ariminum, and took it. It is said that the night before he passed over this river, he dreamed a damnable dream, that he carnally knew his mother.

45. ... [*Caesar overcometh Pompey.*] [The civil war between Caesar and Pompey came to a final test at the battle of Pharsalia, where Pompey made several strategic mistakes.]

46. Then Caesar, entering into Pompey's camp, and seeing the bodies laid on the ground that were slain, and others also that were a-killing said, fetching a great sigh, "It was their own doing, and against my will. For Caius Caesar, after he had won so many famous conquests, and overcome so many great battles, had been utterly condemned notwithstanding, if he had departed from his army." Asinius Pollio writeth, that he spake these words then in Latin, which he afterwards wrote in Greek; and saith furthermore, that the most part of them which were put to the sword in the camp were slaves and bondmen, and that there were not slain in all this battle above six thousand soldiers. As for them that were taken prisoners, Caesar did put many of them amongst his legions, and did pardon also many men of estimation,[1] among whom Brutus was one, that afterwards slew Caesar himself; and it is reported that Caesar was very sorry for him, when he could not immediately be found after the battle, and that he rejoiced again when he knew he was alive, and that he came to yield himself unto him....

48. ... [*The cause of Caesar's war in Alexandria.*] And for the war he made in Alexandria, some say he needed not to have done it, but that he willingly did it for the love of Cleopatra, wherein he won little honor, and besides did put his person in great danger.

... Achillas on the other side saved himself, and fled unto the king's camp, where he raised a marvelous[2] dangerous and difficult war for Caesar, because he, having then but a few men about him, was to fight against a great and strong city. The first danger he fell into was the want of water, for that his enemies had stopped the mouth of the pipes, the which conveyed the water into the castle. The second danger he had was, that seeing his enemies came to take his ships from him, he was driven to repulse that danger with fire, the which burnt the arsenal where the ships lay, and that notable library of Alexandria withal.

---

1 Higher social rank.
2 Very.

The third danger was in the battle by sea, that was fought by the tower of Phars, where meaning to help his men that fought by sea, he leapt from the pier into a boat. Then the Egyptians made towards him with their oars on every side, but he, leaping into the sea, with great hazard saved himself by swimming. It is said that then, holding divers[1] books in his hand, he did never let them go, but kept them always upon his head above water, and swam with the other hand, notwithstanding that they shot marvelously[2] at him, and was driven sometime to duck into the water, howbeit the boat was drowned[3] presently. In fine, the king coming to his men that made war with Caesar, he went against him and gave him battle, and won it with great slaughter and effusion[4] of blood. But for the king, no man could ever tell what became of him after. Thereupon Caesar made Cleopatra his[5] sister queen of Egypt, who, being great with child by him, was shortly brought to bed of a son, whom the Alexandrians named Caesarion.

52. [*Caesar's journey into Africa against Cato and Scipio.*] After the battle of Pharsalia, Cato and Scipio being fled into Africa, King Iuba joined with them, and levied a great puissant[6] army. Wherefore Caesar determined to make war with them, and in the middest of winter, he took his journey into Sicily.... [After hard campaigning in Africa, Caesar eventually defeated Scipio.]

56. [*Caesar Consul the fourth time.*] After all these things were ended, he was chosen Consul the fourth time, and went into Spain to make war with the sons of Pompey, who were yet but very young, but had notwithstanding raised a marvelous great army together, and showed they had manhood and courage worthy to command such an army, insomuch as they put Caesar himself in great danger of his life.... This was the last war that Caesar made. But the triumph he made into Rome for the same did as much offend the Romans and more than anything that ever he had done before, because he had not overcome captains that were strangers, nor barbarous kings, but had destroyed the sons of the noblest man of Rome, whom fortune had overthrown. And because

---

1 Various.
2 Heavily.
3 Sunk.
4 Loss.
5 I.e., the king of Egypt's.
6 Powerful.

he had plucked up his race by the roots, men did not think it meet[1] for him to triumph so for the calamities of his country, rejoicing at a thing for the which he had but one excuse to allege in his defense unto the gods and men, that he was compelled to do that he did.

57. [*Caesar Dictator perpetual.*] This notwithstanding, the Romans, inclining to Caesar's prosperity and taking the bit in the mouth, supposing that to be ruled by one man alone, it would be a good mean[2] for them to take breath a little, after so many troubles and miseries as they had abidden[3] in these civil wars, they chose him perpetual Dictator. This was a plain tyranny, for to this absolute power of Dictator, they added this, never to be afraid to be deposed.... And now for himself, after he had ended his civil wars, he did so honorably behave himself, that there was no fault to be found in him ...

[*Cassius and Brutus Praetors.*] For he pardoned many of them that had borne arms against him, and furthermore, did prefer some of them to honor and office in the commonwealth, as, amongst others, Cassius and Brutus, both the which were made Praetors. And, where Pompey's images had been thrown down, he caused them to be set up again, whereupon Cicero said then, that, Caesar setting up Pompey's images again, he made his own to stand the surer. And when some of his friends did counsel him to have a guard for the safety of his person, and some also did offer themselves to serve him, he would never consent to it, but said: "It was better to die once, than always to be afraid of death." But to win himself the love and goodwill of the people, as the honorablest[4] guard and best safety he could have, he made common feasts again and general distributions of corn.[5]

58. ... Furthermore, Caesar being born to attempt all great enterprises, and having an ambitious desire besides to covet great honors, the prosperous good success he had of his former conquests bred no desire in him quietly to enjoy the fruits of his labors, but rather gave him the hope of things to come, still kindling more and more in him thoughts of greater enterprises and desire of new glory, as if that which he had present were stale and nothing worth. This humor of his was

---

1 Appropriate.
2 Way.
3 Endured.
4 Most honorable.
5 Grain.

no other but an emulation[1] with himself as with another man and a certain contention to overcome the things he prepared to attempt. . . .

60. But the chiefest cause that made him mortally hated was the covetous desire he had to be called king, which first gave the people just cause, and next his secret enemies honest color,[2] to bear him ill-will. . . . When they had decreed divers honors for him in the Senate, the Consuls and Praetors, accompanied with the whole assembly of the Senate, went unto him in the market-place, where he was set by the pulpit for orations, to tell him what honors they had decreed for him in his absence. But he, sitting still in his majesty, disdaining to rise up unto them when they came in, as if they had been private men, answered them, "that his honors had more need to be cut off than enlarged." This did not only offend the Senate but the common people also, to see that he should so lightly esteem of the magistrates of the commonwealth, insomuch as every man that might lawfully go his way departed thence very sorrowfully. Thereupon also Caesar rising departed home to his house, and tearing open his doublet[3]-collar, making his neck bare, he cried out aloud to his friends, "that his throat was ready to offer to any man that would come and cut it." Notwithstanding it is reported, that afterwards, to excuse his folly, he imputed it to his disease, saying, "that their wits are not perfect which have this disease of the falling evil,[4] when standing on their feet they speak to the common people, but are soon troubled with a trembling of their body, and a sudden dimness and giddiness."

61. [*The feast of Lupercalia.*] Besides these occasions and offenses, there followed also his shame and reproach, abusing the tribunes of the people in this sort. At that time the feast of Lupercalia was celebrated, the which in old time men say was the feast of shepherds or herdmen, and is much like unto the feast of the Lycaens in Arcadia. But howsoever it is, that day there are divers noblemen's sons, young men, (and some of them magistrates themselves that govern then), which run naked through the city, striking in sport them they meet in their way with leather thongs, hair and all on, to make them give place.[5] And many

---

1 Competition.
2 Excuse.
3 Close-fitting body garment.
4 Epilepsy.
5 Get out of the way.

noblewomen and gentlewomen also go of purpose to stand in their way and do put forth their hands to be stricken,[1] as scholars hold them out to their schoolmaster to be stricken with the ferula,[2] persuading themselves that, being with child, they shall have good delivery, and so,[3] being barren,[4] that it will make them to conceive with child. Caesar sat to behold that sport upon the pulpit for orations, in a chain of gold, apparelled in triumphant manner. Antonius, who was Consul at that time, was one of them that ran this holy course.[5] So when he came into the market-place, the people made a lane for him to run at liberty,[6] and he came to Caesar, and presented him a diadem[7] wreathed about with laurel. Whereupon there rose a certain cry of rejoicing, not very great, done only by a few appointed for the purpose. But when Caesar refused the diadem, then all the people together made an outcry of joy. Then Antonius offering it him again, there was a second shout of joy, but yet of a few. But when Caesar refused it again the second time, then all the whole people shouted. Caesar having made this proof, found that the people did not like of it, and thereupon rose out of his chair, and commanded the crown to be carried unto Jupiter in the Capitol. After that, there were set up images of Caesar in the city, with diadems upon their heads like kings. Those, the two tribunes, Flavius and Marullus, went and pulled down, and furthermore, meeting with them that first saluted Caesar as king, they committed them to prison. The people followed them rejoicing at it, and called them Brutes, because of Brutus, who had in old time driven the kings out of Rome, and that brought the kingdom of one person unto government of the Senate and people. Caesar was so offended withal, that he deprived Marullus and Flavius of their tribuneships, and accusing them, he spake also against the people, and called them Bruti and Cumani, to wit,[8] beasts and fools.

62. [*Brutus conspireth against Caesar.*] Hereupon the people went straight unto Marcus Brutus, who from his father came of the first Brutus, and by his mother of the house of the Servilians, a noble house

---

1   Struck.
2   Whip, rod.
3   Or.
4   Unable to bear children.
5   Performed this sacred rite.
6   Freely.
7   Crown.
8   That is.

as any was in Rome, and was also nephew and son-in-law of Marcus Cato. Notwithstanding[1] the great honors and favor Caesar showed unto him kept him back, that of himself alone he did not conspire nor consent to depose him of his kingdom. For Caesar did not only save his life after the battle of Pharsalia, when Pompey fled, and did at his request also save many more of his friends besides, but furthermore, he put a marvelous[2] confidence in him. For he had already preferred him to the Praetorship for that year, and furthermore was appointed to be Consul the fourth year after that, having through Caesar's friendship obtained it before Cassius, who likewise made suit for the same, and Caesar also, as it is reported, said in this contention, "indeed Cassius hath alleged best reason, but yet shall he not be chosen before Brutus." Some one day accusing Brutus while he practiced this conspiracy, Caesar would not hear of it, but, clapping his hand on his body, told them, "Brutus will look for this skin," meaning thereby, that Brutus for his virtue deserved to rule after him, but yet that, for ambition's sake, he would not show himself unthankful or dishonorable. Now they that desired change, and wished Brutus only their prince and governor above all other, they durst[3] not come to him themselves to tell him what they would have him to do, but in the night did cast sundry papers into the Praetor's seat, where he gave audience, and the most of them to this effect: "Thou sleepest, Brutus, and art not Brutus indeed."

[*Cassius stirreth up Brutus against Caesar.*] Cassius, finding Brutus's ambition stirred up the more by these seditious bills, did prick him forward and egg him on the more, for a private quarrel he had conceived against Caesar, the circumstance whereof we have set down more at large in Brutus's life. Caesar also had Cassius in great jealousy, and suspected him much, whereupon he said on a time to his friends, "what will Cassius do, think ye? I like not his pale looks." Another time when Caesar's friends complained unto him of Antonius and Dolabella, that they pretended some mischief towards him, he answered them again, "As for those fat men and smooth-combed heads," quoth he, "I never reckon of them; but these pale-visaged and carrion-lean people, I fear them most," meaning Brutus and Cassius.

---

1 Neverthcless.
2 Reposed a great.
3 Dared.

63. [*Predictions and foreshows of Caesar's death.*] Certainly destiny may easier be foreseen than avoided, considering the strange and wonderful signs that were said to be seen before Caesar's death. For, touching the fires in the element, and spirits running up and down in the night, and also the solitary birds to be seen at noondays sitting in the great market-place, are not all these signs perhaps worth the noting, in such a wonderful chance as happened? But Strabo the philosopher writeth, that divers men were seen going up and down in fire, and furthermore, that there was a slave of the soldiers that did cast a marvelous burning flame out of his hand, insomuch as they that saw it thought he had been burnt, but when the fire was out, it was found he had no hurt. Caesar self also doing sacrifice unto the gods, found that one of the beasts which was sacrificed had no heart, and that was a strange thing in nature, how a beast could live without a heart. Furthermore there was a certain soothsayer that had given Caesar warning long time afore, to take heed of the day of the Ides of March, (which is the fifteenth of the month), for on that day he should be in great danger. That day being come, Caesar going unto the Senate-house, and speaking merrily unto the soothsayer, told him, "The Ides of March be come," "So they be," softly answered the soothsayer, "but yet are they not past." And the very day before, Caesar, supping with Marcus Lepidus, sealed certain letters, as he was wont[1] to do, at the board,[2] so talk falling out amongst them, reasoning what death was best, he, preventing their opinions, cried out aloud, "Death unlooked for." Then going to bed the same night, as his manner was, and lying with his wife Calpurnia, all the windows and doors of his chamber flying open, the noise awoke him, and made him afraid when he saw such light, but more, when he heard his wife Calpurnia, being fast asleep, weep and sigh, and put forth many fumbling lamentable speeches, for she dreamed that Caesar was slain, and that she had him in her arms. Others also do deny that she had any such dream, as amongst other, Titus Livius writeth that it was in this sort:[3] the Senate having set upon the top of Caesar's house, for an ornament and setting forth of the same, a certain pinnacle, Calpurnia dreamed that she saw it broken down, and that she thought she lamented and wept for it. Insomuch that, Caesar rising in

---

1 Accustomed.
2 Table.
3 Happened this way.

the morning, she prayed him, if it were possible, not to go out of the doors that day, but to adjourn the session of the Senate until another day. And if that he made no reckoning of her dream, yet that he would search further of the soothsayers by their sacrifices, to know what should happen him that day. Thereby it seemed that Caesar likewise did fear or suspect somewhat, because his wife Calpurnia until that time was never given to any fear and superstition, and that then he saw her so troubled in mind with this dream she had. But much more afterwards, when the soothsayers having sacrificed many beasts one after another, told him that none did like them,[1] then he determined to send Antonius to adjourn the session of the Senate.

64. [*Decius Brutus Albinus's persuasion to Caesar.*] But in the mean time came Decius Brutus, surnamed Albinus, in whom Caesar put such confidence that in his last will and testament he had appointed him to be his next heir, and yet was of the conspiracy with Cassius and Brutus, he, fearing that if Caesar did adjourn the session that day, the conspiracy would be betrayed, laughed at the soothsayers, and reproved Caesar, saying that he gave the Senate occasion to mislike[2] with him, and that they might think he mocked them, considering that by his commandment they were assembled, and that they were ready willingly to grant him all things, and to proclaim him king of all his provinces of the empire of Rome[3] out of Italy, and that he should wear his diadem in all other places both by sea and land. And furthermore, that if any man should tell them from him they should depart for that present time, and return again when Calpurnia should have better dreams, what would his enemies and ill-willers[4] say, and how could they like of his friends' words? And who could persuade them otherwise, but that they would think his dominion a slavery unto them and tyrannical in himself? "And yet if it be so," said he, "that you utterly mislike of this day, it is better that you go yourself in person, and, saluting the Senate, to dismiss them till another time." Therewithal he took Caesar by the hand, and brought him out of his house.

---

1 I.e., the soothsayers did not find any auspicious signs in the entrails of the sacrifices.
2 Find fault.
3 Roman jurisdiction (Rome still being a republic).
4 Ill-wishers.

65. And one Artemidorus also, born in the isle of Cnidos, a doctor of rhetoric in the Greek tongue, who by means of his profession was very familiar with certain of Brutus's confederates, and therefore knew the most part of all their practices against Caesar, came and brought him a little bill,[1] written with his own hand, of all that he meant to tell him. He, marking how Caesar received all the supplications that were offered him, and that he gave them straight to his men that were about him, pressed nearer to him, and said, "Caesar, read this memorial to yourself, and that quickly, for they be matters of great weight, and touch you nearly." Caesar took it of him, but could never read it, though he many times attempted it, for the number of people that did salute him, but holding it still in his hand, keeping it to himself, went on withal[2] into the Senate-house. Howbeit others are of opinion, that it was some man else that gave him that memorial, and not Artemidorus, who did what he could all the way as he went to give it Caesar, but he was always repulsed by the people.

66. [*The place where Caesar was slain.*] For these things, they may seem to come by chance, but the place where the murder was prepared, and where the Senate were assembled, and where also there stood up an image of Pompey dedicated by himself amongst other ornaments which he gave unto the theater, all these were manifest proofs, that it was the ordinance of some god that made this treason to be executed, specially in that very place. It is also reported, that Cassius (though otherwise he did favor the doctrine of Epicurus) beholding the image of Pompey, before they entered into the action of their traitorous enterprise, he did softly call upon it to aid him, but the instant[3] danger of the present time, taking away his former reason, did suddenly put him into a furious passion, and made him like a man half besides himself. Now Antonius, that was a faithful friend to Caesar, and a valiant man besides of his hands, him Decius Brutus Albinus entertained out of the Senate-house, having begun a long tale of set purpose. So Caesar coming into the house, all the Senate stood up on their feet to do him honor. Then part of Brutus's company and confederates stood round about Caesar's chair, and part of them also came towards him, as though they made suit with[4]

---

1 Note.
2 Just the same.
3 Immediate.
4 Furthered the petition of.

Metellus Cimber, to call home his brother again from banishment, and thus prosecuting still their suit, they followed Caesar till he was set in his chair. Who denying their petitions, and being offended with them one after another, because the more they were denied the more they pressed upon him and were the earnester[1] with him, Metellus at length, taking his gown with both his hands, pulled it over his neck, which was the sign given the confederates to set upon him. Then Casca, behind him, strake[2] him in the neck with his sword; howbeit the wound was not great nor mortal, because it seemed the fear of such a devilish attempt did amaze him and take his strength from him, that he killed him not at the first blow. But Caesar, turning straight unto him, caught hold of his sword and held it hard, and they both cried out, Caesar in Latin: "O vile traitor Casca, what doest thou?" and Casca, in Greek, to his brother: "Brother, help me." At the beginning of this stir,[3] they that were present, not knowing of the conspiracy, were so amazed with the horrible sight they saw, they had no power to fly,[4] neither to help him, nor so much as once to make an outcry. They on the other side that had conspired his death compassed him in on every side with their swords drawn in their hands, that Caesar turned him nowhere but he was stricken[5] at by some, and still had naked swords in his face, and was hacked and mangled among them, as a wild beast taken of hunters. For it was agreed among them that every man should give him a wound, because all their parts should be in this murder, and then Brutus himself gave him one wound about his privities.[6] Men report also, that Caesar did still defend himself against the rest, running every way with his body, but when he saw Brutus with his sword drawn in his hand, then he pulled his gown over his head, and made no more resistance, and was driven, either casually or purposedly[7] by the counsel of the conspirators, against the base whereupon Pompey's image stood, which ran all of a gore-blood[8] till he was slain. Thus it seemed that the image took just revenge of Pompey's enemy, being thrown down on

---

1 More earnest.
2 Struck.
3 Violence.
4 Flee.
5 Struck.
6 Private parts.
7 Deliberately.
8 Gory with blood.

the ground at his feet and yielding up the ghost there, for the number of wounds he had upon him. For it is reported, that he had three and twenty wounds upon his body, and divers of the conspirators did hurt themselves, striking one body with so many blows.

67. [*The murderers of Caesar do go to the market-place.*] When Caesar was slain, the Senate (though Brutus stood in the middest[1] amongst them, as though he would have said something touching this fact[2]) presently[3] ran out of the house, and flying, filled all the city with marvelous fear and tumult. Insomuch as some did shut to the doors, others forsook their shops and warehouses, and others ran to the place to see what the matter was, and others also that had seen it ran home to their houses again. But Antonius and Lepidus, which were two of Caesar's chiefest[4] friends, secretly conveying themselves away, fled into other men's houses and forsook their own. Brutus and his confederates on the other side, being yet hot with this murder they had committed, having their swords drawn in their hands, came all in a troupe[5] together out of the Senate and went into the market-place, not as men that made countenance to fly,[6] but otherwise boldly holding up their heads like men of courage, and called to the people to defend their liberty, and stayed to speak with every great personage whom they met in their way.... The next morning, Brutus and his confederates came into the market-place to speak unto the people, who gave them such audience that it seemed they neither greatly reproved nor allowed the fact, for by their great silence they showed that they were sorry for Caesar's death, and also that they did reverence Brutus. Now the Senate granted general pardon for all that was past, and to pacify every man, ordained besides that Caesar's funerals[7] should be honored as a god, and established all things that he had done, and gave certain provinces also and convenient honors unto Brutus and his confederates, whereby every man thought all things were brought to good peace and quietness again.

---

1 Middle.
2 Of Caesar's assassination.
3 Immediately.
4 Closest.
5 Group.
6 Who looked like they were going to run away.
7 Funeral rituals.

68. But when they had opened Caesar's testament, and found a liberal legacy of money bequeathed unto every citizen of Rome, and that they saw his body (which was brought into the market-place) all bemangled with gashes of swords, then there was no order to keep the multitude and common people quiet, but they plucked up forms,[1] tables, and stools, and laid them all about the body, and setting them afire, burnt the corse.[2] Then when the fire was well kindled, they took the fire-brands, and went unto their houses that had slain Caesar, to set them afire. Others also ran up and down the city to see if they could meet with any of them, to cut them in pieces, howbeit[3] they could meet with never a man of them, because they had locked themselves up safely in their houses. There was one of Caesar's friends called Cinna that had a marvelous strange and terrible dream the night before. He dreamed that Caesar bad[4] him to supper, and that he refused and would not go, then that Caesar took him by the hand, and led him against his will. Now Cinna, hearing at that time that they burnt Caesar's body in the market-place, notwithstanding that he feared his dream, and had an ague[5] on him besides, he went into the market-place to honor his funerals. When he came thither, one of the mean sort[6] asked him what his name was? He was straight[7] called by his name. The first man told it to another, and that other unto another, so that it ran straight through[8] them all, that he was one of them that murdered Caesar (for indeed one of the traitors to Caesar was also called Cinna as himself) wherefore taking him for Cinna the murderer, they fell upon him with such fury that they presently dispatched[9] him in the market-place. This stir and fury made Brutus and Cassius more afraid than of all that was past, and therefore within few days after they departed out of Rome, and touching their doings afterwards and what calamity they suffered till their deaths, we have written it at large in the life of Brutus.

---

1 Benches.
2 Corpse.
3 But.
4 Bade, invited.
5 Fever.
6 Commoners.
7 Immediately.
8 Among.
9 Killed.

69. [*Caesar 56 years old at his death*]. Caesar died at six and fifty years of age, and Pompey also lived not passing four years more than he. So he reaped no other fruit of all his reign and dominion, which he had so vehemently desired all his life and pursued with such extreme danger, but a vain name only and a superficial glory, that procured him the envy and hatred of his country.

[*The revenge of Caesar's death.*] But his great prosperity and good fortune that favored him all his lifetime did continue afterwards in the revenge of his death, pursuing the murderers both by sea and land, till they had not left a man more to be executed, of all them that were actors or counselors in the conspiracy of his death. Furthermore, of all the chances that happen unto men upon the earth, that which came to Cassius above all other, is most to be wondered at, for he, being overcome in battle at the journey of Philippes, slew himself with the same sword with the which he strake Caesar.... But above all, the ghost that appeared unto Brutus showed plainly, that the gods were offended with the murder of Caesar. The vision was thus: Brutus being ready to pass over his army from the city of Abydos to the other coast lying directly against it, slept every night (as his manner was) in his tent; and being yet awake, thinking of his affairs (for by report he was as careful a captain and lived with as little sleep as ever man did) he thought he heard a noise at his tent-door, and looking towards the light of the lamp that waxed very dim, he saw a horrible vision of a man, of a wonderful greatness and dreadful look, which at the first made him marvelously afraid. But when he saw that it did him no hurt, but stood by his bedside and said nothing, at length he asked him what he was. The image answered him: "I am thy ill angel, Brutus, and thou shalt see me by the city of Philippes." Then Brutus replied again, and said, "Well, I shall see thee then." Therewithal the spirit presently vanished from him. After that time Brutus, being in battle near unto the city of Philippes against Antonius and Octavius Caesar, at the first battle he wan[1] the victory, and overthrowing all them that withstood him, he drave[2] them into young Caesar's camp, which he took. The second battle being at hand, this spirit appeared again unto him, but spake never a word. Thereupon Brutus, knowing that he should die, did put himself to all hazard in

---

1 Won.
2 Drove.

battle, but yet fighting could not be slain. So seeing his men put to flight and overthrown, he ran unto a little rock not far off, and there setting his sword's point to his breast, fell upon it and slew himself; but yet, as it is reported, with the help of his friend that dispatched him.

2. FROM *LIFE OF BRUTUS*

1. [*The parentage of Brutus.*] Marcus Brutus came of that Junius Brutus, for whom the ancient Romans made his statue of brass to be set up in the Capitol, with the images of the kings, holding a naked sword in his hand, because he had valiantly put down the Tarquins from the kingdom of Rome. But that Junius Brutus, being of a sour stern nature not softened by reason, being like unto sword blades of too hard a temper, was so subject to his choler[1] and malice[2] he bare[3] unto the tyrants, that for their sakes he caused his own sons to be executed. But this Marcus Brutus in contrary manner, whose life we presently[4] write, having framed his manners of life by the rules of virtue and study of philosophy, and having employed his wit, which was gentle and constant, in attempting of great things, me thinks he was rightly made and framed unto virtue. So that his very enemies which wish him most hurt, because of his conspiracy against Julius Caesar, if there were any noble attempt done in all this conspiracy, they refer it wholly unto Brutus; and all the cruel and violent acts unto Cassius, who was Brutus's familiar friend, but not so well given and conditioned as he....

2. [*Brutus's studies.*] Marcus Cato the philosopher was brother unto Servilia, Marcus Brutus's mother, whom Brutus studied most to follow of all the other Romans, because he was his uncle, and afterwards he married his daughter. Now touching the Grecian philosophers, there was no sect nor philosopher of them, but he heard and liked it, but above all the rest he loved Plato's sect best, and did not much give himself to the new or mean[5] Academy (as they call it), but altogether to the old Academy.

---

1 Irascibility, anger.
2 Resentment.
3 Bore.
4 Immediately.
5 Inferior.

[*Brutus's manner of writing his epistles in Greek.*] But for the Greek tongue, they do note in some of his epistles, that he counterfeited that brief compendious manner of speech of the Lacedaemonians. As, when the war was begun, he wrote unto the Pergamenians in this sort: "I understand you have given Dolabella money: if you have done it willingly, you confess you have offended me; if against your wills, show it then by giving me willingly." Another time again unto the Samians: "Your councils be long, your doings be slow, consider the end."

4. Afterwards, when the empire of Rome[1] was divided into factions, and that Caesar and Pompey both were in arms one against the other, and that all the empire of Rome was in garboil[2] and uproar, it was thought then that Brutus would take part with Caesar, because Pompey not long before had put his father to death. But Brutus, preferring the respect of his country and commonwealth before private affection, and persuading himself that Pompey had juster[3] cause to enter into arms than Caesar, he then took part with Pompey, though oftentimes meeting him before, he thought scorn to speak to him, thinking it a great sin and offence in him, to speak to the murderer of his father.

[*Brutus studied in Pompey's camp.*] Brutus, being in Pompey's camp, did nothing but study all day long, except he were with Pompey, and not only the days before, but the selfsame day also before the great battle was fought in the fields of Pharsalia, where Pompey was overcome.

5. [*Julius Caesar loved Servilia, Brutus's mother.*] It is reported that Caesar did not forget him, and that he gave his captains charge before the battle, that they should beware they killed not Brutus in fight; and if he yielded willingly unto them, that then they should bring him unto him, but if he resisted and would not be taken, then that they should let him go, and do him no hurt. Some say he did this for Servilia's sake, Brutus's mother. For when he was a young man, he had been acquainted with Servilia, who was extremely in love with him. And because Brutus was born in that time when their love was hottest, he persuaded himself that he begat[4] him.

6. [*Brutus saved by Julius Caesar after the battle of Pharsalia.*] So, after Pompey's overthrow at the battle of Pharsalia, and that he fled to the

---

1 Jurisdiction of Rome (Rome being still a republic).
2 Turmoil.
3 More just.
4 Fathered.

sea, when Caesar came to besiege his camp, Brutus went out of the camp-gates unseen of any man, and leapt into a marsh full of water and reeds. Then when night was come, he crept out, and went unto the city of Larissa, from whence he wrote unto Caesar, who was very glad that he had escaped, and sent for him to come unto him. When Brutus was come, he did not only pardon him, but also kept him always about him, and did as much honor and esteem him as any man he had in his company.

8. [*Caesar suspected Brutus.*] Now Caesar, on the other side, did not trust him overmuch, nor was without tales brought unto him against him; howbeit[1] he feared his great mind, authority, and friends. Yet, on the other side also, he trusted his good nature and fair conditions. For, intelligence being brought him one day, that Antonius and Dolabella did conspire against him, he answered "That these fat long-haired men made him not afraid, but the lean and whitely-faced[2] fellows," meaning that by Brutus and Cassius.

[*Caesar's saying of Brutus.*] At another time also when one accused Brutus unto him, and bad him beware of him: "What," said he again, clapping his hands on his breast, "think ye that Brutus will not tarry[3] till this body die?" meaning that none but Brutus after him was meet to have such power as he had. And surely, in my opinion, I am persuaded that Brutus might indeed have come to have been the chiefest man of Rome, if he could have contented himself for a time to have been next unto Caesar, and to have suffered[4] his glory and authority, which he had gotten by his great victories, to consume[5] with time.

[*Cassius incenseth[6] Brutus against Caesar.*] But Cassius, being a choleric[7] man, and hating Caesar privately more than he did the tyranny openly, he incensed Brutus against him. It is also reported, that Brutus could evil away with[8] the tyranny, and that Cassius hated the tyrant, making

---

1 Moreover.
2 Pale.
3 Wait.
4 Allowed.
5 Diminish.
6 Stirs up.
7 Hot-tempered.
8 Hated.

many complaints for the injuries he had done him, and amongst others, for that[1] he had taken away his lions from him.

9. [*Cassius enemy of tyrants.*] And this was the cause (as some do report) that made Cassius conspire against Caesar. But this holdeth no water, for Cassius, even from his cradle, could not abide any manner of tyrants....

[*How Brutus was incensed against Caesar.*] But for Brutus, his friends and countrymen, both by divers procurements[2] and sundry rumors of the city, and by many bills[3] also, did openly call and procure[4] him to do that he did. For under the image of his ancestor Junius Brutus, (that drave the kings out of Rome) they wrote: "O, that it pleased the gods thou wert[5] now alive, Brutus!" and again, "that thou wert here among us now!" His tribunal or chair, where he gave audience during the time he was Praetor,[6] was full of such bills: "Brutus, thou art asleep, and art not Brutus indeed." And of all this Caesar's flatterers were the cause, who, beside many other exceeding and unspeakable honors they daily devised for him, in the night-time they put diadems upon the heads of his images, supposing thereby to allure the common people to call him King, instead of Dictator.

10. Now when Cassius felt[7] his friends, and did stir them up against Caesar, they all agreed, and promised to take part with him, so[8] Brutus were the chief of their conspiracy. For they told him that so high an enterprise and attempt as that did not so much require men of manhood and courage to draw their swords, as it stood them upon to have a man of such estimation as Brutus, to make every man boldly think, that by his only presence the fact were holy and just. If he took not this course, then that they should go to it with fainter hearts; and when they had done it, they should be more fearful: because every man would think that Brutus would not have refused to have made one with them, if the cause had been good and honest. Therefore Cassius, considering

---

1   Because.
2   Various solicitations.
3   Notes.
4   Urge.
5   You were.
6   Annually elected magistrate.
7   Sounded out.
8   As long as.

this matter with himself, did first of all speak to Brutus, since they grew strange together for the suit they had for the praetorship.[1]

[*Brutus first to help him to put down the tyrant.*] So when he was reconciled to him again, and that they had embraced one another, Cassius asked him if he were determined to be in the Senate house the first day of the month of March, because he heard say that Caesar's friends should move[2] the council that day that Caesar should be called king by the Senate. Brutus answered him, he would not be there. "But if we be sent for," said Cassius, "how then?" "For myself, then," said Brutus, "I mean not to hold my peace, but to withstand it, and rather die than lose my liberty." Cassius being bold, and taking hold of this word, "Why," quoth he, "what Roman is he alive that will suffer[3] thee to die for thy liberty? What? Knowest thou not that thou art Brutus? Thinkest thou that they be cobblers, tapsters, or suchlike base mechanical people,[4] that write these bills and scrolls which are found daily in thy praetor's chair, and not the noblest men and best citizens that do it? No. Be thou well assured that of other praetors they look for gifts, common distributions amongst the people, and for common plays, and to see fencers fight at the sharp,[5] to show the people pastime,[6] but at thy hands they specially require (as a due debt unto them) the taking away of the tyranny, being fully bent[7] to suffer any extremity for thy sake, so that thou wilt show thyself to be the man thou art taken for, and that they hope thou art." Thereupon he kissed Brutus and embraced him, and so each taking leave of other, they went both to speak with their friends about it.

11. [*Brutus maketh Ligarius one of the conspiracy.*] Now amongst Pompey's friends, there was one called Caius Ligarius, who had been accused unto Caesar for taking part with Pompey, and Caesar discharged him. But Ligarius thanked not Caesar so much for his discharge

---

1   Brutus and Cassius were not speaking to each other, because they were in competition for the praetorship. The socially less-prominent patrician therefore first approached the other.

2   Propose to.

3   Endure.

4   Socially inferior manual laborers.

5   With sharpened weapons.

6   Entertainment.

7   Inclined.

as he was offended with him for that[1] he was brought in danger by his tyrannical power, and therefore in his heart he was always his mortal enemy, and was besides very familiar with Brutus, who went to see him being sick in his bed, and said unto him, "Ligarius, in what a time art thou sick?" Ligarius rising up in his bed and taking him by the right hand, said unto him, "Brutus," said he, "if thou hast any great enterprise in hand worthy of thyself, I am whole."

12. [*They do hide the conspiracy against Caesar from Cicero.*] After that time they began to feel[2] all their acquaintance whom they trusted and laid their heads together, consulting upon it, and did not only pick out their friends but all those also whom they thought stout[3] enough to attempt any desperate matter and that were not afraid to lose their lives. For this cause they durst[4] not acquaint Cicero with their conspiracy, although he was a man whom they loved dearly, and trusted best, for they were afraid that he being a coward by nature, and age also having increased his fear, he would quite turn and alter all their purpose, and quench the heat of their enterprise (the which specially required hot[5] and earnest execution), seeking by persuasion to bring all things to such safety as there should be no peril.

[*The wonderful faith and secrecy of the conspirators of Caesar's death.*] Furthermore, the only[6] name and great calling of Brutus did bring on the most of them to give consent to this conspiracy, who having never taken oaths together, nor taken or given any caution or assurance, nor binding themselves one to another by any religious oaths, they all kept the matter so secret to themselves, and could so cunningly handle it, that notwithstanding the gods did reveal it by manifest signs and tokens from above, and by predictions of sacrifices, yet all this would not be believed.

13. Now Brutus, who knew very well that for his sake all the noblest, valiantest, and most courageous men of Rome did venture their lives, weighing with himself the greatness of the danger, when he was out of his house, he did so frame and fashion his countenance and looks that

---

1 Because.
2 Sound out.
3 Brave.
4 Dared.
5 Urgent.
6 Unique.

no man could discern he had anything to trouble his mind. But when night came that he was in his own house, then he was clean changed, for either care did wake him against his will when he would have slept, or else oftentimes of himself he fell into such deep thoughts of this enterprise, casting in his mind all the dangers that might happen, that his wife, lying by him, found that there was some marvelous[1] great matter that troubled his mind, not being wont to be in that taking,[2] and that he could not well determine with himself. His wife Portia (as we have told you before) was the daughter of Cato, whom Brutus married being his cousin, not a maiden, but a young widow after the death of her first husband Bibulus, by whom she had also a young son called Bibulus, who afterwards wrote a book of the acts and gests of Brutus, extant at this present day.

14. Now a day being appointed for the meeting of the Senate, at what time they hoped Caesar would not fail to come, the conspirators determined then to put their enterprise in execution, because they might meet safely at that time without suspicion, and the rather, for that all the noblest and chiefest men of the city would be there, who, when they should see such a great matter executed, would every man set to their hands, for the defense of their liberty. Furthermore they thought also, that the appointment of the place where the council should be kept was chosen of purpose by divine providence, and made all for them. For it was one of the porches about the theater, in the which there was a certain place full of seats for men to sit in, where also was set up the image of Pompey, which the city had made and consecrated in honor of him, when he did beautify that part of the city with the theater he built, with divers[3] porches about it. In this place was the assembly of the Senate appointed to be, just on the fifteenth day of the month March, which the Romans call Idus Martias, so that it seemed some god of purpose had brought Caesar thither to be slain for revenge of Pompey's death.[4] So when the day was come, Brutus went out of his house with a dagger by his side under his long gown, that nobody saw nor knew but his wife only.

---

1 Very.
2 Not usually being like that.
3 Various.
4 March being named for Mars, the god of war.

[*The wonderful constancy of the conspirators in the killing of Caesar.*] But here is to be noted the wonderful assured constancy of these conspirators, in so dangerous and weighty an enterprise as they had undertaken....

15. [*Sundry misfortunes to have broken off the enterprise.*] Notwithstanding this, by chance there fell out many misfortunes unto them, which was enough to have marred the enterprise. The first and chiefest was Caesar's long tarrying, who came very late to the Senate, for, because the signs of the sacrifices appeared unlucky, his wife Calpurnia kept him at home, and the soothsayers bade him beware he went not abroad. The second cause was, when one came unto Casca being a conspirator and taking him by the hand said unto him, "O Casca? thou keptest it close from me, but Brutus hath told me all," Casca being amazed at it, the other went on with his tale, and said, "Why, how now, how cometh it to pass thou art thus rich that thou dost sue to be Aedilis?"[1] Thus Casca being deceived by the other's doubtful words, he told them it was a thousand to one he blabbed not out all the conspiracy. Another Senator, called Popilius Laena, after he had saluted Brutus and Cassius more friendly than he was wont[2] to do, he rounded[3] softly in their ears, and told them, "I pray the gods you may go through with that you have taken in hand, but withal, dispatch, I read[4] you, for your enterprise is bewrayed."[5] When he had said, he presently departed from them, and left them both afraid that their conspiracy would out.[6]

[*The weakness of Portia, notwithstanding her former courage.*] Now in the meantime, there came one of Brutus's men post-haste unto him, and told him his wife was a-dying. For Portia, being very careful[7] and pensive for that which was to come, and being too weak to away with[8] so great and inward grief of mind, she could hardly keep within, but was frighted with every little noise and cry she heard, as those that are taken

---

1 "How did you get to be so rich that you could stand for the aedilship."
2 Accustomed.
3 Spoke.
4 Urge.
5 Exposed.
6 Be found out.
7 Full of care.
8 Throw off.

and possessed with the fury of the Bacchantes,[1] asking every man that came from the market-place what Brutus did, and still sent messenger after messenger, to know what news. At length Caesar's coming being prolonged, Portia's weakness was not able to hold out any longer, and thereupon she suddenly swooned,[2] that she had no leisure[3] to go to her chamber, but was taken in the midst of her house, where her speech and senses failed her. Howbeit she soon came to herself again, and so was laid in her bed, and attended by her women. When Brutus heard these news, it grieved him, as it is to be presupposed, yet he left not off the care of his country and commonwealth, neither went home to his house for any news he heard.

16. Now it was reported that Caesar was coming in his litter,[4] for he determined not to stay in the Senate all that day (because he was afraid of the unlucky signs of the sacrifices) but to adjourn matters of importance unto the next session and council holden, feigning himself not to be well at ease.[5] When Caesar came out of his litter, Popilius Laena (who had talked before with Brutus and Cassius, and had prayed the gods they might bring this enterprise to pass) went unto Caesar, and kept him a long time with a talk. Caesar gave good ear unto him, wherefore the conspirators (if so they should be called) not hearing what he said to Caesar, but conjecturing by that he had told them a little before that his talk was none other but the very discovery of their conspiracy, they were afraid every man of them, and one looking in another's face, it was easy to see that they all were of a mind that it was no tarrying for them[6] till they were apprehended, but rather that they should kill themselves with their own hands.

[*Brutus with his countenance encouraged his fearful consorts.*] And when Cassius and certain other clapped their hands on their swords under their gowns to draw them, Brutus, marking the countenance and gesture of Laena, and considering that he did use himself rather like an humble and earnest suitor than like an accuser, he said nothing to his

---

1 Female worshipers of the god Bacchus, who work themselves into a religious fervor.
2 Fainted.
3 Time.
4 Conveyance suspended from poles carried on the shoulders of slaves.
5 Next session to be held, pretending not to feel well.
6 Agreed that they would not wait.

companion (because there were many amongst them that were not of the conspiracy), but with a pleasant countenance encouraged Cassius. And immediately after Laena went from Caesar, and kissed his hand, which showed plainly that it was for some matter concerning himself that he had held him so long in talk.

17. Now all the Senators being entered first into this place or chapter-house where the council should be kept, all the other conspirators straight[1] stood about Caesar's chair, as if they had had something to say unto him. And some say that Cassius, casting his eyes upon Pompey's image, made his prayer unto it, as if it had been alive. Trebonius on the other side drew Antonius aside, as he came into the house where the Senate sat, and held him with a long talk without. When Caesar was come into the house, all the Senate rose to honor him at his coming in. So when he was set, the conspirators flocked about him, and amongst them they presented one Tullius Cimber who made humble suit for the calling home again of his brother who was banished. They all made as though they were intercessors for him, and took Caesar by the hands and kissed his head and breast. Caesar at the first simply refused their kindness and entreaties, but afterwards, perceiving they still pressed on him, he violently thrust them from him.

[*The murder of Caesar. Casca the first that wounded him.*] Then Cimber with both his hands plucked Caesar's gown over his shoulders, and Casca, that stood behind him, drew his dagger first and strake[2] Caesar upon the shoulder, but gave him no great wound. Caesar, feeling himself hurt, took him straight by the hand he held his dagger in and cried out in Latin: "O traitor Casca, what dost thou?" Casca on the other side cried out in Greek, and called his brother to help him. So divers running on a heap together to fly upon[3] Caesar, he, looking about him to have fled, saw Brutus with a sword drawn in his hand ready to strike at him. Then he let Casca's hand go, and casting his gown over his face, suffered[4] every man to strike at him that would. Then the conspirators thronging one upon another, because every man was desirous to have a cut at him, so many swords and daggers lighting upon one body, one of them hurt another, and among them Brutus caught a blow on his

---

1 Immediately.
2 Struck.
3 Various conspirators, running in a group together to attack.
4 Allowed.

hand, because he would make one in murdering of him, and all the rest also were every man of them bloodied.

18. Caesar being slain in this manner, Brutus, standing in the midst of the house, would have spoken and stayed[1] the other Senators that were not of the conspiracy, to have told them the reason why they had done this fact. But they, as men both afraid and amazed, fled one upon another's neck in haste[2] to get out at the door, and no man followed them. For it was set down and agreed between them that they should kill no man but Caesar only, and should entreat all the rest to look to defend their liberty. All the conspirators but Brutus, determining upon this matter, thought it good also to kill Antonius, because he was a wicked man, and that in nature favored tyranny, besides also, for that he was in great estimation with soldiers, having been conversant of long time amongst them, and especially having a mind bent to great enterprises, he was also of great authority at that time, being Consul with Caesar. But Brutus would not agree to it.

[*Why Antonius was not slain with Caesar.*] First, for that he said it was not honest; secondly, because he told them there was hope of change in him. For he did not mistrust[3] but that Antonius, being a noble-minded and courageous man, (when he should know that Caesar was dead), would willingly help his country to recover her liberty, having them an example unto him to follow their courage and virtue.

[*Brutus with his consorts went into the Capitol.*] So Brutus by this means saved Antonius's life, who at that present time disguised himself and stole away, but Brutus and his consorts, having their swords bloody in their hands, went straight to the Capitol, persuading the Romans as they went to take their liberty again. Now at the first time, when the murder was newly done, there were sudden outcries of people that ran up and down the city, the which indeed did the more increase the fear and tumult. But when they saw they slew no man, neither did spoil or make havoc of[4] anything, then certain of the Senators and many of the people, emboldening themselves, went to the Capitol unto them. There, a great number of men being assembled together one after another, Brutus made an oration unto them to win the favor of

---

1 Stopped.
2 Fled in a hasty tumult.
3 Doubt.
4 Plunder or destroy.

the people and to justify that they had done. All those that were by[1] said they had done well, and cried unto them that they should boldly come down from the Capitol, whereupon Brutus and his companions came boldly down into the market-place. The rest followed in troupe,[2] but Brutus went foremost, very honorably compassed in round about with the noblest men of the city, which brought him from the Capitol, through the market-place, to the pulpit for orations. When the people saw him in the pulpit, although they were a multitude of rakehells[3] of all sorts and had a good will to make some stir,[4] yet being ashamed to do it, for the reverence they bare[5] unto Brutus, they kept silence to hear what he would say. When Brutus began to speak, they gave him quiet audience, howbeit[6] immediately after, they showed that they were not all contented with the murder. For when another, called Cinna, would have spoken, and began to accuse Caesar, they fell into a great uproar among them, and marvelously reviled him, insomuch that the conspirators returned again into the Capitol. There Brutus, being afraid to be besieged, sent back again the noblemen that came thither with him, thinking it no reason that they, which were no partakers of the murder, should be partakers of the danger.

19. ... [*Honors decreed for the murderers of Caesar.*] This being agreed upon, the Senate brake[7] up, and Antonius the Consul, to put them in heart[8] that were in the Capitol, sent them his son for a pledge. Upon this assurance, Brutus and his companions came down from the Capitol, where every man saluted and embraced each other, among the which Antonius himself did bid Cassius to supper to him, and Lepidus also bade Brutus, and so one bade another, as they had friendship and acquaintance together. The next day following, the Senate being called again to council did first of all commend Antonius, for that he had wisely stayed and quenched the beginning of a civil war;

---

1 In attendance.
2 A group.
3 Scoundrels (from "rake hell"; cf. "bottom of the barrel").
4 Cause a disturbance.
5 Bore.
6 But.
7 Broke.
8 Encourage those.

then they also gave Brutus and his consorts great praises; and lastly they appointed them several governments of Provinces.

20. [*Caesar's will and funerals.*] When this was done, they came to talk of Caesar's will and testament[1] and of his funerals and tomb. Then Antonius, thinking good his testament should be read openly and also that his body should be honorably buried (and not in hugger-mugger,[2] lest the people might thereby take occasion to be worse offended if they did otherwise), Cassius stoutly spake[3] against it.

[*Brutus committed two great faults after Caesar's death.*] But Brutus went with the motion, and agreed unto it, wherein it seemeth he committed a second fault. For the first fault he did was when he would not consent to his fellow-conspirators that Antonius should be slain; and therefore he was justly accused, that thereby he had saved and strengthened a strong and grievous enemy of their conspiracy. The second fault was when he agreed that Caesar's funerals should be as Antonius would have them, the which indeed marred all. For first of all, when Caesar's testament was openly read among them, whereby it appeared that he bequeathed unto every citizen of Rome 75 drachmas a man, and that he left his gardens and arbors unto the people, which he had on this side of the river Tiber, in the place where now the temple of Fortune is built, the people then loved him, and were marvelous sorry for him.

[*Antonius's funeral oration for Caesar.*] Afterwards, when Caesar's body was brought into the market-place, Antonius making his funeral oration in praise of the dead, according to the ancient custom of Rome, and perceiving that his words moved the common people to compassion, he framed his eloquence to make their hearts yearn the more, and taking Caesar's gown all bloody in his hand, he laid it open to the sight of them all showing what a number of cuts and holes it had upon it. Therewithal the people fell presently into such a rage and mutiny, that there was no more order kept amongst the common people. For some of them cried out, "Kill the murderers"; others plucked up forms, tables, and stalls about the market-place . . . and having laid them all on a heap together, they set them on fire, and thereupon did put the body of Caesar, and burnt it in the midst of the most holy places. And furthermore, when the fire was thoroughly kindled, some here, some there, took burning

---

1 Caesar's will.
2 Secret.
3 Spoke.

firebrands, and ran with them to the murderers' houses that killed him, to set them on fire. Howbeit the conspirators, foreseeing the danger before, had wisely provided for themselves and fled.

[*The strange dream of Cinna the poet.*] But there was a poet called Cinna, who had been no partaker of the conspiracy but was always one of Caesar's chiefest friends. He dreamed the night before that Caesar bade him to supper with him, and that, he refusing to go, Caesar was very importunate with him, and compelled him, so that at length he led him by the hand into a great dark place, where, being marvelously afraid, he was driven to follow him in spite of his heart. This dream put him all night into a fever, and yet notwithstanding, the next morning, when he heard that they carried Caesar's body to burial, being ashamed not to accompany his funerals, he went out of his house, and thrust himself into the press of the common people that were in a great uproar.

[*The murder of Cinna the poet, being mistaken for another of that name.*] And because some one called him by his name Cinna, the people, thinking he had been that Cinna who in an oration he made had spoken very evil of Caesar, they, falling upon him in their rage, slew him outright in the market-place.

22. [*Octavius Caesar's coming to Rome.*] Now the state of Rome standing in these terms, there fell out another change and alteration, when the young man Octavius Caesar came to Rome. He was the son of Julius Caesar's niece, whom he had adopted for his son,[1] and made his heir, by his last will and testament. But when Julius Caesar, his adopted father, was slain, he was in the city of Apollonia (where he studied) tarrying for him, because he was determined to make war with the Parthians, but when he heard the news of his death, he returned again to Rome, where, to begin to curry favor[2] with the common people, he first of all took upon him his adopted father's name, and made distribution among them of the money which his father had bequeathed unto them. By this means he troubled Antonius sorely, and by force of money got a great number of his father's soldiers together that had served in the wars with him....

23. ... Now the city of Rome being divided in two factions (some taking part with Antonius, others also leaning unto Octavius Caesar),

---

1   I.e., Caesar had adopted Octavius.
2   Ingratiate himself.

and the soldiers making portsale[1] of their service to him that would give most, Brutus, seeing the state of Rome would be utterly overthrown, he determined to go out of Italy, and went on foot through the country of Luke, unto the city of Elea, standing by the sea.

[*Portia's sorrowful return to Rome, for the absence of her husband Brutus.*] There Portia, being ready to depart from her husband Brutus, and to return to Rome, did what she could to dissemble[2] the grief and sorrow she felt at her heart, but a certain painted table bewrayed her[3] in the end, although until that time she showed always a constant and patient mind.

27. [*Octavius Caesar joineth with Antonius.*] So Brutus preparing to go into Asia, news came unto him of the great change at Rome, for Octavius Caesar was in arms, by commandment and authority from the Senate, against Marcus Antonius. But after that he had driven Antonius out of Italy, the Senate began then to be afraid of him, because he sued to be Consul, which was contrary to the law, and kept a great army about him when the empire of Rome had no need of them. On the other side Octavius Caesar, perceiving the Senate stayed not there, but turned unto Brutus that was out of Italy, and that they appointed him the government of certain provinces, then he began to be afraid for his part, and sent unto Antonius to offer him his friendship. Then coming on unto his army near to Rome, he made himself to be chosen Consul, whether the Senate would or not, when he was yet but a stripling or springal[4] of twenty years old, as himself reporteth in his own [*Commentaries*].

[*The Triumvirate.*] After that, these three, Octavius Caesar, Antonius, and Lepidus, made an agreement between themselves, and by those articles divided the provinces belonging to the empire of Rome among themselves, and did set up bills of proscription and outlawry, condemning two hundred of the noblest men of Rome to suffer death, and among that number Cicero was one.

[*Brutus and Cassius do join armies together.*] Cassius believed [Brutus] and returned. Brutus went to meet him, and they both met at the city of Smyrna, which was the first time that they saw [each other] together

---

1   Auction.
2   Hide.
3   Painting gave her away.
4   Youth.

since they took leave each of other at the haven of Piraea in Athens, the one going into Syria, and the other into Macedon.

29. [*The sharp and cruel conditions of Cassius.*] Now Cassius would have done Brutus much honor, as Brutus did unto him, but Brutus most commonly prevented him, and went first unto him, both because he was the elder man as also for that he was sickly of body. And men reputed him [Cassius] commonly to be very skillful in wars, but otherwise marvelous choleric[1] and cruel, who sought to rule men by fear rather than with lenity, and on the other side, he was too familiar with his friends, and would jest too broadly with them.

[*Brutus's gentle and fair conditions.*] But Brutus, in contrary manner, for his virtue and valiantness, was well beloved of the people [in general] and his own [in particular], esteemed of noblemen, and hated of no man, not so much as of[2] his enemies; because he was a marvelous lowly and gentle person, noble-minded, and would never be in any rage, nor carried away with pleasure and covetousness, but had ever an upright mind with him, and would never yield to any wrong or injustice, the which was the chiefest cause of his fame, of his rising, and of the good-will that every man bare[3] him, for they were all persuaded that his intent was good.

[*Brutus's intent good, if he had overcome.*] For they did not certainly believe that, if Pompey himself had overcome Caesar, he would have resigned his authority to the law, but rather they were of opinion that he would still keep the sovereignty and absolute government in his hands, taking only (to please the people) the title of Consul, or Dictator, or of some other more civil office. And as for Cassius, a hot, choleric, and cruel man, that would oftentimes be carried away from justice for gain, it was certainly thought that he made war and put himself into sundry dangers, more to have absolute power and authority than to defend the liberty of his country.

[*Antonius's testimony of Brutus.*] For it was said that Antonius spake it openly divers times, that he thought that of all them that had slain Caesar there was none but Brutus only that was moved to do it as thinking the act commendable of itself, but that all the other conspirators did conspire his death for some private malice or envy that they otherwise

---

1 Hot-tempered
2 Even by.
3 Bore.

did bear unto him. Hereby it appeareth that Brutus did not trust so much to the power of his army as he did to his own virtue, as it is to be seen by his writings.

30. Now whilst Brutus and Cassius were together in the city of Smyrna, Brutus prayed[1] Cassius to let him have some part of his money whereof he had great store, because all that he could rap and rend of his side,[2] he had bestowed it in making so great a number of ships, that by means of them they should keep all the sea at their commandment. Cassius's friends hindered this request and earnestly dissuaded him from it, persuading him, that it was no reason that Brutus should have the money which Cassius had gotten together by sparing and levied with great evil will of the people their subjects,[3] for him to bestow liberally upon his soldiers, and by this means to win their good wills, by Cassius's charge.[4] This notwithstanding, Cassius gave him the third part of this total sum.

34. [*Brutus and Cassius do meet at the city of Sardis.*] About that time Brutus sent to pray Cassius to come to the city of Sardis, and so he did. Brutus, understanding of his coming, went to meet him with all his friends. There both their armies being armed, they called them both [*Emperors*]. Now as it commonly happened in great affairs between two persons, both of them having many friends and so many captains under them, there ran tales and complaints betwixt them.

[*Brutus's and Cassius's complaints one unto the other.*] Therefore, before they fell in hand with any other matter, they went into a little chamber together, and bade every man avoid, and did shut the doors to them. Then they began to pour out their complaints one to the other, and grew hot and loud, earnestly accusing one another, and at length fell both a-weeping. Their friends that were without the chamber, hearing them loud within and angry between themselves, they were both amazed and afraid also, lest it would grow to further matter, but yet they were commanded that no man should come to them.

[*M. Phaonius a follower of Cato.*] Notwithstanding, one Marcus Phaonius, that had been a friend and a follower of Cato while he lived, and took upon him to counterfeit a philosopher, not with wisdom and

---

1 Asked.
2 Scrape together for himself.
3 Gathered by frugality and acquired at the price of his subjects' hatred.
4 At Cassius's expense.

discretion, but with a certain bedlam[1] and frantic motion, he would needs come into the chamber, though the men offered[2] to keep him out. But it was no boot to let[3] Phaonius, when a mad mood or toy[4] took him in the head, for he was a hot hasty man, and sudden in all his doings, and cared for never a senator of them all.

[*Cynic philosophers counted dogs.*] Now, though he used this bold manner of speech after the profession of the Cynic philosophers (as who would say, *Dogs*[5]), yet his boldness did no hurt many times, because they did but laugh at him to see him so mad. This Phaonius at that time, in despite of the door-keepers, came into the chamber, and with a certain scoffing and mocking gesture, which he counterfeited of purpose, he rehearsed the verses which old Nestor said in Homer:

> All lords, I pray you hearken[6] both to me,
> For I have seen mo[7] years than suchie[8] three.

Cassius fell a-laughing at him, but Brutus thrust him out of the chamber, and called him dog, and counterfeit Cynic. Howbeit his coming in brake their strife at that time, and so they left each other.

35. The next day after, Brutus, upon complaint of the Sardians, did condemn and note Lucius Pella for a defamed person, that had been a Praetor of the Romans, and whom Brutus had given charge unto, for that he was accused and convicted of robbery and pilfery[9] in his office.[10] This judgment much misliked Cassius,[11] because he himself had secretly (not many days before) warned two of his friends, attainted[12] and convicted of the like offenses, and openly had cleared them, but yet he did not therefore leave[13] to employ them in any manner of service

---

1 Insane.
2 Tried.
3 Hopeless to prevent.
4 Fantastic act.
5 The Greek word for "dog" had become a nickname for a Cynic philosopher.
6 Listen.
7 More.
8 Any.
9 Theft.
10 On the job.
11 Cassius disliked this judgment.
12 Proved.
13 Cease.

as he did before. And therefore he greatly reproved Brutus, for that he would show himself so straight and severe in such a time as was meeter[1] to bear a little than to take things at the worst.

[*Julius Caesar slain at the Ides of March.*] Brutus in contrary manner answered, that he should remember the Ides of March, at which time they slew Julius Caesar, who neither pilled nor polled[2] the country but only was a favorer and suborner[3] of all them that did rob and spoil, by his countenance and authority. And if there were any occasion whereby they might honestly set aside justice and equity, they should have had more reason to have suffered Caesar's friends to have robbed and done what wrong and injury they had would[4] than to bear with their own men. "For then," said he, "they could but have said we had been cowards, but now they may accuse us of injustice, beside the pains we take, and the danger we put ourselves into." And thus may we see what Brutus's intent and purpose was.

36. [*The wonderful constancy of Brutus in matters of justice and equity. Brutus's care and watching.*] But as they both prepared to pass over again out of Asia into Europe, there went a rumor that there appeared a wonderful sign unto him. Brutus was a careful man, and slept very little, both for that his diet was moderate, as also because he was continually occupied. He never slept in the day-time, and in the night no longer than the time he was driven to be alone, and when everybody else took their rest. But now whilst he was in war, and his head ever busily occupied to think of his affairs and what would happen, after he had slumbered a little after supper, he spent all the rest of the night in dispatching of his weightiest causes; and after he had taken order for them, if he had any leisure left him, he would read some book till the third watch of the night, at what time the captains, petty captains, and colonels, did use[5] to come to him.

[*A spirit appeared unto Brutus in the city of Sardis.*] So, being ready to go into Europe, one night very late (when all the camp took quiet rest) as he was in his tent with a little light, thinking of weighty matters, he thought he heard one come in to him, and casting his eye towards the

---

1 More appropriate.
2 Robbed nor plundered.
3 Supporter.
4 Wanted to.
5 Were accustomed.

door of his tent, that he saw a wonderful strange and monstrous shape of a body coming towards him, and said never a word. So Brutus boldly asked what he was, a god or a man, and what cause brought him thither? The spirit answered him, "I am thy evil spirit, Brutus: and thou shalt see me by the city of Philippi." Brutus being no otherwise afraid, replied again unto it: "Well, then I shall see thee again."

37. [*Cassius's opinion of spirits after the Epicurean sect.*] The spirit presently vanished away, and Brutus called his men unto him, who told him that they heard no noise, nor saw anything at all. Thereupon Brutus returned again to think on his matters as he did before, and when the day brake, he went unto Cassius, to tell him what vision had appeared unto him in the night. Cassius being in opinion an Epicurean, and reasoning thereon with Brutus, spake to him touching the vision thus. "In our sect, Brutus, we have an opinion, that we do not always feel or see that which we suppose we do both see and feel, but that our senses being credulous and therefore easily abused (when they are idle and unoccupied in their own objects) are induced to imagine they see and conjecture that which in truth they do not. For our mind is quick and cunning to work (without either cause or matter) anything in the imagination whatsoever. And therefore the imagination is resembled to clay, and the mind to the potter, who, without any other cause than his fancy and pleasure, changeth it into what fashion and form he will.

[*The cause of dreams.*] "And this doth the diversity of our dreams show unto us. For our imagination doth upon a small fancy grow from conceit[1] to conceit, altering both in passions and forms of things imagined. For the mind of man is ever occupied, and that continual moving is nothing but an imagination. But yet there is a further cause of this in you. For you being by nature given to melancholic discoursing, and of late continually occupied, your wits and senses, having been overlabored, do easilier[2] yield to such imaginations. For to say that there are spirits or angels, and if there were, that they had the shape of men, or such voices or any power at all to come unto us, it is a mockery. And for mine own part, I would there were such, because that we should not only have soldiers, horses, and ships, but also the aid of the gods, to guide and further our honest and honorable attempts." With these

---

1   Idea.
2   More easily.

words Cassius did somewhat comfort and quiet Brutus. When they raised their camp, there came two eagles that, flying with a marvelous force, lighted upon two of the foremost ensigns,[1] and always followed the soldiers, which gave them meat and fed them, until they came near to the city of Philippi, and there, one day only before the battle, they both flew away.

38. ... [*Brutus's and Cassius's camps before the city of Philippi, against Octavius Caesar and Antonius. Brutus's soldiers bravely armed.*] So Caesar came not thither of[2] ten days after, and Antonius camped against Cassius, and Brutus on the other side, against Caesar. The Romans called the valley between both camps the Philippian fields, and there were never seen two so great armies of the Romans, one before the other, ready to fight. In truth, Brutus's army was inferior to Octavius Caesar's in number of men, but for bravery and rich furniture,[3] Brutus's army far excelled Caesar's. For the most part of their armors were silver and gilt, which Brutus had bountifully given them, although, in all other things, he taught his captains to live in order without excess. But for the bravery of armor and weapon, which soldiers should carry in their hands, or otherwise wear upon their backs, he thought that it was an encouragement unto them that by nature are greedy of honor, and that it maketh them also fight like devils that love to get, and to be afraid to lose, because they fight to keep their armor and weapon, as also their goods and lands.

39. ... [*Unlucky signs unto Cassius.*] Notwithstanding, being busily occupied about the ceremonies of this purification, it is reported that there chanced certain unlucky signs unto Cassius. For one of his sergeants that carried the rods[4] before him brought him the garland of flowers turned backward, the which he should have worn on his head in the time of sacrificing. Moreover it is reported also that another time before, in certain sports and triumph where they carried an image of Cassius's victory of clean[5] gold, it fell by chance, the man stumbling that carried it. And yet further, there was seen a marvelous number of

---

1 Military standards.
2 There for.
3 Trappings.
4 The *fasces*, a bundle of sticks with an ax in the middle, carried before Roman magistrates as a symbol of their authority to punish wrongdoers.
5 Pure.

fowls of prey, that feed upon dead carcasses, and bee-hives also were found, where bees were gathered together in a certain place within the trenches of the camp, the which place the soothsayers thought good to shut out of the precinct of the camp, for to take away the superstitious fear and mistrust men would have of it. The which began somewhat to alter Cassius's mind from Epicurus's opinions, and had put the soldiers also in a marvelous fear.

[*Cassius's and Brutus's opinions about the battle.*] Thereupon Cassius was of opinion not to try this war at one battle, but rather to delay time and to draw it out in length, considering that they were the stronger in money, and the weaker in men and armor. But Brutus, in contrary manner, did always before, and at that time also, desire nothing more than to put all to the hazard[1] of battle, as soon as might be possible, to the end[2] he might either quickly restore his country to her former liberty or rid him forthwith of this miserable world, being still troubled in following and maintaining of such great armies together. But perceiving that in the daily skirmishes and bickerings[3] they made, his men were always the stronger and ever had the better,[4] that yet quickened his spirits again, and did put him in better heart. And furthermore, because that some of their own men had already yielded themselves to their enemies, and that it was suspected moreover divers others would do the like, that made many of Cassius's friends which were of his mind before (when it came to be debated in council, whether the battle should be fought or not) that they were then of Brutus's mind.

40. [*Cassius's words unto Messala the night before the battle.*] So Brutus, all supper-time, looked with a cheerful countenance, like a man that had good hope, and talked very wisely of philosophy, and after supper went to bed. But touching[5] Cassius, Messala reporteth that he supped by himself in his tent with a few of his friends, and that all supper-time he looked very sadly and was full of thoughts, although it was against his nature, and that after supper he took him by the hand, and holding him fast (in token of kindness, as his manner was) told him in Greek: "Messala, I protest unto thee, and make thee my witness, that I

---

1 Chance.
2 So.
3 Small-scale encounters.
4 Came off better.
5 As for.

am compelled against my mind and will, as Pompey the Great was, to jeopardy[1] the liberty of our country to the hazard of a battle. And yet we must be lively and of good courage, considering our good fortune, whom[2] we should wrong too much to mistrust her, although we follow evil counsel." Messala writeth that Cassius having spoken these last words unto him, he bade him farewell, and willed him to come to supper to him the next night following, because it was his birthday.

[*Brutus and Cassius talk before the battle.*] The next morning, by break of day, the signal of battle was set out in Brutus's and Cassius's camp, which was an arming scarlet coat,[3] and both the chieftains spake together in the midst of their armies. There Cassius began to speak first, and said: "The gods grant us, O Brutus, that this day we may win the field, and ever after to live all the rest of our life quietly one with another. But sith[4] the gods have so ordained it that the greatest and chiefest things amongst men are most uncertain, and that if the battle fall out otherwise to-day than we wish or look for, we shall hardly meet again, what art thou then determined to do, to fly, or die?"

[*Brutus's answer to Cassius.*] Brutus answered him, being yet but a young man and not over greatly experienced in the world, "I trust, I know not how, a certain rule of philosophy, by the which I did greatly blame and reprove Cato for killing himself, as being no lawful nor godly act, touching the gods, nor concerning men, valiant, not to give place and yield to divine providence, and not constantly and patiently to take whatsoever it pleaseth him to send us, but to draw back and fly, but being now in the midst of the danger, I am of a contrary mind. For if it be not the will of God that this battle fall out fortunate for us, I will look no more for hope, neither seek to make any new supply for war again, but will rid me of this miserable world, and content me with my fortune. For I gave up my life for my country in the Ides of March, for the which I shall live in another more glorious world." Cassius fell a-laughing to hear what he said, and embracing him, "Come on then," said he, "let us go and charge our enemies with this mind. For either we shall conquer, or we shall not need to fear the conquerors."

---

1 Jeopardize, risk.
2 "Fortune" (thinking of the Roman goddess, Fortuna).
3 Scarlet coat of armor.
4 Since.

[*The battle at Philippi against Octavius Caesar and Antonius.*] After this talk, they fell to consultation among their friends for the ordering of the battle. Then Brutus prayed[1] Cassius he might have the leading of the right wing, the which men thought was far meeter[2] for Cassius, both because he was the elder man, and also for that he had the better experience. But yet Cassius gave it him and willed that Messala (who had charge of one of the warlikest legions they had) should be also in that wing with Brutus. So Brutus presently sent out his horsemen, who were excellently well appointed, and his footmen also were as willing and ready to give charge.

41. Now Antonius's men did cast[3] a trench from the marsh by the which they lay, to cut off Cassius's way to come to the sea, and Caesar, at the least his army stirred not.[4] As for Octavius Caesar himself, he was not in his camp because he was sick. And for his people, they little thought the enemies would have given them battle, but only have made some light skirmishes to hinder them that wrought in the trench, and with their darts and slings to have kept them from finishing of their work, but they [Caesar's army], taking no heed to them that came full upon them to give them battle, marveled much at the great noise they heard, that came from the place where they were casting their trench. In the meantime Brutus, that led the right wing, sent little bills[5] to the colonels and captains of private bands, in the which he wrote the word of the battle;[6] and he himself, riding a-horseback by all the troops, did speak to them, and encouraged them to stick to it like men. So by this means very few of them understood what was the word of the battle, and besides, the most part of them never tarried[7] to have it told them, but ran with great fury to assail the enemies, whereby, through this disorder, the legions were marvelously scattered and dispersed one from the other....

42. The other also that had not glanced by, but had given a charge full upon Caesar's battle,[8] they easily made them fly, because they were

---

1 Asked.
2 More appropriate.
3 Dig.
4 Caesar's army did not stir out of its place.
5 Notes.
6 Issued battle orders.
7 Waited.
8 Army.

greatly troubled for the loss of their camp, and of them there were slain by hand three legions. Then, being very earnest to follow the chase of them that fled, they ran in amongst them hand over head[1] into their camp, and Brutus among them. But that which the conquerors thought not of, occasion showed it unto them that were overcome, and that was, the left wing of their enemies[2] left naked and unguarded of them of the right wing, who were strayed too far off, in following of them that were overthrown.[3] So they [Caesar's soldiers] gave a hot charge upon them [Cassius's wing]. But notwithstanding all the force they made, they could not break into the midst of their battle,[4] where they found them that received them and valiantly made head against them. Howbeit they brake and overthrew the left wing where Cassius was, by reason of the great disorder among them, and also because they had no intelligence how the right wing had sped.[5] So they chased them, beating them into their camp,[6] the which they spoiled, none of both the chieftains being present there. For Antonius, as it is reported, to fly the fury of the first charge, was gotten into the next marsh, and no man could tell what became of Octavius Caesar, after he was carried out of his camp.

[*Octavius Caesar falsely reported to be slain at the battle of Philippi. Cassius's misfortune.*] Insomuch that there were certain soldiers that showed their swords bloodied, and said that they had slain him [Caesar], and did describe his face, and showed what age he was of. Furthermore, the forward and the middest of Brutus's battle[7] had already put all their enemies to flight that withstood them, with great slaughter, so that Brutus had conquered all on his side, and Cassius had lost all on the other side. For nothing undid them but that Brutus went not to help Cassius, thinking he had overcome them as himself had done; and Cassius on the other side tarried not for Brutus, thinking he had been overthrown as himself was. . . . Now Brutus returning from the chase, after he had slain and sacked Caesar's men, he wondered much that he could not see Cassius's tent standing up high as it was wont, neither the other

---

1 With aggressive speed.
2 I.e., Cassius's wing on the left of the line.
3 I.e., Brutus's wing had outrun the left wing, commanded by Cassius.
4 Center of their formation.
5 Fared.
6 I.e., Caesar's men chased Cassius's men.
7 Vanguard and center of Brutus's army.

tents of his camp standing as they were before, because all the whole camp had been spoiled, and the tents thrown down, at the first coming of their enemies. But they that were about Brutus, whose sight served them better, told them that they saw a great glistering of harness,[1] and a number of silvered targets,[2] that went and came into Cassius's camp, and were not, as they took it, the armors nor the number of men that they had left there to guard the camp, and yet that they saw not such a number of dead bodies and great overthrow as there should have been, if so many legions had been slain. This made Brutus at the first mistrust that which had happened.[3] So he appointed a number of men to keep[4] the camp of his enemy which he had taken, and caused his men to be sent for that yet followed the chase, and gathered them together, thinking to lead them to aid Cassius, who was in this state as you shall hear.

43. [*Cassius offended with the sundry errors Brutus and his men committed in battle.*] First of all, he was marvelous angry to see how Brutus's men ran to give charge upon their enemies and tarried not for the word of the battle nor commandment to give charge, and it grieved him beside, that after he[5] had overcome them, his men fell straight to spoil,[6] and were not careful to compass in the rest of the enemies behind; but with tarrying too long also, more than through the valiantness or foresight of the captains his enemies, Cassius found himself compassed in with the right wing of his enemy's army. Whereupon his horsemen brake[7] immediately, and fled for life towards the sea....

[*Cassius's valiantness in wars.*] So Cassius himself was at length compelled to fly, with a few about him, unto a little hill, from whence they might easily see what was done in all the plain. Howbeit Cassius himself saw nothing, for his sight was very bad, saving that he saw (and yet with much ado) how the enemies spoiled his camp before his eyes. He saw also a great troupe of horsemen, whom Brutus sent to aid him, and thought that they were his enemies that followed him; but yet he sent Titinnius, one of them that was with him, to go and know what they

---

1 Glistening of armor.
2 Shields.
3 Begin to wonder about what had happened.
4 Occupy.
5 Brutus.
6 Immediately began plundering.
7 Broke formation.

were. Brutus's horsemen saw him coming afar off, whom when they knew that he was one of Cassius's chiefest friends, they shouted out for joy, and they that were familiarly acquainted with him lighted from their horses, and went and embraced him. The rest compassed him in round about on horseback, with songs of victory and great rushing of their harness,[1] so that they made all the field ring again for joy. But this marred all. For Cassius, thinking indeed that Titinnius was taken of the enemies, he then spake these words: "Desiring too much to live, I have lived to see one of my best friends taken, for my sake, before my face."

[*Cassius slain by his man Pindarus.*] After that, he got into a tent where nobody was, and took Pindarus with him, one of his bondsmen (whom he reserved ever for such a pinch since the cursed battle of the Parthians, where Crassus was slain, though he notwithstanding scaped from that overthrow), but then, casting his cloak over his head, and holding out his bare neck unto Pindarus, he gave him his head to be stricken off. So the head was found severed from the body, but after that time Pindarus was never seen more. Whereupon some took occasion to say that he had slain his master without his commandment. By and by they knew the horsemen that came towards them, and might see Titinnius crowned with a garland of triumph, who came before with great speed unto Cassius. But when he perceived, by the cries and tears of his friends which tormented themselves, the misfortune that had chanced to his captain Cassius by mistaking, he drew out his sword, cursing himself a thousand times that he had tarried so long, and so slew himself presently in the field.

44. [*The death of Titinnius.*] Brutus in the mean time came forward still, and understood also that Cassius had been overthrown, but he knew nothing of his death till he came very near to his camp. So when he was come thither, after he had lamented the death of Cassius, calling him the last of all the Romans, being impossible that Rome should ever breed again so noble and valiant a man as he, he caused his body to be buried, and sent it to the city of Thassos,[2] fearing lest his funerals within his camp should cause great disorder. Then he called his soldiers together, and did encourage them again. And when he saw that they had

---

1 Armor.
2 Shakespeare resolved the inconsistency in North's account that Cassius's body was both buried and sent away by having Brutus order simply that it be sent to Thasos (5.3.104, TLN 2594).

lost all their carriage,[1] which they could not brook[2] well, he promised every man of them two thousand drachmas in recompense. After his soldiers had heard his oration, they were all of them prettily[3] cheered again, wondering much at his great liberality, and waited upon him with great cries when he went his way, praising him, for that he only of the four chieftains was not overcome in battle. And to speak the truth, his deeds showed that he hoped not in vain to be conqueror. For with few legions he had slain and driven all them away that made head against him,[4] and if all his people had fought, and that the most of them had not outgone their enemies to run to spoil their goods, surely it was like enough he had slain them all, and had left never a man of them alive.

45. ... But on Brutus's side, both his camps stood wavering, and that in great danger.... Now for the slaves that were prisoners, which were a great number, and went and came to and fro amongst these armed men, not without suspicion, he commanded they should kill them. But for the free men, he sent them freely home, and said that they were better prisoners with his enemies than with him. For with them, they were slaves and servants, and with him, they were free men and citizens.

46. Afterwards Brutus performed the promise he had made to the soldiers, and gave them the two thousand drachmas apiece; but yet he first reproved them, because they went and gave charge upon the enemies at the first battle, before they had the word of battle given them ...

48. [*The evil spirit appeared again unto Brutus.*] The selfsame night, it is reported that the monstrous spirit which had appeared before unto Brutus in the city of Sardis, did now appear again unto him in the self-same shape and form, and so vanished away, and said never a word.

[*Strange sights before Brutus's second battle.*] Now Publius Volumnius, a grave and wise philosopher, that had been with Brutus from the beginning of this war, doth make no mention of this spirit but saith ... that, before the battle was fought, there were two eagles fought between both armies, and all the time they fought there was a marvelous great silence all the valley over, both the armies being one before the other, marking this fight between them; and that in the end, the eagle towards Brutus gave over and fled away....

---

1   Proper conduct of themselves.
2   Endure.
3   Quite.
4   Had attacked him.

49. [*Brutus's second battle.*] Now after that Brutus had brought his army into the field, and had set them in battle ray[1] directly against the voward[2] of his enemy, he paused a long time before he gave the signal of battle.

[*The death of the valiant young man Cato, the son of Marcus Cato.*] There was the son of Marcus Cato slain, valiantly fighting among the lusty[3] youths. For notwithstanding that he was very weary and over-harried, yet would he not therefore fly, but manfully fighting and laying about him, telling aloud his name and also his father's name, at length he was beaten down amongst many other dead bodies of his enemies which he had slain round about him. So there were slain in the field all the chiefest gentlemen and nobility that were in his army, who valiantly ran into any danger to save Brutus's life.

50. [*The fidelity of Lucilius unto Brutus.*] Amongst whom there was one of Brutus's friends called Lucilius, who seeing a troupe of barbarous men making no reckoning of all men else they met in their way, but going all together right against Brutus, he determined to stay them with the hazard[4] of his life; and being left behind, told them that he was Brutus, and because they should believe[5] him, he prayed[6] them to bring him to Antonius, for he said he was afraid of Caesar, and that he did trust Antonius better. These barbarous men, being very glad of this good hap,[7] and thinking themselves happy men, they carried[8] him in the night, and sent some before unto Antonius, to tell him of their coming. He was marvelous glad of it, and went out to meet them that brought him. Others also understanding of it, that they had brought Brutus prisoner, they came out of all parts of the camp to see him, some pitying his hard fortune, and others saying that it was not done like himself, so cowardly to be taken alive of the barbarous people for fear of death. When they came near together, Antonius stayed a while bethinking himself how he should use Brutus. In the meantime Lucilius was brought to him, who stoutly with a bold countenance said: "Antonius, I dare

---

1   Array.
2   Vanguard, foremost division of the army.
3   Vigorous.
4   At the risk.
5   To make them believe.
6   Asked.
7   Good chance.
8   Conveyed.

assure thee, that no enemy hath taken nor shall take Marcus Brutus alive, and I beseech God keep him from that fortune, for wheresoever he be found, alive or dead, he will be found like himself. And now for myself, I am come unto thee, having deceived these men of arms here, bearing them down[1] that I was Brutus, and do not refuse to suffer any torment thou wilt put me to." Lucilius's words made them all amazed that heard him. Antonius on the other side, looking upon all them that had brought him, said unto them, "My companions, I think ye are sorry you have failed of your purpose, and that you think this man hath done you great wrong, but I assure you, you have taken a better booty[2] than that you followed. For instead of an enemy you have brought me a friend, and for my part, if you had brought me Brutus alive, truly I cannot tell what I should have done to him. For I had rather have such men my friends, as this man here, than mine enemies." Then he embraced Lucilius, and at that time delivered him to one of his friends in custody, and Lucilius ever after served him faithfully, even to his death.

51. [*Brutus's flying.*] Now Brutus having passed a little river, walled in on every side with high rocks and shadowed with great trees, being then dark night, he went no further, but stayed at the foot of a rock with certain of his captains and friends that followed him, and looking up to the firmament[3] that was full of stars, sighing, he rehearsed two verses, of the which Volumnius wrote the one, to this effect:

Let not the wight[4] from whom this mischief vent,[5]
O Jove, escape without due punishment:—[6]

and saith that he had forgotten the other. Within a little while after, naming his friends that he had seen slain in battle before his eyes, he fetched a greater sigh than before, specially when he came to name Labio and Flavius, of whom the one was his lieutenant, and the other captain of the pioneers[7] of his camp.... Furthermore, Brutus thought

---

1 Convincing them.
2 Plunder, prize.
3 Sky.
4 Person.
5 Comes forth.
6 From Euripides' *Medea*.
7 Military engineers.

that there was no great number of men slain in battle, and to know the truth of it, there was one called Statilius, that promised to go through his enemies, for otherwise it was impossible to go see their camp, and from thence, if all were well, that he would lift up a torchlight in the air, and then return again with speed to him. The torchlight was lift up as he had promised, for Statilius went thither. Now Brutus seeing Statilius tarry long after that, and that he came not again, he said: "If Statilius be alive, he will come again." But his evil fortune was such that, as he came back, he lighted in his enemies' hands and was slain.

52. [*Brutus's saying of flying with hands and not with feet.*] Now the night being far spent, Brutus as he sat bowed towards Clitus, one of his men, and told him somewhat in his ear. The other answered him not, but fell a-weeping. Thereupon he proved[1] Dardanus, and said somewhat also to him. At length he came to Volumnius himself, and speaking to him in Greek, prayed him for the studies' sake which brought them acquainted together, that he would help him to put his hand to his sword, to thrust it in him to kill him. Volumnius denied his request, and so did many others, and amongst the rest, one of them said there was no tarrying for them there, but that they must needs fly. Then Brutus, rising up, "We must fly indeed," said he, "but it must be with our hands, not with our feet." Then taking every man by the hand, he said these words unto them with a cheerful countenance: "It rejoiceth my heart, that not one of my friends hath failed me at my need, and I do not complain of my fortune, but only for my country's sake; for as for me, I think myself happier than they that have overcome, considering that I leave a perpetual fame of our courage and manhood, the which our enemies the conquerors shall never attain unto by force or money; neither can let their posterity to say[2] that they, being naughty and unjust men, have slain good men to usurp tyrannical power not pertaining to them." Having so said, he prayed every man to shift for himself, and then he went a little aside with two or three only, among the which Strato was one, with whom he came first acquainted by the study of rhetoric. He came as near to him as he could, and taking his sword by the hilt with both his hands, and falling down upon the point of it, ran himself through. Others say that not he, but Strato (at his request) held

---

1 Tried.
2 Can prevent their descendants from saying.

the sword in his hand, and turned his head aside, and that Brutus fell down upon it, and so ran himself through, and died presently.

53. ... Now Antonius having found Brutus's body, he caused it to be wrapped up in one of the richest coat-armors[1] he had. Afterwards also, Antonius understanding that this coat-armor was stolen, he put the thief to death that had stolen it, and sent the ashes of his [Brutus's] body unto Servilia his mother.

[*Portia, Brutus's wife, killed herself with burning coals.*] And for Portia, Brutus's wife, ... she, determining to kill herself (her parents and friends carefully looking to her to keep her from it), took hot burning coals and cast them into her mouth, and kept her mouth so close that she choked herself. There was a letter of Brutus found written to his friends, complaining of their negligence, that, his wife being sick, they would not help her but suffered her to kill herself, choosing to die, rather than to languish in pain.

3. FROM *LIFE OF MARCUS ANTONIUS*

2. ... [*Antonius corrupted by Curio.*] Now Antonius being a fair young man, and in the prime of his youth, he fell acquainted with Curio, whose friendship and acquaintance (as it is reported) was a plague unto him. For he was a dissolute man, given over to all lust and insolency, who, to have Antonius the better at his commandment, trained him on into great follies and vain expenses upon women, in rioting and banqueting: so that in short time he brought Antonius into a marvelous great debt.... His father hearing of it, did put his son from him, and forbade him his house. Then he fell in with Clodius, one of the desperatest and most wicked tribunes at that time in Rome. Him he followed for a time in his desperate attempts, who bred great stir and mischief in Rome: but at length he forsook him, being weary of his rashness and folly, or else for that he was afraid of them that were bent against Clodius. Thereupon he left Italy, and went into Greece, and there bestowed the most part of his time, sometime in wars, and otherwhile in the study of eloquence.

[*Antonius used in his speaking the Asiatic phrase.*] He used a manner of phrase in his speech called Asiatic, which carried the best grace and

---

1   Coats of armor.

estimation at that time, and was much like to his manners and life: for it was full of ostentation, foolish bravery, and vain ambition.

4. [*Antonius's shape and presence.*] But besides all this he had a noble presence, and showed a countenance of one of a noble house: he had a goodly thick beard, a broad forehead, crooked nosed, and there appeared such a manly look in his countenance, as is commonly seen in Hercules, pictures, stamped or graven in metal.

5. [*Antonius tribune of the people and augur.*[1]] Now the Romans maintaining two factions at Rome at that time, one against the other, of the which they that took part with the Senate did join with Pompey, being then in Rome, and the contrary side, taking part with the people, sent for Caesar to aid them, who made wars in Gaul: then Curio, Antonius's friend, that had changed his garments, and at that time took part with Caesar, whose enemy he had been before, he won Antonius, and so handled the matter, partly through the great credit and sway he bore amongst the people, by reason of his eloquent tongue, and partly also by his exceeding expense of money he made which Caesar gave him, that Antonius was chosen tribune, and afterwards made augur.

[*Caesar gave the charge of Italy unto Antonius.*] Then was Antonius straight marvelously[2] commended and beloved of the soldiers, because he commonly exercised himself among them, and would oftentimes eat and drink with them, and also be liberal unto them, according to his ability.

[*Antonius's vices.*] But then in contrary manner, he purchased divers[3] other men's evil wills, because that through negligence he would not do them justice that were injured, and dealt very churlishly with them that had any suit unto him: and besides all this, he had an ill name to intice[4] men's wives. To conclude, Caesar's friends, that governed under him, were cause why they[5] hated Caesar's government (which indeed in respect of himself was no less than tyranny) by reason of the great insolencies[6] and outrageous parts that were committed: amongst

---

1 Roman religious office with significant political influence.
2 Strongly.
3 Various.
4 Bad reputation for seducing.
5 So many other people.
6 Arrogant actions, contempt for inferiors.

whom Antonius, that was of greatest power, and that also committed greatest faults, deserved most blame.

8. [*Antonius's manhood in war.*] Now there were divers hot skirmishes and encounters, in the which Antonius fought so valiantly, that he carried the praise from them all: but specially at two several times, when Caesar's men turned their backs, and fled for life. For he stepped before them, and compelled them to return again to fight, so that the victory fell on Caesar's side.

[*Antonius led the left wing of Caesar's battle at Pharsalia, where Pompey lost the field.*] For this cause he had the second place in the camp among the soldiers, and they spoke of no other man unto Caesar, but of him: who showed plainly what opinion he had of him, when at the last battle of Pharsalia (which indeed was the last trial of all, to give the conqueror the whole empire of the world) he himself did lead the right wing of his army, and gave Antonius the leading of the left wing, as the valiantest man and skillfullest soldier of all those he had about him. After Caesar had won the victory, and that he was created Dictator, he followed Pompey step by step: howbeit, before, he named Antonius general of the horse men, and sent him to Rome.

[*Antonius's abominable life.*] But by this means he got the ill will of the common people; and on the other side, the noblemen (as Cicero saith) did not only mislike him, but also hate him for his naughty life: for they did abhor his banquets and drunken feasts he made at unseasonable times, and his extreme wasteful expenses upon vain light huswives;[1] and then in the day-time he would sleep or walk out his drunkenness, thinking to wear away the fume of the abundance of wine which he had taken over night. In his house they did nothing but feast, dance, and mask: and himself passed away the time in hearing of foolish plays, and in marrying[2] these players, tumblers, jesters, and such sort of people....

12. [*Antonius unwittingly gave Caesar's enemies occasion to conspire against him.*] Antonius, unawares, afterwards gave Caesar's enemies just occasion and color[3] to do as they did, as you shall hear. The Romans by chance celebrated the feast called Lupercalia, and Caesar, being appareled in his triumphing robe, was set in the tribune[4] where they use

---

1 Hussies, prostitutes.
2 Attending to the marriages of.
3 Excuse.
4 Prominent official location (borrowed by the translator from church architecture).

to make their orations to the people, and from thence did behold the sport of the runners. The manner of this running was thus. On that day there are many young men of noble house, and those specially that be chief officers for that year, who running naked up and down the city, anointed with the oil of olive, for pleasure do strike them they meet in their way with white leather thongs they have in their hands.

[*Antonius Lupercian putteth the diadem upon Caesar's head.*] Antonius, being one among the rest that was to run, leaving the ancient ceremonies and old customs of that solemnity, he ran to the tribune where Caesar was set, and carried a laurel crown in his hand, having a royal band or diadem wreathed about it, which in old time was the ancient mark and token of a king. When he was come to Caesar, he made his fellow-runners with him lift him up, and so he did put his laurel crown upon his head, signifying thereby that he had deserved to be king. But Caesar, making as though he refused it, turned away his head. The people were so rejoiced at it, that they all clapped their hands for joy. Antonius again did put it on his head: Caesar again refused it; and thus they were striving off and on a great while together. As oft as Antonius did put this laurel crown unto him, a few of his followers rejoiced at it: and as oft also as Caesar refused it, all the people together clapped their hands. And this was a wonderful thing, that they suffered all things subjects should do by commandment of their kings: and yet they could not abide the name of a king, detesting it as the utter destruction of their liberty. Caesar, in a rage, arose out of his seat, and plucking down the collar of his gown from his neck, he showed it naked, bidding any man strike off his head that would. This laurel crown was afterwards put upon the head of one of Caesar's statues or images, the which one of the tribunes plucked off. The people liked his doing therein so well, that they waited on him home to his house, with great clapping of hands. Howbeit Caesar did turn them out of their offices for it.

[*Brutus and Cassius conspire Caesar's death.*] This was a good encouragement for Brutus and Cassius to conspire his death, who fell into a consort[1] with their trustiest friends, to execute their enterprise, but yet stood doubtful whether they should make Antonius privy to it or not. All the rest liked of[2] it, saving Trebonius only. He told them that,

---

1 Conspiracy.
2 Approved.

when they rode to meet Caesar at his return out of Spain, Antonius and he always keeping company, and lying together by the way, he felt his mind afar off: but Antonius, finding his meaning, would hearken no more unto it, and yet notwithstanding never made Caesar acquainted with this talk, but had faithfully kept it to himself.

[*Consultation about the murder of Antonius with Caesar.*] After that, they consulted whether they should kill Antonius with Caesar. But Brutus would in no wise consent to it, saying, that venturing on such an enterprise as that, for the maintenance of law and justice, it ought to be clear from all villainy. Yet they, fearing Antonius's power, and the authority of his office, appointed certain of the conspiracy, that when Caesar were gone into the Senate, and while others should execute their enterprise, they should keep Antonius in a talk out of the Senate-house.

14. Even as they had devised these matters, so were they executed: and Caesar was slain in the middest[1] of the Senate. Antonius being put in a fear withal, cast a slave's gown upon him, and hid himself. But afterwards when it was told him that the murderers slew no man else, and that they went only into the Capitol, he sent his son unto them for a pledge, and bade them boldly come down upon his word. The selfsame day he did bid Cassius to supper, and Lepidus also bade Brutus. The next morning the Senate was assembled, and Antonius himself preferred[2] a law, that all things past should be forgotten, and that they should appoint provinces unto Cassius and Brutus: the which the Senate confirmed, and further ordained, that they should cancel none of Caesar's laws. Thus went Antonius out of the Senate more praised and better esteemed than ever man was, because it seemed to every man that he had cut off all occasion of civil wars, and that he had showed himself a marvelous wise governor of the common wealth, for the appeasing of these matters of so great weight and importance. But now the opinion he conceived of himself after he had a little felt the good-will of the people towards him, hoping thereby to make himself the chiefest man if he might overcome Brutus, did easily make him alter his first mind. And therefore, when Caesar's body was brought to the place where it should be buried, he made a funeral oration in commendation of Caesar, according to the ancient custom of praising noble men

---

1 Midst.
2 Proposed.

at their funerals. When he saw that the people were very glad and desirous also to hear Caesar spoken of, and his praises uttered, he mingled his oration with lamentable words; and by amplifying of matters did greatly move their hearts and affections unto pity and compassion. In fine,[1] to conclude his oration, he unfolded before the whole assembly the bloody garments of the dead, thrust through in many places with their swords, and called the malefactors cruel and cursed murderers.

[*Antonius maketh uproar among the people, for the murder of Caesar.*] With these words he put the people into such a fury, that they presently[2] took Caesar's body, and burnt it in the market-place, with such tables and forms as they could get together. Then when the fire was kindled, they took firebrands, and ran to the murderers' houses to set them on fire, and to make them come out to fight.

16. [*Variance betwixt Antonius and Octavius Caesar, heir unto Julius Caesar.*] Now things remaining in this state at Rome, Octavius Caesar the younger came to Rome, who was the son of Julius Caesar's niece, as you have heard before, and was left his lawful heir by will, remaining, at the time of the death of his great uncle that was slain, in the city of Apollonia. This young man at his first arrival went to salute Antonius, as one of his late dead father Caesar's friends, who by his last will and testament had made him his heir; and withal, he was presently in hand with him for money and other things which were left of trust in his hands; because Caesar had by will bequeathed unto the people of Rome threescore and fifteen silver drachmas to be given to every man, the which he as heir stood charged withal. Antonius at the first made no reckoning of him, because he was very young, and said he lacked wit and good friends to advise him, if he looked to take such a charge in hand, as to undertake to be Caesar's heir. But when Antonius saw that he could not shake him off with those words, and that he was still in hand[3] with him for his father's goods, but specially for the ready money, then he spake and did what he could against him.

[*Antonious and Octavius became friends. Antonius's dream.*] Antonius, being afraid of it, talked with Octavius in the Capitol, and became his friend. But the very same night Antonius had a strange dream, who thought that lightning fell upon him, and burnt his right hand. Shortly

---

1   Finally.
2   Immediately.
3   Close at hand, urgent.

after word was brought him, that Caesar lay in wait to kill him. Caesar cleared himself unto him, and told him there was no such matter: but he could not make Antonius believe to the contrary. Whereupon they became further enemies than ever they were: insomuch that both of them made friends of either side to gather together all the old soldiers through Italy, that were dispersed in divers towns: and made them large promises, and sought also to win the legions on their side, which were already in arms.

18. Now their intent was to join with the legions that were on the other side of the mountains, under Lepidus's charge: whom Antonius took to be his friend, because he had holpen[1] him to many things at Caesar's hand, through his means.

19. [*The conspiracy and meeting of Caesar, Antonius and Ledipus.*] So Octavius Caesar would not lean to Cicero, when he saw that his whole travell[2] and endeavor was only to restore the commonwealth to her former liberty. Therefore he sent certain of his friends to Antonius, to make them friends again: and thereupon all three met together (to wit Caesar, Antonius, and Lepidus) in an island environed round about with a little river, and there remained three days together. Now as touching all other matters they were easily agreed, and did divide all the empire of Rome[3] between them, as if it had been their own inheritance.

[*The proscription of the Triumviri.*[4]] But yet they could hardly agree whom they would put to death: for every one of them would[5] kill their enemies, and save their kinsmen and friends. Yet at length, giving place to their greedy desire to be revenged of their enemies, they spurned all reverence of blood and holiness of friendship at their feet. For Caesar left Cicero to Antonius's will, Antonius also forsook Lucius Caesar, who was his uncle by his mother: and both of them together suffered Lepidus to kill his own brother Paulus. Yet some writers affirm, that Caesar and Antonius requested Paulus might be slain, and that Lepidus was contented with it. In my opinion there was never a more horrible, unnatural, and crueler change than this was. For thus changing[6] murder for murder, they did as well kill those whom they

---

1 Helped.
2 Travail, effort.
3 Roman jurisdiction (Rome still being technically a republic).
4 Rule by three (literally "three men").
5 Wanted to.
6 Exchanging.

did forsake and leave unto others, as those also which others left unto them to kill: but so much more was their wickedness and cruelty great unto their friends, for that they put them to death being innocents, and having no cause to hate them.

22. [*The valiantness of Antonius against Brutus.*] When they had passed over the seas, and that they began to make war, they being both camped by their enemies, to wit, Antonius against Cassius, and Caesar against Brutus, Caesar did no great matter, but Antonius had always the upper hand, and did all. For at the first battle Caesar was overthrown by Brutus, and lost his camp, and very hardly saved himself by flying from them that followed him. Howbeit, he writeth himself in his Commentaries, that he fled before the charge was given, because of a dream one of his friends had. Antonius on the other side overthrew Cassius in battle, though some write that he was not there himself at the battle, but that he came after the overthrow, whilst his men had the enemies in chase.

[*The death of Cassius. Brutus slew himself.*] So Cassius, at his earnest request, was slain by a faithful servant of his own called Pindarus, whom he had enfranchised: because he knew not in time that Brutus had overcome Caesar. Shortly after they fought another battle again, in the which Brutus was overthrown, who afterwards also slew himself. Thus Antonius had the chiefest glory of this victory, specially because Caesar was sick at that time. Antonius having found Brutus's body after this battle, blaming him much for the murder of his brother Caius, whom he had put to death in Macedon for revenge of Cicero's cruel death, and yet laying the fault more in Hortensius than in him, he made Hortensius to be slain on his brother's tomb.

[*Antonius gave honorable burial unto Brutus.*] Furthermore he cast his coat-armor[1] (which was wonderful rich and sumptuous) upon Brutus's body, and gave commandment to one of his slaves enfranchised, to defray the charge of his burial. But afterwards Antonius hearing that his enfranchised bondman had not burnt his coat-armor with his body, because it was very rich and worth a great sum of money, and that he had also kept back much of the ready money appointed for his funeral and tomb, he also put him to death.

---

1   Coat of armor.

APPENDIX B: MONTAIGNE ON STOICISM AND EPICUREANISM

ENGLISH TRANSLATION BY JOHN FLORIO, 1603

[Michel de Montaigne (1533–92) published a collection of highly original essays in 1580, with revisions and additions in 1588 and again (posthumously) in 1595. Widely read, urbane, and intensely curious about everything, including himself, Montaigne wrote frankly, often daringly, and with irresistible charm about a remarkable array of subjects, including God, self-knowledge, moral realism, and exploration of the New World. His essays, written in French, circulated widely, making their way to England as early as the 1590s, where they were read in the French original by writers and intellectuals such as Francis Bacon and John Donne. An English translation by Edward Aggas, entered in the Stationers' Register in 1595, has not survived, but John Florio's translation of 1603 is famously paraphrased eight years later in Shakespeare's *The Tempest* (2.1.150–59)—the earliest unquestionable allusion to Montaigne by his younger English contemporary. Montaigne is an illuminating contemporary source for two sets of ideas that figure importantly in *Julius Caesar*: Epicureanism and stoicism.

Shakespeare followed Plutarch in making Cassius a philosophical Epicurean and in having him begin to doubt his philosophy toward the end of his life. At the same time, everything about Brutus suggests that Shakespeare conceived of him as a stoic. In practical terms, these two ancient philosophies aimed to achieve a similar way of living one's life, even though the rationale each of them offered for how to live was very different.

Epicureanism was named for its founder, the Athenian philosopher Epicurus (341–270 BCE). Although only fragments of Epicurus' own writing are extant, his ideas were preserved influentially in *De Rerum Natura* ("On the Nature of Things"), a remarkable philosophical poem in six books of Latin hexameters, composed by the Roman poet Lucretius toward the middle of the first century BCE. Epicureans believed that the aim of life is to achieve a calm of mind they called *ataraxia*, and that this calm can best be achieved by avoiding both pain and extreme pleasure (the latter because it only leads to pain). The most calming pleasure, moreover, is intellectual, and a proper understanding of the world involves a recognition that consciousness coexists with the body, because the opposite (belief in an afterlife for the soul) causes more pain than pleasure. Lucretius outlines a materialist physics to support these contentions: the universe is made up exclusively of either atoms or emptiness. ("Atom" is a Greek word used by Epicurus, following Democritus; Lucretius uses a Latin equivalent, *primordium*.) The gods, who are made of the smallest, swiftest, and finest atoms, exist in a state of perfect *ataraxia*, which prevents their having anything to do with human beings and consequently with the imperfect striving for pleasure in which human beings mistakenly engage. The latter doctrine is the one Cassius begins to doubt.

Stoicism originated with Zeno of Cytium at about the turn of the third century BCE. As its ethical outlook owes a great deal to Socrates in the fifth century, however, there is not necessarily a conflict between Shakespeare's imagining Brutus to be a stoic and Plutarch's claim that Brutus favored Plato, who was Socrates' most influential follower. Stoics were also determinists, but their assumptions were not materialistic, like the Epicureans', because stoics were rigorous providentialists, affirming that the gods oversee every aspect of human existence to the point of making everything that happens necessary and unavoidable. As the stoics understand cosmic determinism, however, it does not deny human freedom. On the contrary, human beings are free not only to investigate the precise causes of things but also to adjust their response to external events in such a way as never to be surprised or overwhelmed by anything that happens, because they have no control over it. The stoic idea of controlling one's response to events was so ingrained in early modern popular consciousness that Shakespeare invariably means "stoicism" when he says "philosophy." Friar Laurence thus offers typically stoic advice to Romeo in Shakespeare's *Romeo and Juliet*, cautioning his young friend not to succumb to despair about his banishment ("that word"), after the Prince has ordered Romeo to leave Verona:

> I'll give thee armor to keep off that word,
> Adversity's sweet milk, philosophy,
> To comfort thee, though thou art banishèd. (3.3.54–56)

Romeo can do nothing about being banished, Friar Laurence urges, but he can do something about his response to his misfortune: he can accept his banishment with equanimity and forbearance, so that by bowing to the inevitable with dignity, he can reduce the pain he suffers. Stoics called this cultivated indifference to fated external events *apatheia*, which for all practical purposes in actual human living looks very much like Epicurean *ataraxia*.

While Montaigne titles his most stoic essay from a treatise by Cicero—"to study philosophy is to learn to die," he quotes in the first sentence—the author he quotes most frequently is Lucretius. The rather grim affirmation of the title is equally in keeping with the stoic assumption that while human beings cannot control events, they can control their response to events, and with the Epicurean assumption that consciousness ends with death, so one's ethical efforts ought to be directed to living well. As Montaigne repeatedly affirms in various ways, death is unavoidable, so the most rational response to death is to accept it and live one's life in preparation for it. As his essay makes clear, Montaigne is not counselling resignation and asceticism but moderation and sober-minded realism, and these ideals are fully compatible with both stoicism and Epicureanism, even though Epicureans denied the influence of the gods on human affairs and advocated a materialist determinism rather than the providential destiny of the stoics. Montaigne's easy conflation of stoicism and Epicureanism is typical of his omnivorous and syncretic philosophical imagination. The reduction of pain through philosophical reflection is a goal of both stoicism and Epicureanism, and it is the real goal of Montaigne's essay.

The source annotations to this edition are taken from O.W. Wright's edition of Montaigne's *Works*. The standard modern English translation of Montaigne's essays, by Donald Frame, does not add to the sparse source annotations by Montaigne himself.]

"THAT TO STUDY PHILOSOPHY IS TO LEARN TO DIE".

Cicero says "that to study philosophy is nothing but to prepare one's self to die."[1] The reason of which is, because study and contemplation

---

1 *Tusculan Disputations*, i. 31.

do in some sort withdraw from us our soul, and employ it separately from the body, which is a kind of apprenticeship and a resemblance of death; or, else, because all the wisdom and reasoning in the world do in the end conclude in this point, to teach us not to fear to die. And to say the truth, either our reason mocks us, or it ought to have no other aim but our contentment only, nor to endeavor anything but, in sum, to make us live well, and, as the Holy Scripture says, at our ease.[1] All the opinions of the world agree in this, that pleasure is our end, though we make use of divers[2] means to attain it. They would, otherwise, be rejected at the first motion, for who would give ear to him that should propose affliction and misery for his end? The controversies and disputes of the philosophical sects upon this point are merely verbal:

> Transcurramus solertissimas nugas.[3]

—there is more in them of opposition and obstinacy than is consistent with so sacred a profession; but whatsoever personage a man takes upon himself to perform, he ever mixes his own part with it.

Let the philosophers say what they will, the thing at which we all aim, even in virtue, is pleasure. It amuses me to rattle in ears this word, which they so nauseate to[4] and if it signify some supreme pleasure and contentment, it is more due to the assistance of virtue than to any other assistance whatever. This pleasure, for being more gay, more sinewy, more robust and more manly, is only the more seriously voluptuous, and we ought give it the name of pleasure, as that which is more favorable, gentle, and natural, and not that from which we have denominated it. The other and meaner pleasure, if it could deserve this fair name, it ought to be by way of competition, and not of privilege. I find it less exempt from traverses[5] and inconveniences than virtue itself; and, besides that the enjoyment is more momentary, fluid, and frail, it has its watchings,[6] fasts, and labors, its sweat and its blood; and, moreover,

---

1 Ecclesiastes 3:12.
2 Various.
3 "Let us skip over those subtle trifles."—Seneca, *Epistles*, 117.
4 Get sick at hearing.
5 Impediments, vexations.
6 Duties.

has particular to itself so many several[1] sorts of sharp and wounding passions, and so dull a satiety attending it, as equal it to the severest penance. And we mistake if we think that these incommodities serve it for a spur and a seasoning to its sweetness (as in nature one contrary is quickened by another), or say, when we come to virtue, that like consequences and difficulties overwhelm and render it austere and inaccessible; whereas, much more aptly than in voluptuousness, they ennoble, sharpen, and heighten the perfect and divine pleasure they procure us. He renders himself unworthy of it who will counterpoise its cost with its fruit, and neither understands the blessing nor how to use it. Those who preach to us that the quest of it is craggy, difficult, and painful, but its fruition pleasant, what do they mean by that but to tell us that it is always unpleasing? For what human means will ever attain its enjoyment? The most perfect have been fain to content themselves to aspire unto it, and to approach it only, without ever possessing it. But they are deceived, seeing that of all the pleasures we know, the very pursuit is pleasant. The attempt ever relishes of the quality of the thing to which it is directed, for it is a good part of, and consubstantial with, the effect. The felicity and beatitude that glitters in Virtue, shines throughout all her appurtenances and avenues, even to the first entry and utmost limits.

Now, of all the benefits that virtue confers upon us, the contempt of death is one of the greatest, as the means that accommodates human life with a soft and easy tranquility and gives us a pure and pleasant taste of living, without which all other pleasure would be extinct. Which is the reason why all the rules center and concur in this one article. And although they all in like manner, with common accord, teach us also to despise pain, poverty, and the other accidents to which human life is subject, it is not, nevertheless, with the same solicitude, as well by reason these accidents are not of so great necessity, the greater part of mankind passing over their whole lives without ever knowing what poverty is, and some without sorrow or sickness, as Xenophilus the musician, who lived a hundred and six years in a perfect and continual health; as also because, at the worst, death can, whenever we please, cut short and put an end to all other inconveniences. But as to death, it is inevitable:—

---

1 Various.

Omnes eodem cogimur; omnium
Versatur urna serius ocius
Sors exitura, et nos in aeternum
Exilium impositura cymbae.[1]

—and, consequently, if it frights us, 'tis a perpetual torment, for which there is no sort of consolation. There is no way by which it may not reach us. We may continually turn our heads this way and that, as in a suspected country:

Quae, quasi saxum Tantalo, semper impendet.[2]

Our courts of justice often send back condemned criminals to be executed upon the place where the crime was committed; but, carry them to fine houses by the way, prepare for them the best entertainment you can—

Non Siculae dapes
Dulcem elaborabunt saporem:
Non avium cyatheaceae cantus
Somnum reducent.[3]

Do you think they can relish it, and that the fatal end of their journey being continually before their eyes, would not alter and deprave their palate from tasting these regalios?[4]

Audit iter, numeratque dies, spatioque viarum
Metitur vitam; torquetur peste futura.[5]

The end of our race is death. 'Tis the necessary object of our aim, which, if it fright us, how is it possible to advance a step without a fit of ague?[6]

---

1 "We are all bound one voyage; the lot of all, sooner or later, is to come out of the urn. All must to eternal exile sail away."—Horace, *Odes*, ii. 3, 25.
2 "Ever, like Tantalus' stone, hangs over us."—Cicero, *De Finibus*, i. 18.
3 "Sicilian dainties will not tickle their palates, nor the melody of birds and harps bring back sleep."—Horace, *Odes*, iii. 1, 18.
4 Elegant entertainments.
5 "He considers the route, computes the time of traveling, measuring his life by the length of the journey; and torments himself by thinking of the blow to come."—Claudian, *In Rufinum*, ii. 137.
6 Fever.

The remedy the vulgar[1] use is not to think on't; but from what brutish stupidity can they derive so gross a blindness? They must bridle the ass by the tail:[2]

Qui capite ipse suo instituit vestigia retro.[3]

'Tis no wonder if he be often trapped in the pitfall. They affright people with the very mention of death, and many cross themselves, as it were the name of the devil. And because the making a man's will is in reference to dying, not a man will be persuaded to take a pen in hand to that purpose, till the physician has passed sentence upon and totally given him over, and then betwixt grief and terror, God knows in how fit a condition of understanding he is to do it.

The Romans, by reason that this poor syllable "death" sounded so harshly to their ears and seemed so ominous, found out a way to soften and spin it out by a periphrasis,[4] and instead of pronouncing such a one is dead, said, "Such a one has lived," or "Such a one has ceased to live"[5] for, provided there was any mention of life in the case, though past, it carried yet some sound of consolation. And from them it is that we have borrowed our expression, "The late Monsieur such and such a one." Peradventure,[6] as the saying is, the term we have lived is worth our money.[7] I was born betwixt eleven and twelve o'clock in the forenoon the last day of February 1533, according to our computation, beginning the year the 1st of January,[8] and it is now but just fifteen days since I was complete nine-and-thirty years old; I make account to live, at least, as many more. In the meantime, to trouble a man's self with the thought of a thing so far off were folly. But what? Young and old die upon the same terms; no one departs out of life otherwise than if he had but just before entered into it; neither is any man so old and decrepit, who, having heard of Methuselah,[9] does not think he has yet twenty good years to come.

---

1 Commoners.

2 I.e., they insist on putting the donkey's headgear on its tail.

3 "Who in his folly seeks to advance backwards"—Lucretius, *De Rerum Natura*, iv. 474.

4 Roundabout way of speaking.

5 Plutarch, *Life of Cicero*, c. 22.

6 Perhaps.

7 Said by a debtor who hopes that something will intervene to prevent repayment.

8 This was in virtue of an ordinance of Charles IX in 1563. Previously the year commenced at Easter, so that the 1st January, 1563, became the first day of the year 1563.

9 Methuselah lived 969 years, according to Genesis 5:27.

Fool that thou art! Who has assured unto thee the term of thy life? Thou dependest upon physicians' tales: rather consult effects and experience. According to the common course of things, 'tis long since that thou hast lived by extraordinary favor; thou hast already outlived the ordinary term of life. And that it is so, reckon up thy acquaintance, how many more have died before they arrived at thy age than have attained unto it; and of those who have ennobled their lives by their renown, take but an account, and I dare lay a wager thou wilt find more who have died before than after five-and-thirty years of age. It is full both of reason and piety, too, to take example by the humanity of Jesus Christ Himself, who ended His life at three-and-thirty years. The greatest man, that was no more than a man, Alexander, died also at the same age. How many several ways has death to surprise us?

> Quid quisque, vitet, nunquam homini satis
> Cautum est in horas.[1]

To omit fevers and pleurisies,[2] who would ever have imagined that a duke of Brittany[3] should be pressed to death in a crowd as that duke was at the entry of Pope Clement, my neighbor, into Lyons?[4] Hast thou not seen one of our kings killed at a tilting,[5] and did not one of his ancestors?[6] die by jostle[7] of a hog? Aeschylus, threatened with the fall of a house, got nothing by going into the fields to avoid that danger, for there he was knocked on the head by a tortoise falling out of an eagle's talons in the air.[8] Another was choked with a grape-stone;[9] an emperor killed with the scratch of a comb in combing his head; Aemilius Lepidus with a stumble at his own threshold,[10] and Aufidius with a jostle against the door as he entered the council-chamber. And betwixt the very thighs of women, Cornelius Gallus

---

1 "Be as cautious as he may, man can never foresee the danger that may at any hour befall him." Horace, *Odes*, ii. 13, 13.
2 Chest pains.
3 Jean II, died 1305.
4 Montaigne speaks of him as if he had been a contemporary neighbor, perhaps because he was the Archbishop of Bordeaux. Bertrand le Got was Pope under the title of Clement v, 1305–14.
5 Tournament, referring to Henri II, who died 10 July 1559.
6 Philip, King Louis VII, eldest son of Louis le Gros.
7 Violent thrust.
8 Valerius Maximus, *Factorum*, ix. 12.
9 Anacreon, also in Valerius Maximus, *Factorum*, ix. 12.
10 Pliny, *Natural History*, vii. 33.

the proctor; Tigillinus, captain of the watch at Rome; Ludovico, son of Guido di Gonzaga, Marquis of Mantua; and (an even worse example) Speusippus, a Platonic philosopher, and one of our Popes. The poor judge Bebius gave adjournment in a case for eight days, but he himself, meanwhile, was condemned by death, and his own stay of life expired.[1] Whilst Caius Julius, the physician, was anointing the eyes of a patient, death closed his own;[2] and, if I may bring in an example of my own blood, a brother of mine, Captain St. Martin, a young man, three-and-twenty years old, who had already given sufficient testimony of his valor, playing a match at tennis, received a blow of a ball a little above his right ear, which, as it gave no manner of sign of wound or contusion, he took no notice of it, nor so much as sat down to repose himself, but, nevertheless, died within five or six hours after of an apoplexy[3] occasioned by that blow.

With so frequent and common examples passing every day before our eyes, how is it possible a man should disengage himself from the thought of death, or avoid fancying[4] that it has us every moment by the throat? What matter is it, you will say, which way it comes to pass, provided a man does not terrify himself with the expectation? For my part, I am of this mind, and if a man could by any means avoid it, though by creeping under a calf's skin, I am one that should not be ashamed of the shift;[5] all I aim at is, to pass my time at my ease, and the recreations that will most contribute to it, I take hold of, as little glorious and exemplary as you will:

> Praetulerim ... delirus inersque videri,
> Dum mea delectent mala me, vel denique fallant,
> Quam sapere, et ringi.[6]

But 'tis folly to think of doing anything that way. They go, they come, they gallop, and dance, and not a word of death. All this is very fine while it lasts, when it comes either to themselves, their wives, their

---

1 Pliny, *Natural History*, vii. 53.
2 Pliny, *Natural History*, vii. 53.
3 Stroke.
4 Imagining.
5 Recourse.
6 "I had rather seem mad and a sluggard, so that my defects are agreeable to myself, or that I am not painfully conscious of them, than be wise and captious [crafty]."— Horace, *Epistles*, ii. 2, 126.

children, or friends, surprising them at unawares and unprepared, then, what torment, what outcries, what madness and despair! Did you ever see anything so subdued, so changed, and so confounded? A man must, therefore, make more early provision for it; and this brutish negligence, could it possibly lodge in the brain of any man of sense (which I think utterly impossible), sells us its merchandise too dear. Were it an enemy that could be avoided, I would then advise to borrow arms even of cowardice itself; but seeing it is not, and that it will catch you as well flying and playing the poltroon,[1] as standing to't like an honest man:—

> Nempe et fugacem persequitur virum,
> Nec parcit imbellis juventae
> Poplitibus timidoque tergo.[2]

And seeing that no temper of arms is of proof to secure us:—

> Ille licet ferro cautus, se condat et aere,
> Mors tamen inclusum protrahet inde caput.[3]

—let us learn bravely to stand our ground, and fight him. And to begin to deprive him of the greatest advantage he has over us, let us take a way quite contrary to the common course. Let us disarm him of his novelty and strangeness, let us converse and be familiar with him, and have nothing so frequent in our thoughts as death. Upon all occasions represent him to our imagination in his every shape; at the stumbling of a horse, at the falling of a tile, at the least prick with a pin, let us presently[4] consider, and say to ourselves, "Well, and what if it had been death itself?" and, thereupon, let us encourage and fortify ourselves. Let us evermore, amidst our jollity and feasting, set the remembrance of our frail condition before our eyes, never suffering[5] ourselves to be

---

1 Coward.
2 "He pursues the flying poltroon, nor spares the hamstrings of the unwarlike youth who turns his back"—Horace, *Odes*, iii. 2, 14.
3 "Let him hide beneath iron or brass in his fear, death will pull his head out of his armor."—Propertius iii. 18.
4 Immediately.
5 Allowing.

so far transported with our delights, but that we have some intervals of reflecting upon, and considering how many several ways this jollity of ours tends to death, and with how many dangers it threatens it. The Egyptians were wont to do after this manner, who in the height of their feasting and mirth, caused a dried skeleton of a man to be brought into the room to serve for a memento to their guests:[1]

> Omnem crede diem tibi diluxisse supremum
> Grata superveniet, quae non sperabitur, hora.[2]

Where death waits for us is uncertain; let us look for him everywhere. The premeditation of death is the premeditation of liberty; he who has learned to die has unlearned to serve. There is nothing evil in life for him who rightly comprehends that the privation of life is no evil: to know, how to die delivers us from all subjection and constraint. Paulus Emilius answered him whom the miserable King of Macedon, his prisoner, sent to entreat him that he would not lead him in his triumph, "Let him make that request to himself."[3]

In truth, in all things, if nature do not help a little, it is very hard for art and industry to perform anything to purpose. I am in my own nature not melancholic, but meditative; and there is nothing I have more continually entertained myself withal than imaginations of death, even in the most wanton time of my age:

> "Jucundum quum aetas florida ver ageret."[4]

In the company of ladies and at games, some have perhaps thought me possessed with some jealousy or the uncertainty of some hope, whilst I was only entertaining myself with the remembrance of some-one, surprised, a few days before, with a burning fever of which he died, returning from an entertainment like this, with his head full of idle fancies of love and jollity, as mine was then, and that, for aught I knew, the same destiny was attending me.

---

1 Herodotus, *History*, ii. 78.
2 "Think each day when past is thy last; the next day, as unexpected, will be the more welcome."—Horace, *Epistles*, i. 4, 13.
3 Plutarch, *Life of Paulus Aemilius*, c. 17; Cicero, *Tusculan Disputations*, v. 40.
4 "When my florid age rejoiced in pleasant spring."—Catullus, lxviii.

Jam fuerit, nec post unquam revocare licebit.[1]

Yet did not this thought wrinkle my forehead any more than any other. It is impossible but we must feel a sting in such imaginations as these at first; but with often turning and returning them in one's mind, they at last become so familiar as to be no trouble at all. Otherwise, I, for my part, should be in a perpetual fright and frenzy, for never man was so distrustful of his life, never man so uncertain as to its duration. Neither health, which I have hitherto ever enjoyed very strong and vigorous, and very seldom interrupted, does prolong, nor sickness contract my hopes. Every minute, methinks, I am escaping, and it eternally runs in my mind that what may be done tomorrow may be done today. Hazards and dangers do, in truth, little or nothing hasten our end; and if we consider how many thousands more remain and hang over our heads, besides the accident that immediately threatens us, we shall find that the sound and the sick, those that are abroad at sea, and those that sit by the fire, those who are engaged in battle, and those who sit idle at home, are the one as near it as the other.

Nemo altero fragilior est; nemo in crastinum sui certior.[2]

For anything I have to do before I die, the longest leisure would appear too short, were it but an hour's business I had to do.

A friend of mine the other day turning over my tablets, found therein a memorandum of something I would have done after my decease, whereupon I told him, as it was really true, that though I was no more than a league's distance only from my own house, and merry and well, yet when that thing came into my head, I made haste to write it down there, because I was not certain to live till I came home. As a man that am eternally brooding over my own thoughts, and confine them to my own particular concerns, I am at all hours as well prepared as I am ever like to be, and death, whenever he shall come, can bring nothing along with him I did not expect long before. We should always, as near as we can, be booted and spurred, and ready to go, and, above all things, take care, at that time, to have no business with any one but one's self:—

---

1 "Presently the present will have gone, never to be recalled."—Lucretius, *De Rerum Natura*, iii. 928.
2 "No man is more fragile than another: no man more certain than another of tomorrow."—Seneca, *Epistles*, 91.

Quid brevi fortes jaculamur avo
Multa?[1]

—for we shall there find work enough to do, without any need of addition. One man complains, more than of death, that he is thereby prevented of a glorious victory; another, that he must die before he has married his daughter, or educated his children; a third seems only troubled that he must lose the society of his wife; a fourth, the conversation of his son, as the principal comfort and concern of his being. For my part, I am, thanks be to God, at this instant in such a condition, that I am ready to dislodge, whenever it shall please Him, without regret for anything whatsoever. I disengage myself throughout from all worldly relations; my leave is soon taken of all but myself. Never did any one prepare to bid adieu to the world more absolutely and unreservedly and to shake hands with all manner of interest in it than I expect to do. The deadest deaths are the best:

"Miser, O miser," aiunt, "omnia ademit
Una dies infesta mihi tot praemia vitae."[2]

And the builder,

"Manuet," says he, "opera interrupta, minaeque
Murorum ingentes."[3]

A man must design nothing that will require so much time to the finishing, or, at least, with no such passionate desire to see it brought to perfection. We are born to action:

Quum moriar, medium solvar et inter opus.[4]

I would always have a man to be doing, and, as much as in him lies, to extend and spin out the offices of life; and then let death take me

---

1 "Why for so short a life tease ourselves with so many projects?"—Horace, *Odes*, ii. 16, 17.
2 "'Wretch that I am,' they cry, 'one fatal day has deprived me of all joys of life.'"— Lucretius, *De Rerum Natura*, iii. 911.
3 "The works remain incomplete, the tall pinnacles of the walls unmade."—Virgil, *Aeneid*, iv. 88.
4 "When I shall die, let it be doing that I had designed." —Ovid, *Amores*, ii. 10, 36.

planting my cabbages, indifferent to him, and still less of my gardens not being finished. I saw one die, who, at his last gasp, complained of nothing so much as that destiny was about to cut the thread of a chronicle he was then compiling, when he was gone no farther than the fifteenth or sixteenth of our kings:

> Illud in his rebus non addunt: nec tibi earum
> jam desiderium rerum super insidet una.[1]

We are to[2] discharge ourselves from these vulgar and hurtful humors.[3] To this purpose it was that men first appointed the places of sepulture[4] adjoining the churches, and in the most frequented places of the city, to accustom, says Lycurgus, the common people, women, and children, that they should not be startled at the sight of a corpse, and to the end, that the continual spectacle of bones, graves, and funeral obsequies should put us in mind of our frail condition:

> Quin etiam exhilarare viris convivia caede
> Mos olim, et miscere epulis spectacula dira
> Certantum ferro, saepe et super ipsa cadentum
> Pocula, respersis non parco sanguine mensis.[5]

And as the Egyptians after their feasts were wont to present the company with a great image of death, by one that cried out to them, "Drink and be merry, for such shalt thou be when thou art dead," so it is my custom to have death not only in my imagination, but continually in my mouth. Neither is there anything of which I am so inquisitive, and delight to inform myself, as the manner of men's deaths, their words, looks, and bearing; nor any places in history I am so intent upon; and it is manifest enough, by my crowding in examples of this kind, that

---

1 "They do not add, that dying, we have no longer a desire to possess things."—Lucretius, *De Rerum Natura*, iii. 913.
2 Should.
3 Moods.
4 Graveyards.
5 "It was formerly the custom to enliven banquets with slaughter, and to combine with the repast the dire spectacle of men contending with the sword, the dying in many cases falling upon the cups, and covering the tables with blood."—Silius Italicus, *Punica*, xi. 51.

I have a particular fancy for that subject. If I were a writer of books, I would compile a register, with a comment, of the various deaths of men: he who should teach men to die would at the same time teach them to live. Dicaearchus made one, to which he gave that title; but it was designed for another and less profitable end.[1] Peradventure, someone may object, that the pain and terror of dying does indeed so infinitely exceed all manner of imagination that the best fencer will be quite out of his play when it comes to the push.[2] Let them say what they will: to premeditate is doubtless a very great advantage; and besides, is it nothing to go so far, at least, without disturbance or alteration? Moreover, Nature herself assists and encourages us: if the death be sudden and violent, we have not leisure to fear; if otherwise, I perceive that as I engage further in my disease, I naturally enter into a certain loathing and disdain of life. I find I have much more ado to digest this resolution of dying when I am well in health than when languishing of a fever; and by how much I have less to do with the commodities of life, by reason that I begin to lose the use and plea-sure of them, by so much I look upon death with less terror. All of which makes me hope, that the further I remove from the first, and the nearer I approach to the latter, I shall the more easily exchange the one for the other. And, as I have experienced in other occurrences, that, as Caesar says, things often appear greater to us at distance than near at hand,[3] I have found, that being well, I have had maladies in much greater horror than when really afflicted with them. The vigor wherein I now am, the cheerfulness and delight wherein I now live, make the contrary estate appear in so great a disproportion to my pres-ent condition, that, by imagination, I magnify those inconveniences by one-half, and apprehend them to be much more troublesome, than I find them really to be, when they lie the most heavy upon me; I hope to find death the same.

Let us but observe in the ordinary changes and declinations we daily suffer, how nature deprives us of the light and sense of our bodily decay. What remains to an old man of the vigor of his youth and better days?

---

1   Cicero, *De Officiis*, ii. 5. Cicero says the book was called *On Human Destruction*, with the claim that human conflict had killed far more people than natural disasters had.

2   Practicing will be so exhausting that the fencer won't be able to survive the match.

3   *Gallic Wars*, vii. 89.

Heu! senibus vitae portio quanta manet.[1]

Caesar, to an old weather-beaten soldier of his guards, who came to ask him leave that he might kill himself, taking notice of his withered body and decrepit motion, pleasantly answered, "Thou fanciest, then, that thou art yet alive."[2] Should a man fall into this condition on the sudden, I do not think humanity capable of enduring such a change, but nature, leading us by the hand, an easy and, as it were, an insensible pace, step by step conducts us to that miserable state, and by that means makes it familiar to us, so that we are insensible of the stroke when our youth dies in us, though it be really a harder death than the final dissolution of a languishing body, than the death of old age; forasmuch as the fall is not so great from an uneasy being to none at all, as it is from a sprightly and flourishing being to one that is troublesome and painful. The body, bent and bowed, has less force to support a burden, and it is the same with the soul; and therefore it is, that we are to raise her up firm and erect against the power of this adversary. For, as it is impossible she should ever be at rest, whilst she stands in fear of it, so, if she once can assure herself, she may boast (which is a thing as it were surpassing human condition) that it is impossible that disquiet, anxiety, or fear, or any other disturbance, should inhabit or have any place in her:

> Non vulnus instants Tyranni
> Mentha cadi solida, neque Auster
> Dux inquieti turbidus Adriae,
> Nec fulminantis magna Jovis manus.[3]

She is then become sovereign of all her lusts and passions, mistress of necessity, shame, poverty, and all the other injuries of fortune. Let us, therefore, as many of us as can, get this advantage; 'tis the true and sovereign liberty here on earth, that fortifies us wherewithal to defy violence and injustice, and to contemn prisons and chains:

---

1   "Alas, to old men what portion of life remains!"—Maximian, *Elegies*, i. 16.
2   Seneca, *Epistles*, 77.
3   "Not the menacing look of a tyrant shakes her well-settled soul, nor turbulent Auster, the prince of the stormy Adriatic, nor yet the strong hand of thundering Jove, such a temper moves."—Horace, *Odes*, iii. 3, 3.

In manicis et
Compedibus saevo te sub custode tenebo.
Ipse Deus, simul atque volam, me solvet. Opinor,
Hoc sentit; moriar; mors ultima linea rerum est.[1]

Our very religion itself has no surer human foundation than the contempt of death. Not only the argument of reason invites us to it—for why should we fear to lose a thing, which being lost, cannot be lamented?—but, also, seeing we are threatened by so many sorts of death, is it not infinitely worse eternally to fear them all, than once to undergo one of them? And what matters when it shall happen, since it is inevitable? To him that told Socrates, "The thirty tyrants have sentenced thee to death," "And nature them," said he.[2] What a ridiculous thing it is to trouble ourselves about taking the only step that is to deliver us from all trouble! As our birth brought us the birth of all things, so in our death is the death of all things included. And therefore to lament that we shall not be alive a hundred years hence, is the same folly as to be sorry we were not alive a hundred years ago. Death is the beginning of another life. So did we weep, and so much it cost us to enter into this, and so did we put off our former veil in entering into it. Nothing can be a grievance that is but once. Is it reasonable so long to fear a thing that will so soon be dispatched? Long life and short are by death made all one; for there is no long nor short to things that are no more. Aristotle tells us that there are certain little beasts upon the banks of the river Hypanis, that never live above a day: they which die at eight of the clock in the morning, die in their youth, and those that die at five in the evening, in their decrepitude:[3] which of us would not laugh to see this moment of continuance put into the consideration of weal or woe? The most and the least, of ours, in comparison with eternity, or yet with the duration of mountains, rivers, stars, trees, and even of some animals, is no less ridiculous.[4]

---

1   "I will keep thee in fetters and chains, in custody of a savage keeper. A god will when I ask him, set me free. This god I think is death. Death is the term of all things."—Horace, *Epodes*, i. 16, 76.
2   Diogenes Laertius, *Lives*, ii. 35; Cicero, *Tusculan Disputations*, i. 40.
3   Cicero, *Tusculan Disputations*, i. 39.
4   Seneca, *Ad Marciam de Consolatione*, c. 20.

But Nature compels us to it. "Go out of this world," says she, "as you entered into it; the same pass you made from death to life, without passion or fear, the same, after the same manner, repeat from life to death. Your death is a part of the order of the universe, 'tis a part of the life of the world.

> Inter se mortales mutua vivunt
>
> ...
>
> Et, quasi cursores, vitai lampada tradunt.[1]

"Shall[2] I exchange for you this beautiful contexture of things? 'Tis the condition of your creation; death is a part of you, and whilst you endeavor to evade it, you evade yourselves. This very being of yours that you now enjoy is equally divided betwixt life and death. The day of your birth is one day's advance towards the grave:

> Prima, quae vitam dedit, hora carpsit.[3]
> Nascentes morimur, finisque ab origine pendet.[4]

"All the whole time you live, you purloin[5] from life and live at the expense of life itself. The perpetual work of your life is but to lay the foundation of death. You are in death, whilst you are in life, because you still are after death, when you are no more alive; or, if you had rather have it so, you are dead after life, but dying all the while you live; and death handles the dying much more rudely than the dead, and more sensibly and essentially. If you have made your profit of life, you have had enough of it. Go your way satisfied.

---

1 "Mortals, amongst themselves, live by turns, and, like the runners in the games, give up the lamp, when they have won the race, to the next comer."—Lucretius, *De Rerum Natura*, ii. 75, 78.

2 The open quotation marks for this paragraph (and those that follow) indicate the imagined voice of Nature, which begins in the previous paragraph and concludes in the penultimate paragraph of the essay.

3 "The first hour that gave us life took away also an hour."—Seneca, *Hercules Furens*, 3 Chorus 874.

4 "As we are born we die, and the end commences with the beginning."—Manilius, *Astronomica*, iv. 16.

5 Steal.

Cur non ut plenus vita; conviva recedis?[1]

"If you have not known how to make the best use of it, if it was unprofitable to you, what need you care to lose it, to what end would you desire longer to keep it?

Cur amplius addere quaeris,
Rursum quod pereat male, et ingratum occidat omne?[2]

"Life in itself is neither good nor evil; it is the scene of good or evil as you make it. And, if you have lived a day, you have seen all: one day is equal and like to all other days. There is no other light, no other shade; this very sun, this moon, these very stars, this very order and disposition of things, is the same your ancestors enjoyed, and that shall also entertain your posterity:

Non alium videre patres, aliumve nepotes
Aspicient.[3]

"And, come the worst that can come, the distribution and variety of all the acts of my comedy are performed in a year. If you have observed the revolution of my four seasons,[4] they comprehend the infancy, the youth, the virility, and the old age of the world: the year has played his part, and knows no other art but to begin again; it will always be the same thing:

Versamur ibidem, atque insumus usque.[5]
Atque in se sua per vestigia volvitur annus.[6]

---

1 "Why not depart from life as a sated guest from a feast?"—Lucretius, *De Rerum Natura*, iii. 951.
2 "Why seek to add longer life, merely to renew ill-spent time, and be again tormented?"—Lucretius, *De Rerum Natura*, iii. 945.
3 "Your grandsires saw no other thing; nor will your posterity."—Manilius, *Astronomica*, i. 529.
4 I.e., Nature's four seasons.
5 "We are turning in the same circle, ever therein confined."—Lucretius, *De Rerum Natura*, iii. 1093.
6 "The year is ever turning around in the same footsteps."—Virgil, *Georgics*, ii. 402.

"I am not prepared to create for you any new recreations:

> Nam tibi praeterea quod machiner, inveniamque
> Quod placeat, nihil est; eadem sunt omnia semper.[1]

"Give place to others, as others have given place to you. Equality is the soul of equity. Who can complain of being comprehended in the same destiny, wherein all are involved? Besides, live as long as you can, you shall by that nothing shorten the space you are to be dead; 'tis all to no purpose; you shall be every whit as long in the condition you so much fear, as if you had died at nurse:

> Licet quot vis vivendo vincere secla,
> Mors aeterna tamen nihilominus illa manebit.[2]

"And yet I will place you in such a condition as you shall have no reason to be displeased.

> In vera nescis nullum fore morte alium te,
> Qui possit vivus tibi to lugere peremptum,
> Stansque jacentem.[3]

"Nor shall you so much as wish for the life you are so concerned about:

> Nec sibi enim quisquam tum se vitamque requirit.
> ...
> Nec desiderium nostri nos afficit ullum.[4]

"Death is less to be feared than nothing, if there could be anything less than nothing.

---

1   "I can devise, nor find anything else to please you: 'tis the same thing over and over again."—Lucretius, *De Rerum Natura*, iii. 957.
2   "Live triumphing over as many ages as you will, death still will remain eternal."—Lucretius, *De Rerum Natura*, iii. 1103.
3   "Know you not that, when dead, there can be no other living self to lament you dead, standing on your grave."—Lucretius, *De Rerum Natura*, iii. 898.
4   "Then none shall mourn his person or his life ... And all regret of self shall cease to be."—Lucretius, *De Rerum Natura*, iii. 932.

Multo ... mortem minus ad nos esse putandium,
Si minus esse potest, quam quod nihil esse videmus.[1]

"Neither can it any way concern you, whether you are living or dead: living, by reason that you are still in being; dead, because you are no more. Moreover, no one dies before his hour: the time you leave behind was no more yours than that was lapsed and gone before you came into the world; nor does it any more concern you.

Respice enim, quam nil ad nos anteacta vetustas
Temporis aeterni fuerit.[2]

"Wherever your life ends, it is all there. The utility of living consists not in the length of days, but in the use of time; a man may have lived long, and yet lived but a little. Make use of time while it is present with you. It depends upon your will, and not upon the number of days, to have a sufficient length of life. Is it possible you can imagine never to arrive at the place towards which you are continually going? And yet there is no journey but hath its end. And, if company will make it more pleasant or more easy to you, does not all the world go the self-same way?

Omnia te, vita perfuncta, sequentur.[3]

"Does not all the world dance the same brawl[4] that you do? Is there anything that does not grow old, as well as you? A thousand men, a thousand animals, a thousand other creatures, die at the same moment that you die:

Nam nox nulla diem, neque noctem aurora sequuta est,
Quae non audierit mistos vagitibus aegris
Ploratus, mortis comites et funeris atri.[5]

---

1   "For us, death must be thought less than nothing, if anything can be less than nothing."—Lucretius, *De Rerum Natura*, iii.939.
2   "Consider how as nothing to us is the old age of times past."—Lucretius, *De Rerum Natura*, iii. 985.
3   "All things, then, life over, must follow thee."—Lucretius, *De Rerum Natura*, iii. 981.
4   French dance.
5   "No night has followed day, no day has followed night, in which there has not been heard sobs and sorrowing cries, the companions of death and

"To what end should you endeavor to draw back, if there be no possibility to evade it? You have seen examples enough of those who have been well pleased to die, as thereby delivered from heavy miseries; but have you ever found any who have been dissatisfied with dying? It must, therefore, needs be very foolish to condemn a thing you have neither experimented in your own person, nor by that of any other. Why dost thou complain of me and of destiny? Do we do thee any wrong? Is it for thee to govern us, or for us to govern thee? Though, peradventure, thy age may not be accomplished, yet thy life is: a man of low stature is as much a man as a giant; neither men nor their lives are measured by the ell.[1] Chiron refused to be immortal, when he was acquainted with the conditions under which he was to enjoy it, by the god of time itself and its duration, his father Saturn. Do but seriously consider how much more insupportable and painful an immortal life would be to man than what I have already given him. If you had not death, you would eternally curse me for having deprived you of it. I have mixed a little bitterness with it, to the end, that seeing how convenient it is, you might not too greedily and indiscreetly seek and embrace it. And that you might be so established in this moderation as neither to nauseate[2] life nor have any antipathy for dying, which I have decreed you shall once do, I have tempered the one and the other betwixt pleasure and pain. It was I that taught Thales, the most eminent of your sages, that to live and to die were indifferent; which made him, very wisely, answer him [who asked], why, then, he did not die. 'Because,' said he, 'it is indifferent.'[3] Water, earth, air, and fire, and the other parts of this creation of mine, are no more instruments of thy life than they are of thy death. Why dost thou fear thy last day? It contributes no more to thy dissolution than every one of the rest: the last step is not the cause of lassitude: it does not confess it. Every day travels towards death; the last only arrives at it." These are the good lessons our mother Nature teaches.

I have often considered with myself whence it should proceed, that in war the image of death, whether we look upon it in ourselves or in others, should, without comparison, appear less dreadful than at home

---

funerals."—Lucretius, *De Rerum Natura*, v. 579.

1 Measured like fabric or other yard goods; an ell was about 45 inches.
2 Deplore.
3 Diogenes Laertius, *Lives*, i. 35. Indifference is a virtue alike for the stoic, the Epicurean, and the skeptic.

in our own houses (for if it were not so, it would be an army of doctors and whining milksops), and that being still in all places the same, there should be, notwithstanding, much more assurance in peasants and the meaner sort of people, than in others of better quality. I believe, in truth, that it is those terrible ceremonies and preparations wherewith we set it out, that more terrify us than the thing itself: a new, quite contrary way of living; the cries of mothers, wives, and children; the visits of astounded and afflicted friends; the attendance of pale and blubbering servants; a dark room, set round with burning tapers; our beds environed with physicians and divines; in sum, nothing but ghost-liness and horror round about us. We seem dead and buried already. Children are afraid even of those they are best acquainted with, when disguised in a visor,[1] and so 'tis with us: the visor must be removed as well from things as from persons, that being taken away, we shall find nothing underneath but the very same death that a mean servant or a poor chambermaid died a day or two ago, without any manner of apprehension. Happy is the death that deprives us of leisure for preparing such ceremonials.

---

1   Mask.

WORKS CITED

Alvis, John. "Liberty and Responsibility in Shakespeare's Rome." *The Inner Vision: Liberty and Literature*. Ed. Edward B. McLean. Wilmington: ISI Books, 2006. 13–35.

Barroll, J. Leeds. "Shakespeare and Roman History." *Modern Language Review* 53 (1958): 327–43.

Barthory, Dennis. "'With Himself at War': Shakespeare's Roman Hero and the Republican Tradition." *Shakespeare's Political Pageant: Essays in Literature and Politics*. Ed. Joseph Alulis and Vickie B. Sullivan. Lanham, MD: Rowman and Littlefield, 1996. 237–61.

Bartlett, Henrietta C. "Quarto Editions of *Julius Caesar*." *The Library*, 3rd series, 4 (1913): 122–32.

Bate, Jonathan, ed. *The Romantics on Shakespeare*. London: Penguin, 1992.

Bellringer, A.W. "*Julius Caesar*: Room Enough." *Critical Quarterly* 12 (1970): 31–48.

Berger, Harry. *Making Trifles of Terrors: Redistributing Complicities in Shakespeare*. Ed. Peter Erickson. Stanford, CA: Stanford UP, 1997.

Bevington, David M., ed. *Complete Works of Shakespeare*. 5th ed. New York: Pearson Longman, 2004.

Blayney, Peter. *The First Folio of Shakespeare*. Washington, DC: Folger Shakespeare Library, 1991.

——, ed. *The Norton Facsimile. The First Folio of Shakespeare*. 2nd ed. New York: W.W. Norton, 1996.

Blits, Jan H. "Caesarism and the End of Republican Rome: *Julius Caesar*, Act I, scene i." *The Journal of Politics* 43 (1981): 40–55.

——. *The End of the Ancient Republic: Essays on "Julius Caesar."* Durham, NC: Duke UP, 1982.

Bloom, Allan. "The Morality of the Pagan Hero *Julius Caesar*." *Shakespeare's Politics*. Ed. Allan Bloom and Henry Jaffa. New York: Basic Books, 1964.

Braden, Gordon. *Renaissance Tragedy and the Senecan Tradition: Anger's Privilege*. New Haven: Yale UP, 1985.

Bradley, A.C. *Shakespearean Tragedy* (1904). New York: Fawcett, 1965.

Burke, Kenneth. "Antony in Behalf of the Play." Ed. Scott Newstock. *Kenneth Burke on Shakespeare*. West Lafayette, IN: Parlor P, 2007. 38–48.

Cantor, Paul. *Shakespeare's Rome Republic and Empire*. Ithaca, NY: Cornell UP, 1976.

Cavell, Stanley. *Disowning Knowledge in Seven Plays by Shakespeare*. Cambridge: Cambridge UP, 2003.

Charney, Maurice. *Shakespeare's Roman Plays: The Function of Imagery in the Drama*. Cambridge, MA: Harvard UP, 1961.

Cox, John D. *Seeming Knowledge: Shakespeare and Skeptical Faith*. Waco, TX: Baylor UP, 2007.

Daniell, David, ed. *Julius Caesar*. Walton-on-Thames: Thomas Nelson for the Arden Shakespeare, 1998.

Dent, Robert William. *Shakespeare's Proverbial Language*. Berkeley and Los Angeles: U of California P, 1981.

Dessen, Alan C. and Leslie Thomson. *A Dictionary of Stage Directions in English Drama, 1580–1642*. Cambridge: Cambridge UP, 1999.

Dorsch, T.S., ed. *Julius Caesar*. London: Methuen for the Arden Shakespeare, 1955.

Epictetus. *Handbook of Epictetus*. Trans. Nicholas White. Indianapolis: Hackett, 1983.

Granville-Barker, Harley. *Prefaces to Shakespeare*. London: Sidgwick and Jackson, 1927.

Greenblatt, Stephen. "Shakespeare and the Exorcists." *Shakespearean Negotiations: The Circulation of Social Energy in Renaissance England*. Berkeley and Los Angeles: U of California P, 1988. 94–128.

Henze, Richard. "Power and Spirit in Julius Caesar." *The University Review* 26 (1970): 307–14.

Hinman, Charlton, ed. *The Norton Facsimile. The First Folio of Shakespeare*. New York: W.W. Norton, 1968.

Holmes, Christopher. "Time for the Plebs in *Julius Caesar*." *Early Modern Literary Studies* 7 (2001). Web.

Horace. *Satires, Epistles and ArsPoetica*. Trans. Rushton Fairclough. Cambridge, MA: Harvard UP for the Loeb Classical Library, 1926.

Humphreys, Arthur R., ed. *Julius Caesar*. Oxford: Oxford UP, 1994.

Ichikawa, Mariko. "'Enter Brutus in his Orchard': Garden Scenes in Early Modern English Plays." *Shakespearean International Yearbook* 9 (2009): 214–47.

Johnson, Samuel. *Johnson on Shakespeare*. Ed. Arthur Sherbo. Vols. 7 and 8 of The Yale Edition of the Works of Samuel Johnson. New Haven: Yale UP, 1968.

Jonson, Ben. *Ben Jonson*. Ed. C.H. Herford and Percy Simpson. 11 vols. Oxford: Clarendon, 1925–52.

Jowett, John. "Ligature Shortage and Speech-prefix Variation in *Julius Caesar*." *The Library*, 6th ser., 6 (1985): 244–53.

Kahn, Coppèlia. *Roman Shakespeare: Warrior, Wounds, and Women*. London and New York: Routledge, 1997.

Kastan, David Scott. *Shakespeare and the Shapes of Time*. Hanover, NH: UP of New England, 1982.

Kaula, David. "'Let Us Be Sacrificers': Religious Motifs in *Julius Caesar*." *Shakespeare Studies* 14 (1981): 197–214.

Kayser, John R. and Ronald J. Lettieri. "'The Last of All the Romans': Shakespeare's Commentary on Classical Republicanism." *Clio* 9 (1980): 197–227.

Kirschbaum, Leo. "Shakespeare's Stage Blood and Its Critical Significance." *PMLA* 64 (1949): 517–29.

Knight, G. Wilson. *The Imperial Theme*. 1931. London: Methuen, 1965.

Knights, L.C. "Shakespeare and Political Wisdom: A Note on the Personalism of *Julius Caesar* and *Coriolanus*." *Sewanee Review* 61 (1953): 43–55.

Liebler, Naomi Conn. "'Thou Bleeding Piece of Earth': The Ritual Ground of *Julius Caesar*." *Shakespeare Studies* 14 (1981): 175–96.

Long, John H. *Shakespeare's Use of Music: The Histories and Tragedies*. Gainesville: U of Florida P, 1971.

MacCallum, M.W. *Shakespeare's Roman Plays and Their Background*. 1910; London: Macmillan, 1967.

Maxwell, J.C. "Shakespeare's Roman Plays: 1900–1956." *Shakespeare Survey* 10 (1957): 1–11.

Miles, Geoffrey. *Shakespeare and the Constant Romans*. Oxford: Clarendon, 1996.

Miller, Anthony. "The Roman State in *Julius Caesar* and *Sejanus*." *Jonson and Shakespeare*. Ed. Ian Donaldson. Atlantic Highlands, NJ: Humanities P, 1983. 179–201.

Miola, Robert. "*Julius Caesar* and the Tyrannicide Debate." *Renaissance Quarterly* 38 (1985): 271–89.

Montaigne, Michel de. *The Complete Essays of Montaigne*. Trans. Donald M. Frame. Stanford: Stanford UP, 1958.

———. *Works*. Trans. W. Hazlitt. Ed. O.W. Wright. 4 vols. Boston: Houghton Mifflin, 1859.

Müller, Wolfgang G. *Die Politische Rede bei Shakespeare*. Tübingen [Germany]: Gunter NarrVerlag, 1979.

New Variorum Julius Caesar. Ed. H.H. Furness. Philadelphia: Lippincott, 1913.

Parker, Barbara L. "From Monarchy to Tyranny: *Julius Caesar* among Shakespeare's Roman Works." *Julius Caesar: New Critical Essays*. Ed. Zander Horst. New York: Routledge, 2005. 111–26.

Paster, Gail Kern. "'In the spirit of men there is no blood': Blood as Trope of Gender in *Julius Caesar*." *Shakespeare Quarterly* 40 (1989): 284–98.

Patterson, Annabel. *Shakespeare and the Popular Voice*. Cambridge, MA: Blackwell, 1989.

Phillips, J.E. *The State in Shakespeare's Greek and Roman Plays*. New York: Columbia UP, 1940.

Picard, Liza. *Elizabeth's London*. London: Weidenfeld and Nicolson, 2003.

Rabkin, Norman. *Shakespeare and the Common Understanding*. New York: Free P, 1967.

——. "Structure, Convention, and Meaning in *Julius Caesar*." *Journal of English and Germanic Philology* 63 (1964): 240–54.

Ribner, Irvin. "Political Issues in *Julius Caesar*." *Journal of English and Germanic Philology* 56 (1957): 10–22.

Ricoeur, Paul. *Freud and Philosophy*. Trans. Denis Savage. New Haven: Yale UP, 1970.

Ringler, William. "*Poeta Nascitur non Fit*: Some Notes on the History of an Aphorism." *Journal of the History of Ideas* 2 (1941): 497–504.

Ripley, John. *Julius Caesar on Stage in England and America, 1599–1973*. Cambridge: Cambride UP, 1980.

Rose, Mark. "Conjuring Caesar: Ceremony, History, and Authority in 1599." *English Literary Renaissance* 19 (1989): 291–304.

Rymer, Thomas. *A Short View of Tragedy*. New York: A.M. Kelley, 1970.

Schanzer, Ernest. *The Problem Plays of Shakespeare*. New York: Schocken Books, 1963.

——. "Thomas Platter's Observations on the Elizabethan Stage." *Notes and Queries* 201 (1956): 465–67.

Shapiro, James. *A Year in the Life of William Shakespeare: 1599*. New York: HarperCollins, 2005.

Simmons, J.L. *Shakespeare's Pagan World: The Roman Tragedies.*
Charlottesville: UP of Virginia, 1973.

Sinfield, Alan. "Theaters of War: Caesar and the Vandals." *Faultlines: Cultural Materialism and the Politics of Dissident Reading.* Ed. Alan Sinfield. Berkeley: U of California P, 1992. 1–28.

Spurgeon, Caroline. *Shakespeare's Imagery and What It Tells Us.* Cambridge: Cambridge UP, 1939.

Taylor, Gary. "*Musophilus, Nosceteipsum,* and *Julius Caesar.*" *Notes and Queries* 229 (1984): 191–95.

Theobald, Lewis, ed. *Works of Shakespeare.* 7 vols. London: Printed for A. Bettesworth and C. Hitch, J. Tonson, F. Clay, W. Feales, and R. Wellington, 1733.

Tillyard, E.M.W. *The Elizabethan World Picture.* New York: Macmillan, 1944.

——. *Shakespeare's History Plays.* New York: Barnes and Noble, 1944.

Velz, John W. "Clemency, Will, and Just Cause in *Julius Caesar.*" *Shakespeare Survey* 22 (1969):109–118.

——. "'If I Were Brutus Now...': Role-Playing in *Julius Caesar.*" *Shakespeare Studies* 4 (1968): 149–59.

——. "*Orator* and *Imperator* in *Julius Caesar*: Style and the Process of Roman History." *Shakespeare Studies* 15 (1982): 55–75.

——. "Undular Structure in 'Julius Caesar.'" *Modern Language Review* 66 (1971): 21–30.

Vickers, Brian. *Shakespeare: The Critical Heritage.* 5 vols. London: Routledge and Kegan Paul, 1974–79.

Weinberg, Bernard. *A History of Literary Criticism in the Italian Renaissance.* 2 vols. Chicago: U of Chicago P, 1961.

Wells, Stanley. *Re-editing Shakespeare for the Modern Reader.* Oxford: Clarendon, 1984.

—— and Gary Taylor, with John Jowett and William Montgomery. *William Shakespeare: A Textual Companion.* Oxford: Oxford UP, 1987.

Wilson, John Dover, ed. *Julius Caesar.* Cambridge: Cambridge UP, 1949. Vol 15. *The Works of Shakespeare.* 39 vols. 1921–66.

from the publisher

A name never says it all, but the word "broadview" expresses a good deal of the philosophy behind our company. We are open to a broad range of academic approaches and political viewpoints. We pay attention to the broad impact book publishing and book printing has in the wider world; we began using recycled stock more than a decade ago, and for some years now we have used 100% recycled paper for most titles. As a Canadian-based company we naturally publish a number of titles with a Canadian emphasis, but our publishing program overall is internationally oriented and broad-ranging. Our individual titles often appeal to a broad readership too; many are of interest as much to general readers as to academics and students.

Founded in 1985, Broadview remains a fully independent company owned by its shareholders—not an imprint or subsidiary of a larger multinational.

If you would like to find out more about Broadview and about the books we publish, please visit us at **www.broadviewpress.com**. And if you'd like to place an order through the site, we'd like to show our appreciation by extending a special discount to you: by entering the code below you will receive a 20% discount on purchases made through the Broadview website.

Discount code: **broadview20%**

Thank you for choosing Broadview.

Please note: this offer applies only to sales of bound books within the United States or Canada.

Cascades | **ENVIRONMENTAL CALCULATOR**
GREEN BY NATURE™

DETAILED REPORT

LIST
of products used:

1,098 lb(s) of Rolland Enviro100 Print
100% post-consumer

Generated by : www.cascades.com/calculator

Sources : Environmental Paper Network (EPN)
www.papercalculator.org

RESULTS
Based on the Cascades products you selected
compared to products in the industry made with
100% virgin fiber, your savings are:

9 trees

9,084 gal. US of water
98 days of water consumption

1,148 lbs of waste
11 waste containers

2,985 lbs CO_2
5,660 miles driven

14 MMBTU
70,792 60W light bulbs for one hour

9 lbs NOx
emissions of one truck during 12
days